Perfect 10

The University of Georgia GymDogs and The Rise of Women's College Gymnastics in America

Suzanne Yoculan and Bill Donaldson

HILL STREET PRESS
ATHENS, GEORGIA

A HILL STREET PRESS BOOK

Published in the United States of America by Hill Street Press LLC
191 East Broad Street, Suite 216, Athens, Georgia 30601-2848 USA
706-613-7200 • info@hillstreetpress.com • www.hillstreetpress.com

Hill Street Press is committed to preserving the written word. Every effort is made to print books on acid-free paper with a significant amount of post-consumer recycled content.

Our best efforts have been used to obtain proper copyright clearance and credit for each of the images in this book. If an unavoidable and inadvertent credit error has occurred it will be corrected in future editions upon notification. Photographers hold copyrights to their work.

Hill Street Press books are available in bulk purchase and customized editions to institutions and corporate accounts. Please contact us for more information.

Text design by Brandi Goodson • Jacket design by Jenifer Carter and Brandi Goodson
Front top photo: Suzanne Yoculan © Radi Nabulsi
Front bottom photos, left to right: Jenny Hansen (UK Sports Information), Mohini Bhardwaj (UCLA Sports Information), Hope Spivey (UGA Sports Communications)
Back top photo: Suzanne Yoculan and GymDogs (UGA Sports Communications)
Back bottom photos, left to right: Jamie Dantzscher (UCLA Sports Information), Theresa Kulikowski (U of U Staff Photos), Kim Arnold (UGA Sports Communications), Lucy Wener (UGA Sports Communications), Suzanne Yoculan (courtesy of Suzanne Yoculan)

Printed in the United States of America.
    Yoculan, Suzanne.
        Perfect 10 : the UGA GymDogs and the rise of women's college gymnastics in America / by Suzanne Yoculan and Bill Donaldson; foreword by Mary Lee Tracy
        p. cm.
    Includes bibliographical references and index.
    ISBN 1-58818-111-1 (alk. paper)
    1. University of Georgia--Gymnastics. 2. Gymnastics for women--Georgia.
    I. Donaldson, Bill, 1927-   II. Title. III. Title: Perfect ten.
      GV468.U55Y63 2005
      796.44'09758'18--dc22   2005000773

ISBN-10: 1-58818-111-1
ISBN-13: 978-1-58818-111-4

10 9 8 7 6 5 4 3 2 1
First Printing

Contents

v	Foreword
ix	Introduction
1	Ten Years to the Top 1983–1993
37	Journey to Georgia
45	Over-the-Hill at Eighteen—Not!
69	Eat or Get Out of My Gym
91	Winning's *Not* the Only Thing
107	Two Hundred to Ten Thousand
127	Chemistry
143	Putting It All Together
157	On the Plateau
209	Gender Equity
237	Problems and Progress
249	Acknowledgements
251	Index

Foreword

Since I started the Cincinnati Gymnastics Academy I've been connected primarily with the Junior Olympics and the elite (Olympic-level) programs. As I began climbing the steps in the gymnastics business, one of my first encounters with a college coach was with Suzanne Yoculan from the University of Georgia. About 1994, she and Assistant Coach Jay Clark were recruiting—along with just about every other major college coach in the country—three of my athletes who were contenders for the 1996 Olympics.

At the time I really didn't have a lot of information on what college gymnastics was all about. It was then I realized that, after all the years of hard work by the gymnasts and their parents, college gymnastics was, in a lot of ways, a payoff for their dedication and commitment to the sport. Just look at the financial value of a college scholarship. A lot of times parents have used some of the money they would have put away for a college education to get their kids through gymnastics, so when an athletic scholarship pays for four years of college—sometimes even a fifth year—it's huge.

My three athletes being recruited so heavily in 1994 were Amanda Borden, Sam Muhleman, and Karin Lichey. As they considered the various schools that were pursuing them, they realized that a lot about Georgia felt like Cincinnati. There was a female head coach at Georgia and two male assistant coaches, and the coaching styles seemed similar to those here. As we all got to know Suzanne and Jay, Georgia and Cincinnati seemed to fit more and more. Then after Amanda, Sam, and Karin visited Georgia, they came back saying it felt a lot like being at home.

Athens wasn't that far from Cincinnati. A lot of kids from the Midwest tend to like to stay on this side of the country. So because of the coaching, the city, the area, the school environment, and the other athletes on the team, Georgia became a place where a lot of the Cincinnati athletes have gone. Much of my assessment of college gymnastics, then, is based on my observations of the GymDogs' program and my former gymnasts' incredible experiences at Georgia.

While I feel like college gymnastics, in general, is a reward and payoff for hard work; more important, I think it's a good transitional step for coming out into the real world. The gymnasts are living on their own for the first time, and college gymnastics is just a good avenue to get them connected with people, to teach them a lot of skills in communication and networking with people in the real world, the big world. All the universities do that. But that's an asset I think Suzanne has been particularly good with—preparing gymnasts for their adult lives.

Now let's examine some of the characteristics of college gymnastics. First, nearly all of the gymnasts in college graduate. It goes along with the sport being so disciplined. Kids who hang in there and persevere through the physical, mental, and emotional challenges of gymnastics find the other challenges of college much easier than the challenges of the sport, which they've already learned to meet. For someone who's never been in a sport like gymnastics, excelling in college may be a much bigger challenge.

For elite athletes especially, and even for some of the higher level J.O. kids who've been used to training twenty-five to thirty-five hours a week, college gymnastics is not just lighter on the hours, it's also lighter on their bodies. As they become women, it's nice that in college the rules allow them to do fewer skills than they did in the elite program. So a lot of girls look forward to college gymnastics because it'll be a relief, physically, while allowing them to continue to pursue what has been for them a life-long passion.

But don't get the idea college gymnastics isn't challenging or exciting. It's elite-quality gymnastics, and in some ways it's even higher level than elite in maturity of performance. Girls get stronger as they mature, so a lot of the skills are bigger. Frequently the skills are more crowd-pleasing and sometime even more fun. But because college gymnasts don't have to earn as many points to get a 10.0 start value, they don't have to do as many of the skills. For example, in elite they may be doing four tumbling passes on floor while in college they're doing three. They may have to have five release moves on bars in elite and only three in college. But the skills in college actually may be bigger. I find college gymnastics every bit as exciting to watch as Olympic level gymnastics and sometimes more fun to watch, because there's a lot more team spirit, team energy, and a little less intensity.

I would guess at least eighty percent of the top 100 gymnasts in the USA will get college scholarships, including those who compete in the Olympics. For me, coaching the Gold Medal Olympic team of 1996 was a rare, unbelievable moment in time. My guess is the girls on the 1996 Magnificent Seven Tour got somewhere between a half million and a million dollars. Since then there just hasn't been the opportunity to make that kind of money—enough money to make it worth giving up a college scholarship. So aside from the very few who take money or for some other reason give up the sport, almost all of the top elite gymnasts are going to compete in college. About a thousand gymnasts are now on college scholarships.

And nowadays, if a gymnast is among the top gymnasts in the country, she's also among the top gymnasts in the world. For the longest time everybody tried to be like the Russians and the Romanians, but now it's a complete reversal, especially since the communist countries split up. Today, the USA is definitely looked on as the strongest force in gymnastics. There are probably no more than two or three teams, other than the USA, that have a chance of winning the Gold in the Olympics. So when two of the top college teams in America meet, the girls in the starting lineup for each team will be Olympic caliber. And because they are older and stronger, there is more power and amplitude in their routines. But the biggest thing I see when I go to a college meet is the level of performance, the ability to entertain the crowd, to pull the crowd in. That's what really puts college gymnastics in a class by itself. The larger crowds probably help the performance level too.

I think Suzanne is one of the best spokespersons for college gymnastics, because she believes in it so much. For years and years she's watched young women come out of high school and become very successful young women. She has produced not just successful athletes but successful people. I think the similarity between the philosophies in my book, *Living the Gold-Medal Life,* and the philosophies of college gymnastics is that the lessons you deal with and learn about in sports are the same ones you encounter in life. The lessons of "failing forward," the perseverance before you finally get to where you want to get, time-management—all of those things—would be lessons hard to learn until you're an adult and you're set right in the middle of them, unless you've been involved in a sport as challenging as gymnastics.

So I'm delighted that Suzanne has decided to share her experiences and to record the history of college gymnastics since it became a part of the NCAA. She discusses the mental as well as the physical side of college gymnastics and dispels the myths about the sport. And her coauthor, Bill Donaldson, provides the perspective of a fan, to help those of you who have yet to discover the sport see what you've been missing.

—MARY LEE TRACY

Introduction

G eorgia is a "football school." What's a football school? Well, let me explain it by saying that North Carolina is a "basketball school." That's sort of just the way it is. If the good Lord had intended it to be the reverse, He would have sent Michael Jordan to Georgia and Herschel Walker to North Carolina. At many colleges one sport seems to dominate the character of the athletic program. For example, the University of Alabama is also considered a football school, and Kentucky, on the other hand, a basketball school. Each has won several national championships in the respective sports. The University of Georgia has been a football school since football displaced baseball as the most popular sport—about the time Sanford Stadium was built in 1929, with a seating capacity twelve times the 1929 student enrollment of about 2500.

I grew up in Georgia, and my Georgia football roots are deep. So living in Georgia with a hundred years of Georgia football in my family background, it was almost preordained that I would be a University of Georgia football fan.

When I was discharged from the Navy at the end of World War II, I transferred from the college I attended previously to the University of Georgia. Had it not been that Charlie Trippi, one of the greatest football players of all time, had returned from military service to play for Georgia, I might have gone elsewhere.

Attending the University of Georgia is not merely educational, it's an experience that stays with you for life. Any graduate who ever wants to leave Athens just didn't get fully inoculated. In 1966 my wife, Barbara, our two children, and I were living in Virginia, where I was head of the laboratories in DuPont's largest facility in Virginia. The United States Environmental Protection Agency was building a research facility adjacent to the university in Athens, and I was offered a professionally exciting position there. Our children were in elementary school, and the university town of Athens seemed like a perfect place to raise them. It was. So everything pointed to my return to Athens in 1966.

Saturday afternoons at Sanford Stadium—with the tailgating, the colorful bands, and Southeastern Conference football—constituted one of my most entertaining experiences. My children, now both alumni of the University of Georgia, attended every Georgia football game every year with Barbara and me when they were young. I even told my children, in jest, that they should always ascertain the location of a prospective spouse's family's renewable football seats before seriously considering matrimony. When the children were first married, they and their spouses—also Georgia alumni, what else?—joined Barbara and me to tailgate at every game. Like thousands of other fans, the addiction to Georgia football had me firmly in its grasp. I'm sure there are college football fans of other schools all over the country with addictions similar to mine.

Was there any other sport at Georgia? Contributors to the renewable season ticket program for football were also given priority seating at basketball games, perhaps to improve attendance, which has never been particularly good at Georgia. Remember, Georgia is a football school. Some contributors who lived near Athens bought season tickets to basketball games just because they had already paid for priority seating. So I did attend some basketball games in the "off-season." But about the only time the arena was filled for basketball was when Kentucky, a perennial national power, came to town.

I was at a Georgia basketball game in the mid-1980s when my half-time conversation was interrupted by a pretty young woman from New Jersey, announcing (too close to the microphone) descriptions of the unbelievable tricks her gymnasts were performing on the balance beam for the half-time show. She was Suzanne Yoculan, the relatively new women's gymnastics coach at the University of Georgia. I had seen Olga Korbut and Nadia Comaneci on television in the Olympics a few years earlier. It seemed to me these young women on the coliseum floor were doing things even more daring than what I recalled Olga and Nadia did. Actually, they were. They attracted attention. You could hear the crowd's gasps as the performers did more daring tricks.

At the next basketball game those same young dare devils were bouncing through the stands, dressed in their colorful nylon warm-ups, passing out gymnastics schedule cards. I recall trying to start a conversation by asking one who seemed to be particularly short how tall she was. She cocked her head back, with a twinkle in her eye and a mischievous, broad smile. Then quick as a flash she retorted, "Hi, I'm Debbie Greco from Cos Cob, Connecticut, and I'm five-feet, seven." The Georgia GymDogs media guide said Debbie is four-feet, eight.

I decided that if these vivacious young women could do more of the stuff they had provided a sample of the previous week on the coliseum floor and look as pretty as they did up close, maybe I should attend a gymnastics game—I soon learned it's called a gymnastics meet. The team had been coached by Suzanne Yoculan only a couple of years, but I read in the paper that they were already causing rumblings about their high national rankings. Attending a gymnastics meet could be a more entertaining diversion from football than the basketball games during the off-season.

When I returned home I convinced Barbara that women's gymnastics might be a sport she could enjoy, for the sport itself—not just for the tailgate party. So she and I went to a meet. And another. And then another. We haven't missed a home meet in over seventeen years, and we even traveled as far as Salt Lake City, twice, to national championships. We'd never traveled farther than the Sugar Bowl in New Orleans for football—1980, a good year. Herschel Walker led Georgia to the national championship. It began to dawn on me that my addiction to football was being arrested, or at least replaced, by a new addiction to gymnastics.

Why? What is so tantalizing about Georgia women's gymnastics that it could replace a life-long, inherent, traditional dedication to football? While the examples I use are all related to Georgia gymnastics, most of them can also apply to any of the major teams: Utah, Alabama, UCLA, Michigan, Florida, Nebraska, LSU, Stanford, Arizona State, etc.

First, there are more seconds of exhilarating apprehension in a college gymnastics meet than in any other sport. A ball isn't passed around, waiting for someone to shoot. There are no 2-yard gains at midfield, wondering when a significant play will develop. And certainly none of the waiting for a pitcher to toss a ball that may not even be swung at. I've found myself alternating TV channels between two "traditional" sports and still found an awful lot of dead time. But from the beginning of a gymnastics routine, to the dismount, every second and every move the gymnast makes are significant. If she "hits" the skill, she scores points. If she misses, she loses points. And if she falls—well, the whole meet could be blown in one split second. There is no way to make up for a mistake, once it's made. You can't put on a full court press or a two-minute offense. So the suspense is continuous.

Just think about it—there are less than ten minutes of activity for both teams combined, from snap to whistle, in a football game. In a dual gymnastics meet there are about forty-five minutes from mounting the apparatus to dismount, for all gymnasts combined. In a televised football coach's show, he can get in every play easily in a thirty-minute telecast. A gymnastics coach has to choose fewer than half the routines, or show only parts of them in a thirty-minute telecast.

Second, the athleticism of the gymnasts surpasses that of athletes in any other sport. Prior to coming to college, they train thirty-five to forty hours a week under highly qualified coaches for eight to ten years to perfect their skills. Only the best make it to a team like Georgia's. In no other sport does a five-foot, one-inch missile project herself seven or eight feet off the floor while flipping twice, with a full twist before landing on her feet with a "kerplunk," not moving a toe. And that's a reasonably common feat among the best.

Then there are unique skills, like the one Lori Strong, former Georgia gymnast, developed and performed on the uneven bars at the 1989 World Gymnastics Championships and the 1988 and 1992 Olympics. It's named for her, "The Strong." No other gymnast in the world has ever mastered it, although I'm told one in Romania tried. The Strong is described in the code of points this way: "From hang (facing low bar) underswing with 540 degree twist and flight over the low bar to hang on." Lori looks like a projectile spun by the rifling of a cannon, with her body fully straightened out, and then somehow she "hangs on." after she passes over the low bar. I've seen thousands of spectators from Alabama to Utah, caught in a spontaneous, resonant gasp of astonishment whenever she performed it. Many college gymnasts have their own signature skills, although they may not be unique.

Gymnasts at the better college programs today perform skills as difficult and exciting as those of any gymnasts. Their skills are fully equivalent to the ones performed by Olympians. The difference between watching their routines and watching those of the Olympians is that it costs about fifty times more for spectators to see the Olympics than it does to attend a college meet.

I'm hooked on gymnastics because you don't depend on subjective polls to see who's best. Every team is judged in every meet against the same scoring standards. You can compare a team competing on Friday on the east coast with one competing on Saturday, two weeks later, on the west coast. Throughout the season and at season's end, the cumulative averages clearly demonstrate who's best. Furthermore, you can see who the best individuals are by the same measure. (There's still some work to be done to make all scores comparable, but it can be done.) Perhaps the best thing about gymnastics scores is that both teams can feel good at the end of the meet, if they both hit their routines, regardless of which team has the higher score. Was Grantland Rice thinking of gymnastics when he penned that most famous of sports poems, which ended, "It's not that you won or lost, but how you played the game."?

And the focus is on the moment. College gymnastics is the ultimate level in team competition. There is no professional competition. There is no speculation about how this athlete would perform "on Sundays" or "at the next level." You enjoy what's happening now.

There is suspense throughout the meet with regard to records. There are team records at the conference, regional, and national levels. There are individual records at the same levels. Then there are season highs and career highs. There are records on each of the four events and for the highest individual who performs on all four events (the all-around). Fans track the gymnasts' progress toward breaking selected records during the meet, making every individual performance statistically meaningful.

There's variety. Each event has its own character. The vault is almost all athletic, requiring a sprinter's speed to build momentum and a diver's aerialist skills, while suspended in the air. The floor exercise entwines exquisite dance movements with acrobatic tumbling passes. The balletic movements are elegant, and the choreography is clever. And, in college, they are performed by mature gymnasts—not the pixies you see on national television performing watered-down routines in exhibitions.

The uneven bars routines are more like the movements of a trapeze artist, and the balance beam is a floor exercise performed on a four-inch-wide wooden weapon. Each fan has his or her own favorite apparatus. Because of the agony of watching the beam routines, few consider it their favorite. I know one fan who leaves the arena when the GymDogs are on the beam. It's not for the faint of heart!

If you like to be lifted up by observing things done right, watch the demeanor of the gymnasts. Neat attire and grooming are built into gymnastics performance. A gymnast can loose points for a torn leotard, dowdy hair, or painted nails—finger or toe. She must smile in addressing the judge. And under no circumstance can she show displeasure at her performance. If she falls from the beam, drawing an egg-sized knot on her cheek as it encounters the solid wood device, she has but a few seconds to regain her composure and remount to continue her exercise. Smiling. Excruciating pain disguised. Courage? You bet!

Neither can a gymnast "showboat." There's no need for a celebration rule. That characteristic, by itself, may attract a lot of fans.

And you just know that these young women are not dumb jocks. They become fully integrated into the collegiate environment, socially and academically. They are experts at time management. Having spent thirty-five to forty hours a week on gymnastics prior to coming to college and less than twenty a week in college, they devote a significant part of their new-found extra time to academics. They all graduate, most in challenging curriculums—for example ten percent of Georgia gymnastics alumnae are physicians or in medical school. In 2003, two Georgia gymnasts (fifteen percent) were in the honors program, compared to ten percent for the entire undergraduate student body.

College gymnastics fans demonstrate that enthusiasm and propriety are not mutually exclusive. They respect all of the athletes, not just their own. There is no waving of cylinder-shaped balloons to distract a free-throw shooter. No organized roar to prevent a signal caller from audiblizing at the line of scrimmage. But they can bring the house down displaying their enthusiasm.

Now what sets the GymDogs apart from other teams is their coach, Suzanne Yoculan. She left the Penn State gymnastics team as a freshman in 1971 because college gymnastics in those days bored her. She earned money to complete college by teaching gymnastics—from two-year- olds to elite-level gymnasts, and then owned and operated her own gym. Most of her time between her freshman year in college and her first year of college coaching, Suzanne was involved in various significant coaching and management tasks with the world famous Woodward Gymnastics Camp. But all the while she had a vision about the potential of college gymnastics—that college gymnastics could be an exciting, challenging, and beautiful spectator sport; and, when she became a coach, she turned women's college gymnastics on its ear, bringing the first former U.S. Olympian into its ranks, and upgrading the difficulty of skills from the mundane, conservative ones to exciting Olympic levels.

Flamboyant, vivacious, articulate, and animated are characteristics often used in describing Suzanne Yoculan. Chris Marlowe, the ESPN announcer, called her "the most enthusiastic coach I've ever seen in any sport." Her club-level mentor, Ed Isabelle, told me, "She lives on the edge; she always has and always will." And Anne Vexler, who was her teammate in club gymnastics said, "You didn't have to be looking to know when she came into the gym." When Suzanne noticed that spectators were fascinated with her attire at meets, she exploited her world-class legs by wearing tastefully short skirts. And she can maneuver in four-inch heels better than most of us can in athletic shoes.

The performance of Suzanne's team's has become second to none. A substantiation of this claim is in the afterword, but just a couple of statistics stand out: She has the highest winning percentage of any female college coach in any sport. Her team is the only one in college gymnastics to go through an entire season undefeated—and they've done it three times, against the toughest competition she could schedule.

When it was revealed that one of her gymnasts was losing weight at an alarming pace because of severe anorexia, Suzanne attacked the problem like she does every other problem. She assembled a team of experts in anorexia: nutritionists, trainers, psychologists, and—

perhaps the most important element—other members of her team. She harnessed the same motivating force that enabled the anorexia and turned it into a force that reversed it.

Through experience she learned the difference between the acrobatic pixies and more mature college gymnasts—the ratio of their strength and conditioning to their weight. So she led her competitors to follow her in making the mature gymnasts just as acrobatic as the pixies, making college gymnastics even more spectacular than Olympic gymnastics.

Cheating—a harsh term, perhaps, but accurate—by some of her peer coaches who selected judges showing favor to their gymnasts was repugnant to Suzanne. To change this she first lobbied successfully for using four judges for each event, rather than two, at the Southeastern Conference Championships and then having an NCAA representative select judges for all SEC meets.

Within a few short years she raised attendance at GymDog meets from two hundred to ten thousand. As attendance grew, Suzanne enhanced fairness of seat assignments and increased revenues by establishing the first renewable season ticket program in college gymnastics. To promote her sport further, she brought her vivaciousness and articulateness to weekly television with the first gymnastics coach's television show.

With the influx of fans from sports where intimidation of competitors is part of the game, fan behavior at some gymnastics meets became distracting to gymnasts, endangering them. Suzanne started a campaign to correct this practice at college gymnastics meets by publishing her philosophy and her "Fans' Code of Conduct" in the *NCAA News*.

Perhaps Suzanne's most challenging adventure has been her successful struggle in advancing the recognition and fair treatment of coaches and players, both men and women, of the nonrevenue-producing sports in college. Nearly every time I meet a coach of college gymnastics, she reminds me of her appreciation for what Suzanne has done for her and her sport.

I can continue, but I think that the story of Suzanne Yoculan, the evolution of college women's gymnastics as the exciting sport she envisioned a few years ago, and her experiences in accomplishing all that she has can be told much better in her own words. So buckle up, as you take this trip with Suzanne. With her at the helm it will be more like travel in a rocket ship than in a more conventional means of travel.

—BILL DONALDSON

Ten Years to the Top 1983–1993

The Super Six?

Forget that noise.

On Friday night, only one team deserved to be called super.

And you could have called them superhuman, and not gotten any argument.

Georgia.

Everybody else was merely mortal.

The top-seeded Bulldogs obliterated the record book by posting an NCAA-meet record score of 198.000—that's no misprint, folks—to convincingly capture the 1993 NCAA Women's Gymnastics Championship at Gill Coliseum.

Georgia scored five 10.0s and averaged 9.9 for twenty routines. It crushed Utah's year-old NCAA meet scoring standard of 195.65 and shattered championship marks on every apparatus except beam.

The excerpt above comes from an article titled, "A League of Their Own"—the same title Sarah Gilbert had given her book just a year earlier about the All-America Girls Baseball League formed during World War II. But this article was about gymnastics, and the author was apparently looking for a way to express his astonishment. It was by Brooks Hatch, writing in the *Corvallis Gazette Times*, Saturday, April 17, 1993.

"GymDogs" is what the late Clyde Bohler, one of our biggest fans, named the Georgia gymnastics team in the early nineties. The students quickly adopted the term, then the media.

The GymDogs had won our third national championship at Oregon State University the night before. The team liked Brook's writing so much we had his article laminated and hung in our gym back in Athens.

Later in the article Brooks continued, "The Bulldogs started out higher than Yoculan's heels and hemline and rocketed into orbit from there to thoroughly stun a crowd of 5,502 that had anticipated a three-way showdown between Georgia, Utah, and Alabama."

"Super Six" refers to the top-six teams from the preliminary meets the previous day, competing for the national team championship on Friday—like the "Final Four" in basketball.

"Yoculan's heels and hemline" relates to the media's fascination with my attire—it was beginning to get as much attention as the team's achievements. Brooks' analogy was a good one. The gymnasts were certainly soaring high. And I had worked long and hard to promote our program, capitalizing on almost anything that caught the media's fascination—including my high heels and short skirts.

As I read Brook's article, on Saturday morning, I was still "in orbit." We really did have the best night ever in collegiate gymnastics. We hit twenty-four of twenty-four routines—and *threw out* a bars score of 9.875!

But a reporter's assessment, no matter who he is, isn't quite as meaningful as the assessments of a coach's peers. And the one fellow coach whose reaction would be most important to me was Greg Marsden of Utah. His team won the first five NCAA Women's Gymnastics Championships—1982-1986. Covering the 1993 championships for the *Salt Lake Tribune,* Dick Rosetta quoted Greg Marsden: "You just witnessed the best collegiate gymnastics team ever." You have to realize that in those days Greg Marsden was known for his candor—not his diplomacy—to fully appreciate the significance of his assessment.

The GymDogs had, indeed, reached a pinnacle far above what any gymnastics expert would have admitted could be reached. In retrospect, it wasn't a pinnacle, but the leading edge of a plateau the GymDogs have been on ever since. Take a look at the Regional Qualifying Scores (RQS):

REGIONAL QUALIFYING SCORES
(A modification of season average scores)

Year	Georgia	# 2 Team	# 2 Score	Difference
1994	196.381	Utah	194.594	1.787
1995	196.725	Utah	196.075	0.650
1996	197.287	Alabama	196.806	0.481
1997	197.927	Michigan	196.892	1.035
1998	197.081	Michigan	196.337	0.774
1999	197.444	Alabama	197.088	0.356
Average Difference	0.847			

What makes the GymDogs' performance even more impressive is that we were "throwing" the most difficult tricks in college gymnastics—really putting on a show—and we didn't miss a single routine. And many of our tricks or skills—the terms are used to refer to individual moves during a routine—were every bit as difficult as those performed by Olympians of the day. When I say, "of the day," I'm referring to difficulty that would not even have been dreamed of by the best gymnasts in the world just ten years earlier. For example, in 1972 Olga Korbut startled the world by doing a back somersault on the beam. In 1993, at Corvallis, several GymDogs did two in a row, preceded by a back handspring. In 1972 nobody was doing double back somersaults in floor exercise. In the GymDogs' 1993 routines, Hope Spivey did a tucked double back with a full twist added, and Heather Stepp went one step further doing a piked double back with a full twist. I could go on. And I won't even try to describe Lori Strong's trick on the uneven bars. People who saw it don't believe it.

There were warning signs the dominance was coming. As indicated before, Coach Greg Marsden's Utah Utes had owned all the NCAA Championships since their inception in 1982. But in 1987, an upstart, fifth-seeded GymDog team slipped through the back door, in Marsden's own gym, to win the first NCAA National Championship by any team other than Utah. And we had the gall to do it again just two years later, when we were also seeded fifth.

In a couple more years the GymDogs began to come into the championships with season-average scores near the top every year, although mistakes opened the door for either Utah to come back or Alabama to begin flexing its muscles. But in 1993 the GymDogs not only came in seeded first, we came in undefeated, a first in women's collegiate gymnastics and a feat only matched, so far, by—who else?— the 1998 and 1999 GymDogs.

Where did the GymDogs come from? Only ten years before, in 1983, the University of Georgia Athletic Association was considering the elimination of women's gymnastics. The team had never won an SEC Championship or qualified for the first two NCAA Championships. Fewer than 200 fans (the gymnasts' boyfriends, roommates, and families) attended home meets. The coach, Rick Walton, resigned to take a job at Nebraska, where gymnastics was traditionally a popular sport.

The athletic association at Georgia was headed by Football Coach Vince Dooley, and he has always been considered frugal. On the football field, he coached a national championship team using a conservative, ball-control game. And he was the same way as a tight-fisted administrator. Gender equity was staring him in the face, and he needed lots of scholarships for women in sports that didn't cost much per participant. Gymnastics didn't fit this bill.

But I was so excited about the opportunity to accept my first college coaching job that none of that mattered when my husband, Sam, my five-year-old son, Adam, and I drove into Athens in our Toyota Corolla on a steamy, hot August day in 1983. Once I made up my mind I wanted the job, everything happened pretty fast. We drove down from Pennsylvania and looked for a place to rent.

It was August after the 1983 Sugar Bowl game in which Penn State beat Georgia for the national championship in football. The game was

Herschel Walker's last at Georgia. Sam and I were riding around town with Sam wearing a Penn State cap, and he was getting a lot of hand signs (birds) and people saying, "You need to take off that hat." We didn't realize what the problem was for a while. We didn't understand why people were so unfriendly. Was this the "Southern hospitality" we'd heard so much about? Then we realized it was the Penn State cap.

Actually, you have to know University of Georgia students to appreciate their reaction. They are pretty sophisticated. Although they are ardent supporters of their teams, they seem to jab at fans of their opponents with a sense of humor. So the "birds" were a type of recognition, "Okay, so you won. Big deal! I'd rather be a Dawg who lost than a Nittany Lion who won."

Sam and I hadn't come to appreciate the fans when we attended our first football game—with everybody barking. I thought, I don't know about this. Maybe it's time to go back north. I really only knew Georgia as a state you go through to visit relatives in Florida—that, and Jimmy Carter and peanuts. The coaching job was a great opportunity, but besides the fact that the University of Georgia was here, it wasn't exactly the place in the country I wanted to be. Now, I love it, but I just didn't know about Athens then.

In 1983, there was a men's gymnastics team here as well as a women's team, and the men and women practiced together in the gym. I didn't know any of the gymnasts. I hadn't recruited any of them. Kathy McMinn was the only senior on the team. Kathy had a great reputation and had been All-American for the three consecutive years before. She was one of the best gymnasts in the nation.

Steve Bonham was the men's coach at the time, and the men's team was very good. I had only one assistant coach. Carl Leland had worked with me during summers at Woodward Camp in Pennsylvania, so I asked him to come with me when I got the job. Actually he was only part-time, because he was attending graduate school.

My son, Adam, was starting kindergarten. One of the things I knew for sure was that it was important for a mother to be there after school. So the very first year, I established a schedule that would allow me to spend time with Adam after school. I held Tuesday practice at night and took Wednesdays off, which allowed me to pick Adam up from school on Tuesdays and Wednesdays.

The gym was in a converted, all-purpose facility (basketball court, auditorium, etc.) in the old women's physical education building, built in the 1920s. A stage, about four to five feet above the gym floor, was at one end of the gym, but a wall had been installed across the front so that only about two feet of the stage was still exposed. Old-timers tell me that fraternity and sorority dances were held there in the 1940s.

I loved our gym. I loved it because I could flip the switch and have an instantly warm training facility in the middle of the winter. Coming from Pennsylvania, I was tired of being in a freezing cold gym.

I loved it because it was cozy—actually crowded. The men's and women's teams were in the gym at the same time, which meant we had to have more equipment. None of the equipment was common to both men's and women's gymnastics except for the floor mat. I love that it was a "working gym" and everyone associated with either team did his or her part. In 1983, a lot of gyms didn't even have pits, filled with foam rubber to practice dismounts and landings. But before I came here, the athletes got in the gym and dug the pit themselves and did the concrete work. They did this under Lee Cunningham, a former coach, who was extremely helpful during my first five years here.

There were windows above the pit. At the end of practice, some of the team members would go over and unlock the windows so that they could climb the outside of the building and come back through at night. They'd jump into the pit and have parties in the gym. They thought I didn't know it was going on, but I used to come back behind them and lock the windows. Then they'd climb up the outside and not be able to get in.

Kathy McMinn remembers those days: "One of the nice things about going to a school and being on a team like that is you immediately have friends—there was the men's team and our team and we got along real well. We were always doing things together. So, on New

Year's Eve or somebody's birthday, we were always getting together. It was really nice. It was like having twenty or thirty friends instantly."

The gym was dirty. It was dusty. It was chalky. It was old. But we loved it, because it was ours. And there was something about being old versus being new. No one cared what we did in there. There was no one trying to control the facility. No one cared when we came. No one cared when we left. No one cared how loud we played the music. We had slumber parties in there. We had birthday parties. We did what we wanted.

It worked out great to have both gymnastics teams in the gym. Everybody helped each other. A lot of the girls dated the guys on the men's team. Steve Bonham, the men's coach, helped the woman's team, and I used to spot the guys in tumbling. And even though we often practiced at the same time, we seemed to have enough room, and we made it work.

I have nothing but great memories of those years. Steve was a very different person from me. He was detailed and focused, while I looked at the big picture. Together, we accomplished a lot.

My office back then was in the old trophy room on the main level of the coliseum. It housed about sixteen coaches of "nonrevenue-producing" sports in little cubicles. The room was maybe 25 by 50 feet, maybe 1,250 square feet. The gymnastics team, alone, has a suite of offices larger than that today. The cubicles were just partitioned off with barriers about five-feet high, so there was no privacy. And the cubicles were just big enough to fit a chair and a desk in.

My most vivid memory of the cubicles was of Sid Feldman, the volleyball coach. He occupied the cubicle just behind mine. Sid was from "up North" too, and he had what the Southerners describe as a typical, loud, Yankee voice. He sounded like he was amplified at about 200 watts in normal conversation, and I'm not exactly soft-spoken. At times, it was a problem. I had to come back into the office at night to call recruits in order to reach them at home, and it was difficult to hear if Sid was there too. I really didn't like to come to the coliseum at night because I was the only woman coach. At the time, we couldn't charge long distance calls from home to the university, but Coach Dooley finally changed that and allowed me to charge business calls from home. I think this was the first request for a policy change I made of him. There were to be many more.

Jack Bauerle was among the coaches in the old trophy room. After being a member of Georgia's swimming team, Jack became the women's swimming and diving coach in 1979 and coach of both women's and men's swimming and diving in 1983. His success has been phenomenal, originally under the absolute worse conditions imaginable: having to swim in the old Stegeman pool. But since he moved to the new Gabrielson Natatorium, adjacent to the gymnastics gym in the Ramsey Student Center, in 1996, the Georgia women swimmers have won four national championships, and five conference championships in the powerful SEC with other powerhouses such as Florida and Auburn. He's produced lots of Olympians—even gold medalists—and coached the women in the 2000 Olympics in Australia and in the World Championships in Spain in 2003.

Jack said, "All the coaches of the women's sports and other nonrevenue-producing sports had a special relationship in the early years. They say familiarity breeds contempt, but we had a pretty nice bond. We knew that we were all at the beginning of something very important— women's sports at the University of Georgia. Liz Murphey picked a lot of good people to be her coaches in the women's athletic program."

At the time, I thought my cubicle was the most wonderful office in the world. I didn't sit there and say, "Look at this small cubicle—this lack of space. How am I supposed to do my job?" To me, it was wonderful. It was an office. It was a place to work, and it provided an opportunity to do something and make something happen.

I didn't see any negatives at all when I first came here. I find that interesting, contrasting it with the new coaches today with the attitude, "What are you going to do for me? I can't build a program without more money. Sure, I could draw 10,000 people, like Suzanne, if I had her budget." But it's not about the budget. It's about the person. In all those years, I didn't see anything to discourage me or prevent me from being successful.

I didn't consciously think about negativism as being so terrible at the time. But it really is an impediment to progress. Recently Heather Whitestone McCallum, the 1995 Miss America who is totally deaf, said in a presentation at the University or Georgia, "A negative attitude is the worst handicap in the whole world." Who should know better than she?

There were three freshmen on the 1984 team. Jana Jackson and Jodi Thompson were recruited by Rick Walton, the previous coach. Terri Eckert came with me. I had coached Terri since she was nine years old. Two weeks after Sam and I moved, in August, Carolyn and Lee Eckert, Terri's parents, called me on the phone and said, "Terri just can't stay up here. She needs to come with you." So they worked it out with Terri's high school in Pennsylvania for Terri to take correspondence courses from the school, and Terri moved in with us. She lived with us for a couple of months. One amusing aspect of her living with us was that other coaches were recruiting her, but they didn't realize that she was staying at our house. So I'd answer the phone and say, "Just a minute, please." Then I'd whisper, "Terri, it's Greg Marsden."

Sam and I encouraged Terri to visit other schools, and we actually thought it might be best for her to go to a school other than Georgia. The reason for her coming down here was not for her to attend the University of Georgia. She was like a family member. Terri went to the Atlanta School of Gymnastics to practice, and lived with us in Athens. About six weeks after Terri moved here, I got a letter from the NCAA saying that Terri must move out of our house within three days. If she didn't move out, she was not eligible to be recruited by the University of Georgia. They said I was in NCAA violation, even though Sam and I had legal guardianship of Terri. Someone at another team learned that Terri was living with us and reported it to the NCAA. That was my first experience with the NCAA. It was horrible, because Terri didn't know what to do. She cried for three days. She decided to move to Atlanta and live with a family there for two months.

I hadn't planned to sign Terri until after the 1984 season. But she wanted to train with me for an elite meet, and the only way she could do that was to become a GymDog. So when she finished high school by correspondence, she enrolled at the University of Georgia in January 1984, at age seventeen. That's how Terri Eckert became a GymDog on the 1984 team.

I knew right away we had a team of only five or six committed athletes: Jodi Thompson, Jana Jackson, Laurie Jones, Laurie Reiff, Stacy Cook, and Kathy McMinn. And then, of course, Terri. The rest of the girls were "college students doing gymnastics." Stacey Cook was also an elite gymnast. She was great and was from the Atlanta School of Gymnastics.

Before the season, I wanted to make sure the press understood that I had actually inherited a pretty good team. I didn't want to lead them to believe I'd work miracles. In discussing the expectations for success that were being kicked around by the press, I told interviewers, "I think it's very important that this will not be a rebuilding year for our team. We have to reorganize a bit, but we're not rebuilding. Georgia finished eleventh nationally last year, and any team that can be that young and do that well doesn't have to rebuild. The key to our success will be to stay healthy, because we don't have enough depth to lose our gymnasts to injury. The optimism and enthusiasm is extremely high. There's really great unity on this team."

College gymnastics had changed big-time in the twelve years between when I was on the team as a freshman at Penn State and when I came to Georgia. At Penn State, it was like an intramural sport. Anybody could come out for the team. We had forty girls out there. The team at Georgia was a "for-real" team. Scholarships were available and you could recruit. The NCAA limit for scholarships was ten at the time, but we only had seven or eight the first two years I was here, when we finished ninth and seventh in the nation. In going from AIAW (Association of Intercollegiate Athletics for Women) to NCAA, major changes took place in women's college gymnastics.

Because of the good program Georgia had in 1983, many schools wanted to compete against us. We had our work cut out for us with four of the top-ten teams in the country on our schedule in 1984.

Our major goal in 1984 was to just keep everybody healthy. Most gymnastics teams carry twelve people or more. We didn't have a lot of depth. But as I told the press, "We have some great girls, and we don't expect to lose. Florida's favored in our region. Georgia finished fourth in the SEC last year, and we hope to move up to second or third this year. In two or three years, I'd like for Georgia to be among the top-three teams in the country. It takes work, and I've had tremendous support since I've been here. The athletic department has been very, very supportive." The map I laid out was followed precisely, except we actually overshot each goal. My remarks to the press were not just idle boasting. I knew what I wanted to achieve, what I had to do to achieve our goals, and that we could do it.

We lost our first meet—by 0.4 point to Alabama. Back then the team to beat in the SEC was Florida. We didn't beat them in regular season competition for four years. But I remember our winning the "Red and White Classic." Alabama had that invitational for years and years and they always won it. And then we came along and rained on their red-and-white parade.

That might have been the start of what has become the greatest rivalry in women's college gymnastics.

With the toughest schedule I could arrange, the GymDogs won fourteen and lost only three in the regular season, losing to Ohio State and Florida on the road, in addition to that opening home meet to Alabama. And we did move up in the SEC Championship, coming second to Florida, and we came in second to the Gators again in the NCAA Regionals.

Travel in those days was certainly different from what it is today. We always had four people in a room in hotels. We had thirteen people in one van. I can remember traveling back from Gainesville with three or four girls lying on the floor at our feet—at four o'clock in the morning. Terri Eckert was always on the floor, trying to stretch out to sleep. It was dangerous. That's the biggest thing, the fact that it was dangerous. We were traveling at night and everyone was half-asleep. But no one ever complained, because no one ever knew anything different. It was the same for all the nonrevenue-producing sports.

Today, travel is by chartered busses—state-of-the-art models—for meets within a few hours drive, chartered planes for intermediate distances, and travel on scheduled airliners for cross-country trips.

I left three gymnasts at home for the Florida meet in 1984 because they were overweight. I wanted to make a point that you can't compete in gymnastics if you're not strong and in condition. Competing out of condition is contagious, as soon as you allow two or three to compete out of weight limits. We weighed the gymnasts underwater and determined the percent body fat, which determined the upper-weight limit. We only had four gymnasts compete on each event at that Florida meet. That really upset Ernestine Weaver, the Florida coach.

My expectations were a whole lot higher than the girls' expectations were for themselves. When we went to Disney World after regionals at Gainesville, ten of us crowded into and around a phone booth to call to find out if we made it to the NCAA Nationals. There were five regions scattered around the country, and the top-ten scores of all the teams in all the regions combined qualified for nationals. Of course we went in ninth as a team, the first time a University of Georgia team ever went to the NCAA Championships. There was never any doubt in my mind that we would qualify. But the gymnasts were overwhelmed and almost knocked over the phone booth in adulation.

The NCAA Championships had been established only two years prior to 1984. The AIAW Championships existed before that, but qualification procedures were somewhat non-uniform. Most authorities agree that meaningful national championship competition in women's college gymnastics began with the first NCAA-sanctioned Championships in 1982 at Salt Lake City. In team competition only five gymnasts competed on each event, and four scores counted for the 1982 format.

Utah won the 1982 championship going away—148.6 to second

place Cal. State-Fullerton's 144.15. Utah had lost three meets during the season, but as Coach Greg Marsden put it, "We beat the best, and we beat them easily," in the championships.

Megan McCunniff—who later became Megan Marsden and is still her husband Greg's chief assistant coach—was the odds on favorite to win the all-around competition, but an uncharacteristic three falls on the uneven bars knocked Megan out of the meet. However, another Ute, Sue Stednitz, came through and won the all-around. Utes won the individual competition on two other events as well. Stednitz won beam, and Elaine Alfano won vaulting. Lisa Shirk, of Pittsburgh, was the uneven bars champion, and Oregon State gymnast, Mary Ayotte-Law won the floor exercise.

In 1983, the format was changed to count the best five of six scores. Megan McCunniff lived up to expectations this time by winning the all-around with a score of 37.50. Utah's 184.65 won the team championships, while the Ute's Elaine Alfano won the individual championship on vaulting again. Jeri Cameron (Arizona State) won bars, Julie Goewey (Cal. State-Fullerton) won beam, and Kim Neal (Arizona State) was the floor champion.

Although Georgia's 1983 team didn't qualify for nationals, Kathy McMinn, as an individual qualifier, made a splash by coming in third in the all-around. About her floor exercise, *International Gymnast* (*IG*) reported: "She displayed unmatched amplitude in her tumbling and leaps and the best double back of the competition." Kathy made All-American in vaulting, floor, bars, and the all-around at the AIAW, as she did in 1981. She did not compete in the 1982 NCAA Championships.

In 1984 I brought the first college team I had ever coached to the NCAA National Championships, which were held outside Salt Lake City for the first time—at UCLA's Pauley Pavilion. I was unquestionably the new kid on the block, but I wasn't the least bit intimidated by all of my opposing coaches' experience.

Coach	Team	Year As Head Coach
John Spini	Arizona State	fourth
Jim Gault	Arizona	fourth
Bob Ito	Washington	fourth
Jerry Tomlinson	UCLA	fifth
Ernestine Weaver	Florida	fifth
Sarah Patterson	Alabama	sixth
Lynn Rogers	Fullerton	ninth
Greg Marsden	Utah	ninth
Judi Avener★	Penn State	tenth

★*Judi, who coached at Florida from 1993 through 2002, is now Judi Markel.*

In 1984, ten teams went to nationals. The first day was for the team national championship. A team was in either the evening or afternoon session based on its ranking. The second day was for individual finals.

With only seven gymnasts competing, the GymDogs placed ninth, but we let the world of college gymnastics know that we expected to be back. And we have come back *every year.* Freshman Terri Eckert wasn't intimidated either as she placed tenth in the all-around, just 1.05 points behind the repeat winner, Megan Marsden, who also won the vaulting championship. Other individual champions were Jackie Brummer, Arizona State, (bars); Heidi Anderson, Oregon State, (beam); and Maria Anz, Florida (floor). Utah still owned the team championship with a score of 186.05, over 8 points better than the GymDogs' 177.60.

Kathy McMinn repeated her All-American honors on vault and uneven bars.

When I was considering the Georgia job, Rick Walton, the former Georgia coach, told me, "You'll never do anything at Georgia. There's no support there." So it's a bit ironic that Georgia qualified for nationals, and Nebraska, the team Rick left to coach, didn't make it.

All four of the returning GymDogs improved their all-around average score in 1984 over their 1983 score. The team improved its average score by over 3 points, from 178.50 to 181.90.

I recruited my first gymnasts, except for Terri from the year before, for the 1985 season. So we could begin to put together a philosophy and set the direction of the team in terms of expectations.

In recruiting those days we were not allowed in-house visits. We didn't fly up and have contacts, like we do today. We invited the recruits in for an official visit, and the rest was all phone calling. Unlimited phone calls were allowed back then. Paula Maheu, Tanya Schuler, and Gina Bañales were all Pennsylvania kids. I did a lot of recruiting from that area because I knew the coaches and I knew the programs—the carry-over from being a club coach there. That really helped Georgia from the outset in terms of getting some top recruits.

Gina Bañales was an elite gymnast and one of the top kids in the country. I had coached her for years. Back then, signing was always in April.

Of the Pennsylvania gymnasts I mentioned above, only Gina Bañales was a freshman in the 1985 season. Maheu and Schuler came later. Joining Gina in the 1985 class were freshmen Jackie Hastey, Julie Klick, Morgan Lewis, Sydney McAllister, Susie Origer, and Michelle Sessions. Sherri Stryker transferred from Auburn. The two Lauries, Jana, Stacy, Jodie, and Terri returned from the seven-gymnast 1984 team. That's fourteen gymnasts on the roster. I was beginning to get some breathing room. And with future All-Americans Julie, Gina, and Terri, the talent level was going up.

With more gymnasts, I needed more coaches, so I persuaded Kathy McMinn to coach while in graduate school. Herbert Etchison, a former Bulldog gymnast from the men's team, also was an assistant coach. He helped with promotions too. Support staff was limited, relative to today, so every coach had two, three, or more assignments.

Performance was going up too. Perhaps the most impressive statistic was that the GymDogs continued winning at home. We lost only one meet in 1984, beginning a thirty-five and zero home record that extended until the last home meet in 1988, against UCLA. This certainly didn't hurt home-meet attendance. Fans like to win. While the GymDogs were still unable to beat Florida or win a conference championship in 1985, we qualified for the NCAA Championships again.

Dwight Normile, writing for *IG*, described the team's performance at nationals: "Ranked ninth beforehand, Georgia was a pleasant surprise to take seventh place. Suzanne Yoculan has done a lot in building this southeastern power. The daring Gina Bañales made it to the bars finals. Had the team stayed on beam it may have moved up another notch. As a team, the Bulldogs were second only to Florida in tumbling difficulty. Terri Eckert is a name that will be heard in years to come, finishing in tenth place in the all-around for the second year in a row. Eckert also tied for second on bars and took second on beam."

Qualifying for the individual championships made Gina an All-American on the bars and Terri an All-American on bars and beam.

According to *IG*, "Many experts had put their money on Florida to take the team title away from Utah. Coached by Ernestine Weaver, the Gators were undefeated in the 1984-85 dual meet season." But the Utes pulled it out again, with their 188.35 score 4.05 points above third-place Florida and 7.45 above seventh-place Georgia. It was clear that the GymDogs were not even close to being a threat to win it all—yet.

Penny Hauschild (Alabama) won the all-around competition and the bars. Elaine Alfano and Lisa Mitzel (both of Utah) won the vault and floor exercise respectively, and Lisa Zeis (Arizona State) won the beam.

Between the 1985 and 1986 seasons, I made what turned out to be, unquestionably, the most important personnel move in my tenure at Georgia. When I got here I started looking for another assistant coach. I wanted somebody local. I wanted somebody familiar with the clubs and the coaches in the state—to get some support from the developing gym clubs in Georgia. I really thought that would be a big part of the future. Everywhere I went one name came up, Doug McAvinn. Doug, of course, is still with the team. No one will challenge the assertion that today Doug is the most respected assistant coach in college women's gymnastics.

With Doug coming in, my expectations continued to rise, and the talent level of the team continued to rise also. There were no seniors on the 1986 team. Four freshmen joined the team, and they were all potential stars. Debbie Greco came in with international experience. Tanya Schuler was an elite qualifier, and Paula Maheu would make All-American as a freshman. And Lucy Wener was the first heralded gymnast ever to come to Georgia, having been on the 1984 U.S. Olympic Team.

Team performance in the 1986 season was beginning to reflect the new talent level. The GymDogs defeated Florida for the first time in a dual meet. Then we defeated both Florida and Alabama to win the SEC Championship. And we defeated Florida a third time in winning the NCAA Southeast Regional Meet. Julie Klick won the SEC all-around championship.

The NCAA Championships were held in Gainesville, Florida in 1986. All previous championships had been held at the University of Utah, except in 1984, which was at UCLA. Competition was getting tighter. Ultimately some team would dethrone Utah. After the Alabama Crimson Tide scored a 186.35 in the afternoon session, Coach Sarah Patterson sounded the challenge: "I dare another team to go out there and be perfect like we were." The Tide had hit twenty-four routines, but don't ever issue a challenge to Greg Marsden. Utah matched the perfection of Alabama and scored 186.95, just edging out Arizona State's 186.70. Alabama's score was only good enough for third place.

From *IG:* "Georgia (fourth, at 185.45) looked to be in excellent physical and mental condition for its run for the roses. Suzanne Yoculan's team won the floor (46.75), with sophomore Gina Bañales (9.45) and freshman Paula Maheu (whip through to double back, second pass ending in double back, 9.50) advancing to finals. Georgia also tied Fullerton for the top-team score on bars (46.75) thanks to Lucy Wener's 9.70."

Notice that the new talent was beginning to shine. The differential between the GymDogs' team score and the champion's was shrinking. Four GymDogs made All-American: Bañales (floor), Klick (beam), Maheu (floor), and Wener (bars).

Of course, the most treasured prize was Lucy Wener's winning the individual championship on bars. From *IG:* "A knee injury limited Georgia freshman Lucy Wener (1984 U.S. Olympian) to less than competitive vault and floor efforts, but she was superb on bars, leading the field at 9.70." Lucy became the first of what would be many—more than any other team at this writing—GymDog individual national champions.

Alabama's Penny Hauschild repeated as all-around champion, tying Arizona State's Jackie Brummer. Kim Neal (Arizona State) and Pam Loree (Penn State) tied for the vault championship. Burmmer also won the beam, and Hauschild tied with Arizona State's Lisa Zeis on floor.

The GymDogs were beginning to be a force at the NCAA Championships. Contrast the 1986 performance with that of our first year, just two years before. But for me the biggest event of 1986 was the birth of my daughter, Alexis, in the summer.

The men's gymnastics team at Georgia was disbanded after the 1986 season. All of the women's coaches and the gymnasts were sad to see this finally happen, although it had been planned for several years. Gender equity was forcing colleges to eliminate scholarships for some men's teams in order to improve the ratio of women's scholarships to men's. Most schools in the SEC focused on establishing and retaining sports in which there could be competition against other conference teams. There was a uniform agreement. To provide for intraconference competition, each school was encouraged to develop teams in the same sports as the other schools. Because women's gymnastics was expensive in terms of cost per athlete, the outstanding national rankings of its six teams may have been what kept the gymnastics teams alive.

Only two freshmen joined the team for the 1987 season, but they were both superstars. Andrea Thomas was on the 1984 Canadian Olympic Team and placed fourteenth in the all-around at the Olympic Games. Corrinne Wright was a member of the U.S. National Team in both 1985 and 1986. No team in the country had two more highly regarded recruits. We had now recruited gymnasts for three years to be on the team with the lone senior, Terri. We were definitely developing a flavor I had become known for—go-for-broke routines, lots of enthusiasm, and a belief that we could beat any team at anytime.

The 1987 regular season record was our best yet. We lost only to Ohio State with a miserable performance in the opening meet in Columbus, Ohio and to LSU in Baton Rouge. The GymDogs won the SEC for the second consecutive year. Our only other loss for the entire season, prior to nationals, was at the NCAA Regional meet, where we came in second to Florida.

In those days the format for the NCAA Championships seemed to change continually. The number of qualifying teams was increased to twelve. Because of Georgia's poor showing at regionals, we were seeded fifth, behind one-UCLA, two-Alabama, three-Utah, and four-Arizona State. After the fourth rotation in the team competition, UCLA was leading with a score of 94.25, followed by Georgia, 93.85, Utah, 93.25, and Alabama, 92.60. But when the final dust settled, the scoring printouts showed Georgia's 187.90 was barely enough to win, by the second slimmest margin in the short NCAA history, over Utah's 187.55.

Excerpts from *IG*'s report: "1987 marks the end of a five-year Utah dynasty, and, with top elites entering the collegiate ranks each year, the age of the dynasty may well have come to an end . . . While the partisan crowd was at times a bit rough on the visiting teams, the college game atmosphere made this meet unlike any other. Once the team competition was over the fans were very, very fair, even to Georgia. They really do appreciate good gymnastics in Salt Lake City."

Oklahoma's phenomenal Kelly Garrison-Steves won the all-around championship; Yumi Mordre from Washington won the vault and the balance beam; UCLA's Kim Hamilton won the floor exercise; and Lucy repeated as the uneven-bars champion.

Five GymDogs made All-America: Corrinne Wright (all-around, floor), Julie Klick (all-around, floor), Lucy Wener (bars), Terri Eckert (floor), and Andrea Thomas (beam).

Incidentally, Andrea Thomas' beam score of 9.7 during the team competition was higher than Mordre's winning score in the individual competition the next night. But I'm sure Andrea wouldn't trade her championship ring for the individual trophy, and her beam performance was a big factor in the team score.

People told me that my after-the-meet remarks displayed a combination of in-your-face confidence and admission of concern before the meet. To be honest I knew we could win if we hit our routines because our routines had bigger scoring potential. If we did well on vaulting and bars, the other teams could not match our scores. Then when we were on beam, UCLA was on a bye and watching us on what had been their strongest event. When we came off beam with that 47.4 score, I knew we had taken charge of the meet.

After watching UCLA warm up, I thought they were so far ahead of us we couldn't beat them, even with our best performance. But, hey, we did well, and some of their kids fell. It just goes to show you've got to keep on dreaming.

But let's get real about the 1987 team. It should not have been shocking that we won the championship. We had been ranked second most of the year behind either Utah or UCLA, and at the end of the regular season, going into the SEC Championships, we were ranked number one. On March 8, at a home meet, we scored the highest team score in NCAA history, a 191.55. It didn't go into the NCAA record books, however, because only those scores in the NCAA Regionals and the NCAA Nationals, where judges are assigned by the NCAA committee, count as official national records.

On several occasions Sarah Patterson said that she thought Georgia was the best team in the country. It was probably the relatively poor showing at regionals, coming in second, behind Florida, that threw people off guard about our potential. Even that poor showing, which counted as two-thirds of our qualifying score, left us seeded fifth. Nevertheless, winning in Salt Lake City, where Utah had never lost, posed a formidable task for any team.

The icing on the cake came when Lucy's picture was on the cover of the *International Gymnast* July 1987 issue. College gymnastics was beginning to get recognized as an exciting sport with tremendously gifted athletes.

There was a bad news–good news story with regard to coaches between the 1987 and 1988 seasons. Carl Leland left the staff and Scott Bull joined it. Scott had been an assistant at UCLA for six years, so he was the most experienced coach on the staff in terms of coaching at the college level. Scott was a competent coach for any event, but he concentrated primarily on bars, and he and Doug shared responsibilities for the strength and conditioning program.

Terri Eckert was the lone senior on the 1987 team. Everyone else from the national championship team returned for 1988. But, unfortunately only Lynn Messer of the four 1988 freshmen, including Shannon Abel, Debbie DeMasi, and Leigh Herman, returned for the 1989 season. Injuries were the major problem for the team, with as many as seven of the twelve gymnasts hobbling at one point in the season.

Even with all of the misfortunes, the GymDogs managed to establish a record that most teams would envy. We tied eventual national champion Alabama, in Alabama, and defeated them in Athens. The only losses during the season were to LSU in Baton Rouge, UCLA in Athens, and Florida in Gainesville. The SEC meet was held in Tuscaloosa, and Alabama was already beginning to gel for the postseason. Georgia placed second to Alabama in the SEC. Then we won the Southeastern Regional meet and went into nationals seeded fifth again. You may be wondering about the SEC Championships and Regionals. Since 1983, of the six SEC teams, only three are in the region with Georgia—Florida and Kentucky are the other two. In the sixteen years (1984–1999) that the regional championships were comprised exclusively of teams from within the region, Georgia and Florida gobbled up all of the regional championships, with the GymDogs taking thirteen of them.

Alabama, with a score of 190.05, won its first NCAA Championship by 0.55 points over second-place Utah. UCLA was third, LSU fourth, Georgia fifth, and Florida sixth. Four SEC teams were in the top six. The conference was clearly established as the strongest in the country, and it has remained such ever since.

About Georgia's performance *IG* reported: "The defending national championships were not expecting miracles this year. Coach Suzanne Yoculan claims that the team had an inconsistent year both in practice and in meets. They had some injuries and other factors that kept them from being their best throughout the season and in NCAAs. A fifth-place showing is certainly respectable for a struggling year." "Respectable" or not, I wasn't pleased with fifth place, which tied for the lowest GymDogs' finish since 1985.

Troubles continued for the GymDogs even in the individual competition. From *IG:* "Also notable in the finals was two-time defending champion Lucy Wener, who unfortunately came off an in-bar Jeager following her beat uprise straddle vault over high bar to edge grip. The Georgia junior, however, knows how to work the uneven bars."

For the second year in a row, Oklahoma's fabulous Kelly Garrison-Steves won the all-around. She almost swept the individual competition, as she also won the bars and beam. UCLA gymnasts took the other two events, with Jill Andrews winning vaulting and Kim Hamilton winning the floor exercise.

The difference between the winning score and the fifth-place score or the tenth-place score decreased also. This reflected the increase in the number of good teams, increasing the likelihood that the number of teams who have won national championships will increase in years to come.

So many changes took place during my first five years. There was clearly a change in leadership from Utah, alone, to a scramble among several teams. I don't want to place too much emphasis on the national championship as the sole determinant of the strongest team. Indeed, with more parity among the teams developing, the strongest team may win less than half the time. Besides Utah, Georgia, and Alabama, other teams making serious bids for the title were Arizona State, Florida, and UCLA.

Attendance was increasing at venues other than Salt Lake City, and the Georgia-Alabama rivalry was attracting national attention.

New GymDogs in 1989 included Kathy Dwyer, a transfer from Old Dominion, and freshmen Melissa DePaoli, Julie Ponstein, and Chris Rodis. Of the three, Julie had the most impressive credentials. She qualified as an elite gymnast in 1987.

Georgia was to host the 1989 NCAA National Championships. Just prior to the season I said, "Wouldn't it be awesome if we could win it right here in front of our home fans?" Well, it didn't look like that would happen, based on the funk the GymDogs were in at the beginning of the season. We averaged under 188.0 during our first six meets and lost to Cal State-Fullerton (twice), UCLA, and Arizona State. Our national ranking fell all the way to fourteenth midway through the season, the lowest the GymDogs had been ranked since I became coach. But then it appeared as if a different team began competing. The next three scores were 190.0, 191.4, and 191.95. Then our score of 190.4 was only good enough to come in third, behind Florida and Alabama in the tough SEC Championships. But we bounced back by breaking the NCAA scoring record in the regionals, posting a 193.20, 2.15 points better than second-place Florida.

It certainly appeared as if the GymDogs had the momentum to bring that championship back to Georgia, but number-one seed UCLA had been awesome during the season. The team had scored an unbelievable 195.20 in winning the Pac-10 Championship, and Coach Jerry Tomlinson had promised his fans an NCAA Championship. UCLA has won more national championships in NCAA-sanctioned sports than any other school; there was probably pressure on him to add women's gymnastics to the list of teams that had won championships.

There has never been a more dramatic finish to the NCAA Team Championships than what happened in Athens on April 14, 1995. The format still called for all twelve teams to compete in two sessions on Friday. Teams seeded seven through twelve competed in the afternoon, and the one through six seeds competed in the evening. Seeded fifth, Georgia barely made the evening session. Under this format, with the judges holding back in awarding high scores in the afternoon, it was almost impossible for a team competing in the afternoon to win the championship.

Number-one-seed UCLA was the odds-on favorite to win the title. And the team almost did. The drama came on the final rotation. In the previous rotation, UCLA had to count two falls on the balance beam, scoring a 47.30, while Georgia was scoring a sizzling 48.50 on floor. The GymDogs were finished, with a bye on the last rotation, and the Bruins needed a 48.70 on the floor exercise to tie Georgia. The last gymnast to perform was the eventual national champion on the event, Kim Hamilton. Kim would have to score 9.95 to tie Georgia. Her performance was elegant as she matched her career high of 9.90, leaving the Bruins 0.05 point short, the absolute smallest scoring increment at that time.

At least two gymnasts from the 1989 UCLA team are still prominent in collegiate gymnastics. Kim Hamilton, now Kim Anthony, is as near-perfect as a color commentator for gymnastics with ESPN as she was on the floor exercise at UCLA. Tanya Service is now Tanya Chaplin, head coach of the Oregon State Beavers.

Jerry Tomlinson's remarks to *IG* reflected his disappointment at the 1989 championships: "To train so hard and so right it's really hard when the kids come out and do everything so right. It's the best year we've ever had. A lot of our kids did their personal best performances tonight. You'll always have some wins and some losses. It's just really disappointing. We train human beings at UCLA. We try to teach them what will happen when they're done with gymnastics."

IG commented on Georgia's victory: "Suzanne Yoculan expressed it best when she said, 'It's magic.' Magic, indeed, for Georgia was picked by many to finish no higher than third in the Southeastern Conference. But after losing to Florida in the SEC Championships, the Lady Bulldogs raised their performance level above the stratosphere to down the Gators in the NCAA Southeast Regional and claw their way to the national title. And the Lady Bulldog fans in the

Georgia Coliseum barked their approval with each routine. Dogs and gymnastics? Go figure."

Four GymDogs brought home nine All-American honors: Corrinne Wright (all-around, vault, beam, and floor), Andrea Thomas (beam), Lucy Wener (all-around, uneven bars, floor), and Chris Rodis (vault).

Taking a look at the individual championships, one would not have considered the GymDog's team victory a fluke. Georgia's Corrinne Wright won the all-around and tied with UCLA's Kim Hamilton on the floor exercise. The tie was certainly fitting. It would be impossible to choose a clear-cut winner between the two. They had little in common. Kim was slender and willowy, and her floor exercise was graceful and balletic. At four feet ten inches, Corrinne was a little dynamo, with a fiery routine filled with powerful tumbling, the most impressive being her layout double back. GymDog Lucy Wener won her third uneven bars championship. Rounding out the individual championships were Kim Hamilton on vault and Jill Andrews (UCLA) and Joy Selig (Oregon State) tying on the balance beam.

As "magic" as it was, the team championship for the GymDogs might have been anticlimactic had the individual championships been on Friday and the team championships on Saturday, instead of the reverse.

Again from *IG:* "Yoculan's Lady Bulldogs had already won their second team title in three years just twenty-four hours earlier, but Wener's few moments on the bars was the time they'd remember most. Wener concluded a perfect routine with a perfect dismount, and the judges rewarded her with the first 10.00 ever in NCAA Championships history. What can you say? In her four years at Georgia, Wener has been the nation's premier bars performer, and it is unlikely we will see another with the strength and grace of a Lucy Wener for some time to come."

In June of 2000, quite fittingly, Lucy was among the first eighteen University of Georgia athletes selected (from thousands in intercollegiate competition spanning over a hundred years) for the university's highest athletic award, The Circle of Honor. That says worlds for what women's gymnastics has become in this "football school."

The *IG* article on the meet concluded with a statement that confirmed the coming of the GymDog's dynasty: "In its first year as host of the NCAAs, Georgia proved to be a gracious—but very ambitious—one. By taking the team title, all-around title, and two of the four individual titles, Georgia proved that it is a force to be reckoned with—as long as Suzanne Yoculan's leather skirt can stay wrinkle-free."

The 1989 season signaled that the GymDogs had not quite reached the absolute top yet, considering our sub-par performance during the regular season and the razor-thin victory.

Graduation hit the 1989 team hard: Debbie Greco, Paula Maheu, Tanya Schuler, and Lucy Wener. Ouch!

But look at what was coming in: Lisa Alecia (New York), Sandy Rowlette (Florida), and Heather Stepp (Michigan) were elite-level gymnasts with plenty of honors. And Jennifer Carbone (New York), Debbie Still (Georgia), and Traci Tilton (Georgia) were national competitors with a plethora of state championships.

We were beginning to like the feel of winning national championships, and we set a 1990 goal of beginning as the nation's top team and winning the conference, regional, and national championships. It was certainly conceivable that we could meet the challenge, but replacing seniors with freshmen is risky business.

Things started out well for the 1990 season. The GymDogs defeated ten consecutive opponents before losing to Alabama at a three-team meet with Florida, in Tuscaloosa, 191.75 to 190.85. We pasted Florida (185.65) in that meet, but lost to the Gators the following week in Gainesville by a scant 0.05 point. The GymDogs would not lose again until the SEC Championships, where we lost to Alabama and Florida, in Athens. The GymDogs bounced back for the regionals by topping our previous year's record score. The NCAA Championship appeared within our grasp again, but we were no shoe-in.

It was becoming clear that the problem in the college gymnastics scoring system was getting more critical. The system had just not kept up with the caliber of gymnasts who were coming into college gymnastics. Georgia threw the most difficult tricks our gymnasts were capable of performing safely and consistently. But our superior gymnastics was not rewarded. Here's how *IG* explained it:

> Women's college gymnastics has long been criticized for inflated scores and failure to award the best competitors. . . . The problem is readily explainable. First, the NCAA competition I rules, which require only two C moves. Add a couple of tricks with bonus (there are plenty) and a D and you start from a 10.0. And since less difficulty is needed, athletes of this caliber can hit near flawless sets in every meet.
>
> Also the code is interpreted more literally in collegiate meets. A "D" is a "D," whether easy or hard (all D skills are hard), and the distinction is rarely made. Of course a floor set with a double layout and two double backs will score big, but so will one with only one double back, a layout front-full, and an Arabian front-1 1/4. All six passes are of D value and both routines easily exceed the requirements. What's a judge to do?
>
> The Bulldogs' ("Roof! Roof!") difficulty, a trademark of Suzanne Yoculan's high powered program, puts everyone to shame.

The statement addresses what I've been trying to change as long as I've been a coach. But I wish the writer could spell "Woof! Woof!"

There is little of significance about the 1990 NCAA Championships, held at Oregon State, in Corvallis. The teams finished exactly as they were seeded. Number-one-ranked Utah was the only team to defeat number-two-ranked Alabama during the season, and Alabama returned the favor, so each team came in with one loss. In winning the championship, Utah obliterated Georgia's record score (192.65) with a 194.90, only 0.325 ahead of Alabama. Georgia edged

UCLA for third place, with Nebraska and LSU coming in fifth and sixth respectively. Three SEC teams were in the top-six finishers.

A new star was born in Alabama's Dee Dee Foster, a freshman who won the all-around with a new record of 39.30. Michele Bryant (Nebraska) won the vault, Marie Roethlisberger (Minnesota) won bars, and Joy Selig (Oregon State) won beam and floor. Joy's beam championship was her second in a row.

Only two GymDogs made All-American in 1990—Chris Rodis on bars and Corrinne in the all-around.

Scott Bull left the coaching staff after the 1990 season to become co-head coach at UCLA. Jay Clark, a student majoring in exercise and sports science, was working part-time at the sports medicine clinic used by the GymDogs, and became captivated by the gymnastics program. He had played football and tennis in high school, but had no gymnastics experience. During the 1990 season, this "gym rat" began helping the coaches with spotting, and he caught our eye—we recognized his rapport with the gymnasts, his intense interest, and his ability to learn exceptionally fast. Appreciating that these invaluable assets are rare and that Doug and I could teach Jay about gymnastics, we brought him on as a student assistant for the 1991 season. Because of Scott's departure, Jay worked primarily with the uneven bars.

We also took advantage of the availability of another gymnastics enthusiast, Delene Darst. Delene, a member of the National Gymnastics Hall of Fame, has a résumé that would fill half this book. She helped coach the 1984 U.S. Olympic Team, and is considered one of the top judges in the world. Delene commuted from her home in Duluth, Georgia, as a part-time, volunteer coach, working primarily with the balance beam.

Losing Andrea Thomas and Corrinne Wright to graduation was a huge loss to the GymDogs. But Hope Spivey and Kelly Macy constituted the most talented freshman duo in the country in 1991. Kelly was a two-time national team member, and Hope was on the 1988 U.S. Olympic Team. They more than lived up to their billing in their first year.

The GymDogs got off to a good start defeating UCLA, Arizona State, and Washington. But then we lost an unprecedented (for a team I coached) two home meets in a row—to Utah and then to Alabama. The experience made a lasting impression on me. I made up my mind it would not happen again. The GymDogs would not lose another regular season home meet for the next eight seasons.

After a controversy at the Utah meet in Athens, the athletic administration considered canceling the meet with Utah in Salt Lake City on March 9. I was ready to cancel, but when the administration suggested that we should compete, I reluctantly took our team to Salt Lake City. The meet cost the GymDogs more than just a second loss to Utah. Sophomore Heather Stepp was having a stellar year—she had already recorded a 39.25 all-around. The GymDogs were doing touch warm-ups on vault at the Utah meet, when Heather over-rotated on her front handsprings and stuck out her arm to catch herself. She essentially destroyed her elbow. The broken bone was a compression fracture, the most difficult to repair. Back home, Kurt Gelfand, a member of the medical team treating her, said, "It was a mess. Out first thoughts were not gymnastics. Our first thoughts were to get her a good elbow. When I looked in there I doubted that this girl would ever be doing full-scale gymnastics. It was a very complex, severe injury—typically career ending." Heather's injury just devastated the whole team. But what the doctors did not know was that while Heather was still in the hospital after her surgery, she told me that her dream was to be on a championship team and she'd be back to see that that happened.

The GymDogs lost the meet to Utah, and then we finished our regular season by defeating Brigham Young two days later.

But drama wasn't over for the team. At the SEC Championships in Lexington, Kentucky, Georgia was competing on floor last. Alabama had already completed its fourth event and was "sitting in the clubhouse" with a 194.05. Lisa Alicea was nursing a broken toe, so Georgia was planning to use only five gymnasts on floor. Lisa did not even warmup. When Jennifer Carbone fell, Alabama began planning its victory celebration. Without a sixth gymnast, Georgia would have to count Jennifer's low score, and there was no way to make up for it. I'm not sure why I was considering an unlikely contingency, but although Lisa didn't warm up, I had listed her name in the lineup. After Jennifer's fall, I huddled with Lisa and watered-down her routine to one that would provide the needed 9.45 for Georgia to win the championship, but would minimize stress on the broken toe. Still, Lisa had to hit the routine, and she hadn't practiced a full routine for several weeks.

Lisa pulled off the first tumbling pass without a hitch. She began to gain confidence with every skill, while her teammates fidgeted and the coaches winced. Lisa continued the routine, gritting her teeth the whole way, and finished with flying colors. Do I need to say what she scored? Of course a 9.45, giving the GymDogs a 0.05 point SEC Championship.

"This is the happiest moment of my life," Lisa proclaimed after the meet. "To be able to help the team win something this important is great."

The GymDogs won our fourth consecutive Southeast Regional meet, which was held in Athens, and headed for the NCAA Championships in Tuscaloosa, significantly handicapped by the loss of Heather Stepp.

It was fitting that Alabama had a late-season surge to go into the championships ranked number one. But with the exceptional performances from the fabulous freshmen Hope Spivey and Kelly Macy, Georgia loomed as a major contender. Before the meet, Hope told the press, "I don't think at this time we can settle for second." Unfortunately, thanks to three falls on the beam, we had to settle for third. There were lots of bright spots in the team's performance, but not enough to overcome the falls on beam. Ironically, I had solicited the help of the booster club in attempting to create a loud and hostile atmosphere during practice on the beam the two weeks before the meet. I knew that Georgia would be on beam while Alabama was on floor, performing before a large and loud home crowd.

Even the most sportsmanlike crowd at any school is noisiest when its team is on the floor. That's where the excitement is. And the Alabama crowd, knowing that Georgia was its biggest threat to a second championship for the Tide, didn't go out of its way to help Georgia stay on the beam. The predominantly Tide crowd of 7,413 chanting "Roll Tide Roll" could have influenced the performance. But they were yelling for Alabama, not necessarily against Georgia. Any team on the beam on that rotation would have had to deal with the same problem.

Over a period of years I had noticed that a counted fall, on average, cost our team about 0.65 point in the final team score. Even adjusting our score for two counted falls we still came short of Alabama's 195.125. Alabama won the championship; Georgia didn't hand it to them. After the meet at the press conference I said, "Actually we're very pleased with third. We were realistic enough to think that's where we would finish." Utah came in second at 194.375. So, again, the teams finished exactly as they were seeded.

The SEC continued to show its overall strength, with five of the six conference teams finishing in the top-nine positions. In addition to Alabama and Georgia, Florida came in sixth, LSU seventh, and Auburn ninth.

If a team can find consolation in the individual championships, then the GymDogs should have found plenty. Hope Spivey won the all-around, vault, and floor exercise; and Kelly Macy won the uneven bars. Two freshmen from the same team won four of the five individual events. In her junior year, Utah's former Olympian, Missy Marlowe, was finally beginning to rise to her enormous potential, sharing the balance beam championship with Gina Basile of Alabama.

After bringing home only two citations in 1990, the GymDogs got back on track in that department. Four GymDogs garnered nine All-America citations: Kelly Macy (bars), Chris Rodis (floor), Sandy Rowlette (vault and bars), and Hope Spivey (everything).

With no seniors on the team, the freshmen added for the 1992 season would be a total net gain. And what a gain! Agina Simpkins was the consensus number one recruit in the country because of her ranking on the USGF National Team. She was the first alternate for the 1990 Good Will Games. Nneka Logan, who trained with Agina at the Illinois Gymnastics Institute, was also a member of the national team, and she won the Senior Elite Regional all-around title before injuring her Achilles tendon and having to sit out her senior year in high school. She was fully recovered for the beginning of practice with the GymDogs.

Nneka and Agina were generally regarded as equals and were nicknamed "Double Trouble." That nickname was somewhat prophetic in terms of team chemistry later in their careers. The third freshman was Andrea Dewey, a vaulting and uneven-bars specialist, who practically never fell or had a step on a dismount.

Return of the entire 1991 team and addition of these recruits caused Greg Marsden to suggest that the GymDogs would be in a class by themselves for the next few years. Greg knows gymnastics, but he also is good at psyching opposing coaches.

Perhaps a more significant "addition" to the team was the miraculous recovery of Heather Stepp to be "as good as new." Things looked pretty rosy for the GymDogs' 1992 season.

The GymDogs proved Greg prophetic. We breezed through the season, obliterating opponents by 5, 6, 7 points. Only in road meets with Florida and Alabama was the margin of victory less than 3 points. School, conference, regional, and national records fell. The team recorded eight perfect 10s. Individuals broke records. We went all the way to the NCAA National Championships at Minneapolis undefeated. My evaluation to the press at nationals was: "Our team never got a taste of a close, nail-biting competition, because we competed strongly all season, right up until the end."

But in the NCAAs, Murhphy's law came into play. The GymDogs started on bars and had our worst performance of the season, counting two falls. Remember, that's equivalent to 1.3 points given to the opposition. To our credit, the GymDogs came back strong on the other events, posting a meet score of 194.60 coming in second, 1.05 points behind champion Utah and 1.25 points ahead of third place Alabama.

"It was our worst meet all year," I said afterward. "We made mistakes that I can't even explain. After the first event I told them not to come out of the locker room if they were not going to fight back. It's pretty hard when you have three falls on your first event not to just go through the motions. I'm really proud of the team that they didn't do that. They really fought back."

Later I said, "As a team we had a letdown. We went through the whole season without letting down. What was hardest about it was that, if we had competed at our best or even competed at our early-season level, we could have been the national champions." Maybe not. Some Utah fans claim today the 1992 team was Utah's best ever. It lost only one meet during the season. Suffice it to say, it would have been close.

It was certainly fitting that Missy Marlowe, senior at Utah and former Olympian, had an outstanding meet. In her senior year, she finally performed up to her potential, throughout the season, becoming the first college gymnast to score a 10.00 on each event at some time during her career—not in the same meet, however. On winning the all-around, Missy had this to say: "I've come a long way during my career at Utah. That's approximately the same difficulty I competed at the Olympics, and I didn't perform nearly as well then as I did tonight."

Missy, Lucy Wener, Hope Spivey, and Andrea Thomas—all are former Olympians and all are performing better in college.

And Missy almost swept the other individual events, winning the floor exercise, uneven bars, and tying with Alabama's Dana Dobransky on balance beam. The vaulting championship ended in a three-way tie—Kristen Kenoyer (Utah), Tammy Marshall (UMass, an individual qualifier) and Heather Stepp (Georgia).

Heather not only came back to win the vaulting championship, but during the season she scored a school record 39.60 all-around in winning the SEC title. To see Heather come back and compete, to see her up there on the awards platform—it was so impressive. It was amazing that she not only came back, she came back better than before she was injured. It's a tribute to Heather's determination and work ethic that she was so successful. No one was surprised when Heather won the 1992 Honda Inspiration Award, but she still was not part of a national championship team.

Six GymDogs won sixteen All-American citations: Andrea Dewey (vault), Nneka Logan (uneven bars and balance beam), Chris Rodis (floor), Agina Simpkins (all-around, vault, bars, floor), Hope Spivey (all-around, vault, bars, floor), and Heather Stepp (everything). Heather followed Hope from the previous year as Georgia's second five-time All-American in one year.

Even though we didn't win the national championship, you could make a case for titling this chapter, "Nine Years to the Top." The 1992 season certainly indicated that we had done just about everything—everything except win the national championship. But you're not on top when you can't finish it off.

But surely we would reach the top in 1993. We returned four All-Americans on both vault and uneven bars, three on floor, and two on the balance beam—thirteen of the twenty-four slots in the lineup. Perhaps more impressive was one of the two freshmen coming in. Lori Strong, a two-time Canadian Olympian, had won the Canadian national all-around championship three years in a row, and had been selected Canadian female athlete of the year. Lori joined Courtney Snyder, the other freshman, who was a senior elite gymnast from Maryland.

We went through the regular season again winning nearly every meet by 4, 5, or 7 points. Alabama (in Tuscaloosa) came closest, 196.75 to 195.90. Winning by 0.85 points isn't exactly close, but it was close enough to set a fire under the team. They went on a tear, scoring over 197 in each of the next five meets, which included the SEC Championship and the NCAA Southeast Regional Championship.

The NCAA National Championships changed formats again. The new format called for two days of team competition. On Thursday, the six odd-seeded teams would compete in the afternoon and the even-seeded teams in the evening. The scores for the first session determined the national all-around champion. The top-three teams in each session advanced to the "Super Six" on Friday to compete for the team championship.

Georgia, seeded first, won the first session, with Alabama coming in second and UCLA third. Utah, Auburn, and Arizona qualified from the evening session. Of the first session *IG* reported: "The Lady Bulldogs won the session handily, paced by sophomore dynamo Agina Simpkins, senior Heather Stepp, and 1988 Olympian Hope Spivey-Sheeley. Georgia didn't appear to water down any routines. But then that is Coach Suzanne Yoculan's trademark: don't hold anything back." Heather's dream came true.

In the "Super Six," Georgia's 198.00 was 1.175 points better than Alabama's second-place score, which was their highest of the season. Both teams hit twenty-four routines. As mentioned in the beginning of the chapter, the GymDogs set new NCAA Championship records for the team score, vaulting, uneven bars, and the floor exercise—everything but beam.

The meet was the debut for a freshman individual qualifier from Kentucky. In terms of total individual championships won and All-American citations, Jenny Hansen walks away from all other gymnasts in NCAA history. She won her first NCAA all-around at the Corvallis meet. Heather Stepp won the vaulting and tied with UMass' Tammy Marshall and Oregon State's Amy Durham for the floor exercise championship. Agina Simpkins tied with Michigan's Beth Wymer on the uneven bars, and Alabama's Dana Dobransky won the balance beam for the second year in a row.

In another unprecedented accomplishment, Georgia scored five 10.0s in the Super Six. Not only was that a first, it hasn't happened since either. And six 10.0s were scored among the gymnasts competing in the individual championships, resulting in all of those ties for first place. The gymnasts were out-pacing the scoring code again. It would be altered before the 1994 season, but not enough to satisfy me. As large as the gap between the GymDogs and the other teams was in 1992 and 1993, it might have been substantially larger with a more demanding code of points. In completing the first undefeated season in NCAA history, the GymDogs had compiled a two-year won/loss record of sixty-five and one.

And we set yet another record—more All-American gymnasts (seven) and more All-American citations (seventeen) than had been recorded for a team previously: Andrea Dewey (bars), Nneka Logan (floor), Sandy Rowlette (vault, bars, and floor), Agina Simpkins (all-around, vault, bars, and beam), Hope Spivey-Sheeley (vault, beam, floor), Heather Stepp (all-around, vault, bars, floor), and Lori Strong (bars).

After I got back to Athens, I acknowledged to our fans that the 1993 team was the best in NCAA history, as Greg Marsden said, "Without question." But then a sort of sinking feeling hit me. I'm just not comfortable unless I'm climbing mountains. Two near-perfect years, culminating in one championship, wasn't enough. What other mountains were there to climb? It didn't take long to identify them. We had won three championships, but Utah was still way ahead of us. Though the average home-meet attendance was up to nearly 6,000, there were still 4,000 more seats to be filled. And gymnastics at Georgia still depended on revenues from football. I was getting comfortable again, plotting my attack on these new objectives even before the end-of-the-season recognition banquet.

It was at the recognition banquet that I perceived we were finally beginning to get Coach Dooley's attention. You will recall that he had almost eliminated gymnastics at Georgia in 1983. I wasn't sure he recognized it as a major sport, even after a ten-year record that made it the premier program at Georgia in terms of achievements. He had agreed to speak at the banquet. Coach Dooley, the reserved, frugal manager, came up with a lively speech, delivered with verve and animation. He used several quotations from Brooks Hatch's article in the Corvallis paper. At one point he referred to Brook's statement relating to the GymDogs' hitting twenty-four of twenty-four routines: "It was legendary. It might have been the most impressive postseason performance since Bill Walton shot twenty-one for twenty-two against Memphis State in basketball a generation ago." To which Coach Dooley added, "Hell! He missed one!" At that moment, I felt we had made it to the top.

TOP
A picture from my
East Brunswick
(New Jersey) High
School yearbook
shows me practicing
for the Girls
Gymnastics Team,
1971.
(Courtesy of Suzanne Yoculan)

LEFT
With Steve Bonham,
men's gymnastics coach at
Georgia, 1984.
(UGA Sports Communications)

TOP LEFT
Megan McCunniff (Marsden), Utah.
(U of U Staff Photos)

TOP RIGHT
1982 Utah Team, the first NCAA
National Champions; Left to Right,
Front Row: Sue Sednitz, Christa
Canary, Wendy Whiting, Andra Turner;
Middle Row: Linda Kardos, Elaine
Alfano, Cindy Paul, Celeste Harrington;
Top Row: Emily May, Megan
McCunniff, Shannon Coleman.
(U of U Staff Photos)

BOTTOM LEFT
Kathy McMinn, Georgia.
(UGA Sports Communications)

TOP
Georgia Team, 1987 NCAA National
Champions; Left to Right, Front Row:
Corrine Wright; Middle Row: Paula
Maheu, Tanya Schuler, Julie Klick; Top
Row: Lucy Wener, Terri Eckert, Gina
Banales, Susie Origer, Michelle Sessions.
(UGA Sports Communications)

LEFT
Terri Eckert, Georgia.
(UGA Sports Communications)

CAA WOMEN'S NATIONA

TOP
Georgia Team, 1989 NCAA National
Champions: Left to Right, Front Row:
Paula Maheu, Andrea Thomas, Debbie
Greco, Corrinne Wright, Sophia Royce,
Julie Ponstein, Lynn Messer, and Chris
Rodis; Back Row: Melissa DePaoli,
Kathy Dwyer, Tanya Schuler, and
Lucy Wener.
(UGA Sports Communications)

BOTTOM
Cheering for the GymDogs during
the NCAA National Championships,
Athens, 1989.
(UGA Sports Communications)

Alabama Team, 1991 NCAA National Champions: Left to Right, Front Row: Tina Rinker, Shea McFall, Kim Masters; Middle Row: Keri Duley, Katherine Kelleher, Sheryl Dundas, Dee Dee Foster, Dana Dobransky; Top Row: Gina Basile, Marti Watson, Kara Stilp.
(UA Media Relations)

Hope Spivey, Georgia.
(UGA Sports Communications)

Kelly Macy, Georgia.
(UGA Sports Communications)

TOP
Utah Team, 1992 NCAA National Champions:
Left to Right, Front Row: Merdith King,
Missy Wells, Aimee Trepanier, Traci Richards;
Back Row: Kristen Kenoyer, Shelley Shaerrer,
Missy Marlowe, Jenny Donaldson, Kelly Wolsey,
Suzanne Metz.
(U of U Staff Photos)

BOTTOM LEFT
Missy Marlowe, Utah.
(U of U Staff Photos)

BOTTOM RIGHT
Heather Stepp, Georgia.
(UGA Sports Communications)

Journey to Georgia

When I was growing up in East Brunswick, New Jersey in the 1960s, there were practically no organized sports available to girls—only basketball and track. I started taking modern dance, ballet, and tap dancing lessons at a very young age, and dance was a passion for me back then. My mother, Doris Allen, encouraged all four daughters to dream big, so I dreamed of being a Rockette and commuted to New York City to study dance at a higher level. But, during my freshman year at East Brunswick High School, I was introduced to gymnastics and joined the gymnastics team. High school gymnastics was really big back then. At that time, there were no clubs, so gymnastics was not a year-round sport, but I started putting more and more into the sport and getting more and more out of it—just in terms of rewards and feeling of accomplishment. I felt like I was competing against myself to learn a skill. I was constantly challenged to succeed and inspired in a different way from anything else. I began doing more and more gymnastics, which I loved, and less and less dance. However, I still wanted to keep dance as part of my life, and when I went to college I majored in dance and movement therapy.

My dad, Bill Allen, instilled a strong work ethic in me. He always said, "I will not tolerate laziness or disrespect," and he didn't. Those words stayed with me throughout my life and inspired me to work hard in gymnastics.

I spent the summers at Sokal Woodlands gymnastics camp. I won my first all-around state championship my senior year, 1971, at the AAU High School State meet after Anne Burmeister, a teammate, graduated. Anne won everything until she graduated in 1970 and then she went to UMass, where she met and married Norm Vexler. They are the parents of Talya Vexler, a recent GymDog All-American and graduate of UGA. The men practiced with us as well, and we had many top gymnasts in our high school programs back then.

I looked at all the schools with gymnastics and decided on Northeastern University because at the time my first choice, Penn State, didn't accept freshmen to attend the main campus at University Park unless you were an athlete, and initially I was not recruited by them. My dad had already paid my admission fees at Northeastern when, at the last minute, coach Beth Hanley at Penn State called and made arrangements for me to be admitted there in the summer as an athlete and stay on the main campus.

In 1972, Penn State didn't have a gymnastics program like they do today. They didn't give scholarships; it was more of an intramural-type program. This differed from my high school gymnastics experience with Don Weider, where I felt challenged. Practice at Penn State felt like PE class. We were always standing around waiting for a turn and that drove me crazy. I don't have the patience for that. To me, gymnastics was about developing high-level skills, pushing yourself to do high-level routines, and trying new things. That was what attracted me to the sport in the first place—trying to do things I couldn't do and trying to learn new things. Repeating basics bored me.

I felt like I was wasting my time, so I quit. I never even went to a competition. I stayed on the team maybe two months. I started teaching gymnastics at Nittany Gymnastics, a club down the road. I just walked in and asked if they needed any extra teachers—just three or four hours a week, something part time. Ed Isabelle owned the gym, but he's not the one who hired me initially, when I was in college. I started teaching more and more. I loved teaching—couldn't get enough of it.

Then I was asked to be an instructor at a gym club in Altoona, forty-five minutes from Penn State. The gymnastics program was run by the parents, who had rented the building, put in equipment, and then had lost their instructor. I started teaching the kids a couple of days a week, and they approached me to be the owner of the gym. All I had to do was take over the loans for the equipment. This happened just before I married Sam Yoculan in 1975. Because we're both Geminis, we named the gym Gemini Gymnastics.

We built the program's base from 60 to 400 kids. After a few years, we had kids achieving at a high level. In fact, the United States Association of Independent Gymnastics Clubs (USAIGC) program picked the top-ten kids in the country (under twelve years old) for a program they call TOPs (Talent Opportunity Program) today; and one of our kids, Julie Walters from Altoona, made that program. That basically changed my life, right there. I was then invited to several national coaching clinics with her—for the top-ten kids. And the top coaches in the nation—Dick Mulvahill, for example—were teaching the coaches what to teach the kids. I could not learn enough.

I was able to go to these clinics, where I learned how to spot Julie, what to do with her, and how to train her. Over the next couple of years we had eight national-level kids in my gym. Jodie Twoey was one of them. She eventually went to the University of Nebraska on scholarship. I was the only coach in the gym. Prior to attending these clinics, I didn't know anything about high-level gymnastics. All I did was make sure I stayed one step ahead of what the athlete needed.

I relied a lot on Danny Warbutton at GymDandys in Washington, Pennsylvania. I would take Julie and Jody and my top kids and travel around the state to other gyms. We'd go down and work with Ted Jackson in South Hampton, Pennsylvania, at Carole Ide's gym, where Penny Hauschild was on the team. She later became one of the top gymnasts at Alabama. Terri Eckert, another high-level gymnast, was also on my team. I stayed one step ahead of what these kids needed. When they needed to learn a double back, I went somewhere and learned to teach a double back. I did the best I could to give them what they needed.

Then one day we received an offer from someone who wanted to buy our gym. He would pay us, take over the debt, and keep me on as head coach. I could have more time at home with my son, Adam, who was born in 1978. I thought an angel from heaven had come down. All I had to do now was coach the team kids. But two weeks after he bought the gym, he fired me. He wanted to be the coach, and he didn't like it because the kids relied on me and not him.

So I called Ed Isabelle and asked him if I could bring my top-ten kids over to his gym, Nittany Gymnastics. I would drive the kids four days a week to State College, and I'd be their coach at his gym. This was about 1979, and three or four of the kids were on the national team. They were some of the top kids in the country.

Terri Eckert was one of the kids I coached while I was in college at Penn State. When I started my own gym in Altoona, her mother brought her to me. Then when I went back to State College, she went with me. Gina Bañales, who was one of the top kids in the state, was also on the team. In the summer I started working full time at Nittany. They made me director of the Woodward Gymnastics Camp shortly thereafter. Ed owned both Nittany and Woodward.

I did a lot of managerial things at Woodward. I worked as co-director with Mark Stevenson, who's now the head coach at North Carolina State. We scheduled classes and tested the kids and we had spotting clinics for the coaches. The Nebraska men's team was training at Woodward prior to the 1984 Olympics, and they told me Nebraska was in search of a women's gymnastics head coach.

When the Nebraska job opened, Ed convinced me to apply, but I didn't get the interview they promised me. I was devastated. I want people to do what they tell me they're going to do. They actually hired Rick Walton, the coach of women's gymnastics at Georgia, and canceled my interview. Rick left Georgia, telling anyone who would listen that UGA would never have a good gymnastics team. He said there was no support from the administration.

Meanwhile, at Georgia, they were trying to decide whether to drop gymnastics altogether. Liz Murphey, then women's athletic director at Georgia, recounted the story to me:

> Coach Dooley and I got a shock when the Athletics Director at Nebraska called and said, "I've got someone here in my office who's one of your coaches, and we'd like to hire him." Coach Dooley and I looked at each other like, "Uh Oh! What is this all about?" We had been told by Rick (Walton), the women's gymnastics coach, that he might be looking for another job, but he had not told us definitely that he was. At that point Coach Dooley brought up the fact that the insurance to cover injuries per athlete was higher in gymnastics than it was even in football at that time. We were having a lot of injuries, and Coach Dooley said, "I think we should just drop the sport." Of course I said, "Oh, Coach, we don't want to do that. This sport is up-and-coming."
>
> It took a very special young woman, Kathy McMinn, who was a three-time All-American at that time, to convince Coach Dooley to keep the sport. Kathy McMinn went with me to see Coach Dooley, and he realized that this was a chance for her to be the first four-time All-American (four years) in women's sports at Georgia. Kathy became a part of the search committee, because she knew more about women's gymnastics than anyone else on campus. And we really did advertise.

Then the Georgia job opened, and Ed wanted me to apply. He told me that I was a natural for college gymnastics and that I should go for an interview, but I was fed up with the rejection I had received from Nebraska and I told Ed, "No way!" So Ed forged my signature and sent my application to Georgia, without my knowledge, and Liz Murphey called me up. I said, "I'm not interested, I did not even apply." Then Liz said, "Well, we have your application right here," and she talked me into visiting. Liz had to talk me into making the trip, but she didn't have to talk me into taking the job after I visited the university.

I have always been spontaneous. Athens and the University of Georgia felt right. Ed Isabelle changed my life.

I learned later that Lee Cunningham, former men's gymnastics coach at Georgia and one of the biggest and most influential boosters of both men's and women's gymnastics at Georgia, had contacted Ed Isabelle to learn more about me. Ed's a good salesman, and he must have been pretty convincing because I was invited for the interview at Georgia.

The search continued and Liz recounted it to me:

We wanted to find a quality person. We were narrowing down the numbers when we had an interview with a little gal who ran her own gym at Penn State. It was Suzanne, of course.

When Suzanne came to the campus, Kathy McMinn said, "Wait a minute, none of us has ever been coached by a woman. I just don't think that's gonna work, Coach Murphey." So I told her we were going to meet Suzanne, just to see what she was like.

All candidates who were interviewed were asked to go to the gym to meet the girls. When Suzanne entered the gym, both the men's and the women's teams were working out because they shared the gym. When the male gymnasts saw her, all of the guys who she knew from summers at Woodward Camp went running over saying, "Suzanne, Suzanne, come spot us." And the girls looked at each other saying, "How do these guys know her?" It was quite exciting to see her kick off her high heels and run out on to the middle of the mat. They were doing all sorts of complicated things, and Suzanne began spotting them. In fact, she was one of the few women in the country who knew how to spot. She actually taught a class in spotting to other coaches.

The girls looked at one another and said, "How can this woman do all these things?" I think that did it right there. That convinced the team to support her candidacy. It was really pretty exciting to all of us to have her accept the job because she had already demonstrated that she was going to come in and be a real mover and shaker.

Kathy, of course, had made a very emotional appeal to Coach Dooley to retain the sport. He realized that here was a quality young woman who is so skilled and has an opportunity to be a four-time All-American, and she wanted to complete her degree at Georgia. She was really devastated when she learned that Coach Walton was leaving, because he had coached her in club gymnastics in Alabama before either of them came here. So it was a real experience for her to have a woman coach her final year. But Suzanne and Kathy became very close. Suzanne has a wonderful way of communicating with her gymnasts. It was very heart warming to see Kathy doing gymnastics her senior year and for her to have Suzanne's support throughout the years, even through medical school and on.

Liz and Kathy weren't the only ones campaigning to keep women's gymnastics at Georgia. Jackie Clifton was a gymnast at UGA, and her career was ending because of multiple knee injuries. Her mother, Judy Clifton, was spending sleepless nights because of her concern over losing the sport. So Judy met with Coach Dooley and appealed to him not to drop women's gymnastics, telling him how the sport was growing rapidly at the club level throughout the state, going from one or two clubs in the seventies to over a hundred in the early eighties. At the time Judy was a United States Gymnastics Federation (USFG) judge, so she had a great feel for its growth. Apparently Judy hit home. Coach Dooley told her to get her materials together, and he would arrange for her and her husband Johnny, a former baseball letterman at Georgia, to meet with the president of the university, Fred Davison.

Judy prepared charts and graphs to get her points about the growth in importance of women's gymnastics across, especially its growth in Georgia, and about the status of women's varsity sports teams in other schools in the South. And, as Coach Dooley promised, she made her presentation to Dr. Davison and his Vice President for Finance and Business, Alan Barber, with Coach Dooley and Johnny at her side.

Judy later told me that there was also a letter-writing campaign to Coach Dooley from people around the state supporting the sport. Needless to say, she was delighted when she heard a few weeks later that a new coach had been hired and she has turned out to be one of Georgia gymnastics' biggest supporters through all my years here.

I remember, while on the interview trip, going downtown and looking up through the arch on Old Campus, and it reminded me of Penn State with the downtown bordering the campus, and it just felt right. It didn't matter that the gym was a dungeon. It didn't matter that Coach Dooley was going to pay me only around $12,000. I ended up right in the middle of a place I'd hardly heard of before.

I didn't even know that much about collegiate gymnastics—and this is an important point—because a lot of club coaches even today are not that familiar with collegiate gymnastics. You tend to get in your own world, and club gymnastics and collegiate gymnastics are totally separate. There's no overlap. And back then there was no TVcoverage for college gymnastics, so if you were a club coach, you didn't hear who won the national championship. I didn't even know that Utah won the national championship the first year there was an NCAA title in 1982.

But I was here. I was confident that my training over the past ten years, my passion for coaching and for the sport, and my vision that college gymnastics could be the most exciting and beautiful level of the sport would serve me well. And I was raring to go!

Over-the-Hill at Eighteen—Not!

In 1985, just before my second season at Georgia, I read that over half of all college gymnasts were freshmen. It was generally accepted back then that college gymnasts rarely get better as they get older. Many gymnasts would come in as freshmen and be high in the starting lineup, and by the time they were seniors, they were hardly making the lineup. Up until I came to Georgia, I had dealt with gymnasts below the college age, and the idea that these gymnasts would "peak" and then go downhill while in college was unacceptable.

I was proud that, in 1985, we actually had two seniors who were competing in their fourth year. At that time, there were few girls who did that. Some of the best gymnasts in the country would do two years of college and then give up and then start downhill or actually get out of the program. But Laurie Reiff and Laurie Jones, even though they were seniors and even though the odds were against them, were competing very strong and were in the lineup all year. Of course Kathy McMinn was the GymDogs' best gymnast as a senior the year before.

At that time, I wasn't really thinking about why Kathy and the two Lauries were different from most other gymnasts. Kathy was extremely disciplined and dedicated. I'm sure that had something to do with her longevity. But within her discipline there was something else that I wasn't being analytical enough to figure out.

As Terri Eckert and the freshmen who came in 1985 progressed to higher classes, nearly all of them seemed to get better too. Terri made All-American on the floor exercise her senior year. Gina Bañales made All-American on vault her senior year. And Julie Klick made All-American on bars her junior year.

Perhaps the biggest surprise at that time was Lucy Wener. As mentioned earlier, she came to Georgia for the 1986 season, after making the U.S. Olympic Team in 1984. Unfortunately she was injured just before the Olympics and was unable to compete. She came here pretty well worn out both physically and mentally after about ten years of intensive training and competing at the national level. But she was a senior when she scored the first-ever perfect 10.00 in NCAA Championships competition and won her third NCAA National Individual Championship on bars. Also, as a senior, she vaulted for the first time in five years, which allowed her to compete in the all-around, and she came in second in the all-around at the NCAA Championships in 1989.

What was going on? These "over-the-hill" gymnasts weren't supposed to get better. At that time, the Olympic gymnasts were getting younger and smaller, not older and larger.

But that wasn't always the case. The format for Olympic competition in women's gymnastics as we know it today—bars, beam, floor, and vaulting—began with the 1952 Olympics. That year, Agnes Keleti of Hungary won the gold medal on the floor exercise and the bronze on the uneven bars. She was thirty-one years old. Four years later she won another gold medal at age thirty-five. In 1956, the average age of the gymnasts on the U.S. Olympic Team was nineteen and the average weight was 124 pounds.

But changes had taken place that made it more difficult for the older gymnasts to compete. Although, in terms of events, the present format for women's Olympic gymnastics began with the 1952 Olympics, the skills performed have become progressively more difficult—ever since Olga Korbut, from the Soviet Union, did the first back flip on the balance beam in 1972. At that time, her back flip on the beam was considered daring. It even became controversial as being too dangerous.

I can remember Anne Burmeister, who was on my club team in

New Jersey, trying to learn a back flip with a spotting belt around her waist with the equipment hoisting her up to do the back flip. That was about 1970. Today, you would never teach somebody a back flip on the beam with a spotting belt. Thousands of kids can do a back flip, and it's not even considered a high-level skill today. I'm talking about a simple back tuck—no hands.

Kim Arnold, a senior on our 1998 team did *three connected in the laid-out position, following a back handspring.* So not only have the gymnasts changed, *gymnastics* has changed—so much so that the Olympic routines of 1972 are done by beginners today.

Olga Korbut was only about five-feet tall and weighed only eighty or ninety pounds in 1972. There may have been a hint back then that tiny gymnasts performed the more athletic-type gymnastics better. But it wasn't until 1976 that everyone got the idea that the best gymnasts *had* to be tiny and young. That's when Bela Karolyi introduced Nadia Comaneci and the other young and tiny gymnasts on the Romanian National Team, which won the Olympic Team gold medal.

The irony of all of this is that Bela probably knew better. According to his book, *Feel No Fear,* he didn't select these young, tiny pixies because he had decided they would be better gymnasts than more mature athletes. He had no option. When he first began training young students in the coal mining village of Vulcan, Romania, the only students available to him were elementary school kids. His concentration on gymnastics wasn't even premeditated. Bela was a physical education instructor. He taught the youngsters soccer, volleyball, and rugby. But when cold weather set in, he had to move inside, so he began to teach the kids gymnastics.

And he taught them a new kind of gymnastics, based on his background in physical conditioning and strength training. Bela called it "physical gymnastics." He recognized that strength and conditioning were essential to good performance in the dynamic type of gymnastics he was teaching. The reason that college gymnasts were retiring early, as the more physical gymnastics became popular, was that they weren't strong enough for their bodies. Olga Korbut's coach, Renald Knysh, and Bela really changed gymnastics, and the college gymnasts weren't prepared for the new physical gymnastics.

After Bela's team won its first Olympic championship in 1976, the Romanian government took his team away from him to put them on exhibition. So he had to start over. Again he had only young gymnasts to work with. While the 1976 national team was getting out of condition, his new, younger team was getting strong and well-conditioned. Bela's new pixies won the Romanian championship away from the former champions in 1980, defeating a team composed largely of out-of-shape gymnasts from his 1976 national team. Were they really over-the-hill? No, they were out of condition.

However, one member of the 1976 national team had joined Bela's team of youngsters. She was nineteen years old and thirty pounds overweight when she rejoined the team. But with intensive physical conditioning and training, Nadia Comaneci was able to regain her championship form, a better gymnast at nineteen than she was at fifteen.

Because the other members of Bela's 1980 Romanian team were pixies, like the 1976 team, suddenly the whole world of gymnastics thought that gymnasts had to be tiny and young. The Soviets and East German gymnasts were getting smaller and smaller, copying what they thought had made Bela so successful. And the United States gymnastics coaches followed suit. By 1992, the average age of the U.S. Olympic Team was down to sixteen, and the average weight was less than ninety pounds.

But at Georgia, our gymnasts were consistently getting better as they got older, and they certainly weren't pixies. Across the country, other college teams were experiencing the same thing—Megan Marsden at Utah and Penny Hauschild at Alabama were among the early seniors to excel. And then our Lucy Wener and Utah's Missy Marlowe were among the early former Olympians to have their best years as seniors, four or five years beyond their appearance in the Olympics. Yes, even former Olympians were improving during their college years. I can't put my finger on any specific time when

I realized the keys to longevity in gymnastics. We didn't sit down and carefully analyze how we were training. But, without question, our gymnasts were getting better as they got older, and this was happening at about the same time the movement in the Olympics to concentrate on younger and smaller gymnasts was in full force. But we were going in the opposite direction.

Check out these GymDogs who were national individual champions in their senior years:

GYMNAST	SENIOR YEAR
Lucy Wener*	1989
Heather Stepp	1993
Hope Spivey*	1994
Lori Strong*	1996
Leah Brown	1997
Kim Arnold	1998

*Former Olympic Team members before entering college.

It didn't take long for people to get concerned about what the intensive training of female gymnasts so young might do to their health—both physical and mental. Gymnasts as young as eight to ten years of age were training as many as forty hours a week. This concern has been exploited in Joan Ryan's best-selling book, *Little Girls in Pretty Boxes.* But I didn't buy into all the alarms being sounded. In the August 2002 issue of the *Journal of Pediatrics,* Emma Laing and Rick Lewis reported that adolescent gymnasts participating in competitive artistic gymnastics had higher levels of bone mass density, bone mineral content, and fat-free soft tissue mass than girls of the same age who did not participate in competitive sports. So it looks like a lot of the concern over physical damage to young gymnasts may not be well-founded.

However, I do believe that intensive training of young athletes can be detrimental to their mental well-being. That, in itself, is enough reason for concern.

The NCAA has published information indicating that intensive exercise alone is not dangerous. They point out that physical activity should be encouraged since it promotes cardiovascular fitness, bone strength, and longevity. However, an energy deficit, in which calorie intake does not match energy expenditure, is a risk factor. Proper nutrition, then, is important. This should come as a surprise to no one.

Unfortunately there is a temptation to put winning in competitive sports of all types above the welfare of the athletes. The temptation exists in competitive gymnastics. Many of the gymnasts who come to the University of Georgia have been engaged in international competition for several years, and their bodies reflect the results. Broken bones, stress fractures, and torn ligaments are common among competitive gymnasts. Perhaps one reason Georgia gymnasts perform better during their junior and senior years is that they spend their freshman and sophomore years being rehabilitated from the injuries they brought with them. Often, they come here either needing surgery, postponed in order to compete, or recovering from surgery.

Four gymnasts in the GymDogs' senior class of 1999 are examples of what I'm talking about—Jennie Beathard, Stacey Galloway, Karin Lichey, and Sam Muhleman, all with backgrounds in international competition. One competed with pain throughout her freshman year because of bone chips in her ankles, which were removed after the season. Two were recovering from knee surgery. It was revealed midway through the season that the fourth came to Georgia with stress fractures in her back. So we ran a rehabilitation unit for the four. Even though they comprised the best recruiting class in the history of college gymnastics at the time, their contribution to the team during the first two years was minimal. But they began to come on strong during their junior year, winning two individual national championships and compiling ten All-American honors among them. And they really peaked in their senior year, garnering a total of twenty-two All-American honors during their careers with an overall record of 126-6-1—the best overall ever. In addition, they were part of our 1998 and 1999 back-to-back NCAA Championship Teams.

I must add here that two members of the GymDogs class of 1999 were from Mary Lee Tracy's Cincinnati Gymnastics Academy. Mary Lee was the coach of the first U.S. Olympic Gymnastics Team to win the team gold medal, so her credentials as a coach are well-established. But she is also as concerned—maybe even more concerned—about the physical and sociological welfare of her gymnasts. One of her alumnae who came to Georgia was beaten up in other gyms before she transferred to Cincinnati.

The vast majority of club coaches are caring and considerate of their gymnasts. But the requirements of competing in all-around and performing compulsory routines, before compulsories were eliminated from the Olympics, made extensive training necessary in the eyes of elite-level coaches. Everyone had to get ahead of everyone else. More hours in the gym had to be the answer.

No one in the world loves gymnastics more than I do. It's a wholesome activity for young women. But teaching gymnastics to our children is not nearly as important as guiding them into wholesome activities that they are interested in and are well suited for. My daughter, Alexis, attended my gymnastics camps for a few summers. She's a terrific athlete, and she was doing well, but she decided that gymnastics was not for her. She competed on the varsity soccer and basketball teams at her high school, as well as club soccer in the Gwinnett Soccer Association. She now plays soccer on athletic scholarship at Vanderbilt. But it would be fine with me if she didn't enjoy organized sports at all, as long as she engages in activities that develop her morally, physically, and emotionally.

Gymnastics does, however, provide an excellent starting point for young girls to gain an early sense of the body that may be transferred to other sports and/or cultural activities. And if they do well in gymnastics and like it, by all means they should continue as long as they enjoy it. Gymnastics is the sport built on the mind/body concept developed by the early Greeks. Consider these psychological attributes developed in gymnastics: high self-esteem, physical courage, determination, perseverance, expressiveness, reliance, and self-confidence.

So gymnastics is a wonderful, comprehensive, developmental activity, but parents shouldn't push their young daughters into any sport. They should encourage them to spend their time away from school in whatever activities they enjoy, as long as they are beneficial.

Early intensive training tends to shorten the years that a gymnast can compete. It cheats her out of some wonderful experiences later, and experts seriously question even the athletic value of training beyond a reasonable amount of time per week.

To me, you have a certain amount of longevity in the sport of gymnastics. If you start at age eight and train forty hours a week, you may not have much left by age eighteen or twenty. But if you start at age eight and train twenty hours a week, you have a better chance of going on to college and continuing to learn. For example, before Melinda Baimbridge came to Georgia as a freshman in 2001, she was spending six hours a day on the uneven bars shortly after shoulder surgery, which she had no business doing that soon after an injury. She had to retire before she even competed one routine at Georgia. It wasn't because she was too old. It was because her shoulders were too old.

The amount of time for training at which a gymnast reaches the point of diminishing return in performance is probably much lower than the amount of time that some elite-level gymnasts train. The GymDogs' normal schedule calls for four hours a day in the gym, four days a week.

Too many repetitions in gymnastics training can be detrimental to development of good technique if there is insufficient oversight by the coach. Repeating the wrong technique over and over tends to ingrain it into the gymnast's performance. It is important for a coach to observe gymnasts closely enough to make sure they are repeating good technique.

So part of extending the longevity of gymnasts is avoidance of over-training at an early age. Concern about over-training has resulted in raising the age at which gymnasts can compete in the Olympics. And that's good. The International Gymnastics Federation (IGF) changed the age to sixteen, beginning with the 2000 Olympics. In the 1970s it was fourteen, and it was raised to fifteen in the 1980s. Many authorities argue that it should be raised to seventeen or eighteen. They cite psychological as well as physical benefits.

It's been our experience that a gymnast gets stronger mentally as she gets older. She can deal with the pressures; she can deal with the distractions. She can be more consistent, and she has more confidence. If you are stronger mentally, then why don't we want to have you stronger physically as you get older too? It doesn't make any sense to try to peak physically at sixteen, when the gymnast is stronger mentally at twenty-two. Development of the gymnast both physically and mentally needs to be coordinated.

When Kimmie Arnold was on the U.S. National Team, she rarely hit an entire meet. She never stayed on the equipment. Every year she went to championships, and she should have been one of the top kids in the country, but she never was because she could not stay on. As she matured mentally and caught up to her physical ability, she began to hit. At twenty and twenty-one years of age, her consistency level was so good and so high because she was mentally stronger and more confident. Kim won the all-around in the NCAA Championships in both her junior and senior years (1997 and 1998).

Competing every week also gave her confidence because she was doing the repetitions under pressure on a regular basis. So why wouldn't you want to parallel that and get athletes physically at their best at the same time they're mentally at their best and have those kids on the Olympic Team. A lot of people are figuring that out—not just Georgia. Greg Marsden probably figured it out with his kids before I did. So let's train them to be at their best physically when they're juniors and seniors.

Although I can't be totally sure how we learned to help gymnasts at Georgia extend their longevity, I do know some of the things that we now recognize. For example, it stands to reason that as females mature from age fifteen to eighteen, the age at which most enter college, they gain weight. While this enhances the potential for grace and elegance in performance, it presents other problems. The simple laws of physics tell us that it takes more strength to propel 125 pounds into the air than it does 95 pounds. So a logical deduction is that heavier gymnasts have to be stronger. Their muscle mass was naturally high when they were leaner, so the need for developing strength for younger gymnasts was not as obvious. It came along with the technique training.

But college-aged women don't have naturally low body fat. The average body fat for college-aged women who are not athletes is about 28 percent. That is not reflective of a strong body. The average body fat for our team is usually about 15 percent. Gymnasts don't have to be skinny; they have to be lean and strong. They attain a low body fat through strength training and proper nutrition.

Collegiate gymnasts have to be strong and durable because they compete every week for over three months. The age-group of the elite gymnasts (the highest level, which is scored by Olympic standards) compete in only three or four events per year. If collegiate gymnasts are not strong and durable, they will have a higher incidence of injuries. Strong gymnasts can also recover more effectively from mistakes during a performance.

Nowhere is the importance of strength and stamina more obvious than in the floor exercise. The exercise consists of a minute and a half of extensive physical exertion in which the gymnast is required to perform at least two tumbling passes, and all of our gymnasts perform three. In tumbling passes, the gymnast has to propel herself into the air, and while suspended there, perform various acrobatic moves, such as flips and twists. If she gets tired, she can't propel herself far enough into the air and, therefore, doesn't have time to complete all of her acrobatic moves while suspended. So what happens? She comes down partially through a move, not in an upright position and not prepared for a proper landing. The result is obvious. She falls. The fall costs her a big deduction. But worse, it may cause injury. Even if the gymnast is able to avoid a fall, she lands in an awkward position, which increases the likelihood of injury.

So it's becoming apparent that college gymnasts must be strong and have good endurance. We spend about four hours a week on strength and conditioning activities—weight training for strength and aerobic exercises to build stamina. Now we mix it up to include Pilates, some yoga, kick boxing, and spinning. It's important that whatever activities we choose change on a regular basis to prevent monotony.

The NCAA wisely limits the time a student athlete can spend training to twenty hours a week. After all, these young women are college students. At Georgia, as I stated earlier, we spend only sixteen hours a week in the gym, including strength and conditioning time—four hours a day, four days a week. We have found through the years that we can prepare for the season and be successful with sixteen hours of training per week.

We are able to do this because a strong gymnastics foundation has already been established by the time a gymnast reaches a major college program. If a gymnast is deficient in some foundation characteristic, we accept the fact that she doesn't have time to correct that deficiency. Some deficiencies aren't correctable, such as limited flexibility. So we build her routines around her stronger skills. We "accentuate the positive and eliminate the negative."

And we devote time to teaching new skills, an activity that is more motivating to the gymnasts, instead of spending time trying to reshape a gymnast's basic performance characteristics.

The question of what new skills to teach has evoked a lot of discussion among college coaches. It is human nature to look for things to criticize when a team has almost instant success, as the GymDogs had in the mid-1980s. So critics looked at what the GymDogs were doing differently from other teams. One difference stood out. The GymDogs were "throwing" more difficult skills than other teams. I had coached high-level gymnasts for nine years before coming to UGA. They perform the same skills the Olympic gymnasts perform. A lot of elite gymnasts were beginning to perform on college teams.

The code of points for scoring collegiate gymnastics was a modified Junior Olympic code, designed to allow gymnasts to attain a 10.0 stat value in order to maintain interest on the part of both the gymnasts and spectators. But the modified code was at a level approximately two levels below what elite gymnasts had been accustomed to. A former level-10 and elite-level gymnast who performs the same routines she had been performing before she came to college wouldn't get extra points for a lot of the difficulty in her routines.

Understandably, the Georgia gymnasts didn't want to regress. All accomplished people want to advance. A musician who has mastered the more difficult classical compositions doesn't want to revert to playing exercises for beginners. He wants to be challenged by playing even more difficult pieces. So that's what we did with our gymnasts. The coaches encouraged them to take on new challenges—to continue to grow in their gymnastic skills. Even the former Olympians learned new and more challenging skills, and they were excited about learning them. The satisfaction of meeting the challenge was a tremendous motivation.

Coaches of teams who have difficulty qualifying for the NCAA Championships want to make it easier to attain high scores, so they want a less-demanding code of points. They argue that the more challenging codes will cause coaches to pressure gymnasts to perform skills they are not capable of performing safely, that the stricter codes will lower scores and reduce spectator interest, and that the disparity among team average scores will increase. They use words like "safety" and "parity" to put forth their arguments. In reality, they are simply trying to place a handicap on the teams capable of performing more challenging routines.

After the 1996 Olympics, Greg Marsden wrote an article against a significantly more challenging code for the NCAA News. He suggested that a more challenging code would lead to more injuries because gymnasts would be encouraged to perform skills more difficult than they could do safely. Greg was also interested in having more teams be competitive—maintaining the interest of gymnasts and coaches of teams that had difficulty making scores that interested fans. I was asked to write an article in response to Greg's, making a case for a more challenging code. Here's part of what I wrote:

The objectives and goals of women's intercollegiate gymnastics should be to promote the true spirit of competitive sports, putting the physical and mental welfare of the student athlete and the fostering of high standards of ethics and fairness above all else. Programs should encourage continued improvement of performance and pursuit of excellence in women's gymnastics in a way that will convey the wholesome aspects of competition in all walks of our athletes' lives.

We must put the responsibility for safety where it will be effective in achieving our safety goals. The collegiate gymnastics coaches are the individuals best-equipped to determine what is safe for their gymnasts. They are the only ones who have sufficient knowledge of the capabilities and needs of the individual athletes to make these determinations. Attempting to "legislate" safety through a set of regressive scoring standards cannot work, will not provide the highest degree of safety, and interferes with the pursuit of excellence in a way that takes into consideration the abilities and limitations of the individual athlete. Suggesting that injuries can be reduced by manipulating the scoring system, encouraging the selection of less-challenging skills, could distract us from the real factors that influence safety and cause a false sense of security.

The performance level of collegiate gymnasts is growing by leaps and bounds. The winning NCAA team championship score went from 184.65 to 198.00 in just ten years, from 1983 to 1993. College-aged gymnasts are now among the best in the world. To suggest that collegiate gymnasts should regress to a lower standard of scoring than many of them have already advanced beyond runs countercurrent to the desires of the athletes themselves and to the fans who support them and thrill to them. Change is essential now because we have already outgrown the present system. When a team compiles a vault score of 49.925, and a gymnast scores four perfect 10.0s in one meet, it's past time to change. These are both records posted by the GymDogs. There must be room to improve.

At the same time gymnasts want the achievement of perfect scores to be reachable for a significant percentage of gymnasts in order to maintain the excitement of perfect-score expectations for themselves and for the fans.

For the 1998 season, the standards were tightened somewhat. The start value, from which bonus points must be added to reach a potential score of 10.0, was lowered to 9.5 from 9.6. At the time, I wanted it lowered to 9.2. Already, nearly all of the gymnasts on the top-ranked teams had routines with start values of 10.0, causing scores for the better gymnasts to be bunched between 9.800 and 10.00. This doesn't leave much room for judges to distinguish performance and separate routines.

But I've actually changed my thinking in that area now—at least from the standpoint of keeping more teams competitive and increasing parity. I am closer to Greg's point of view. If we don't keep a lot of teams competitive, we're going to have more schools dropping out of college gymnastics. Part of the reason men's college gymnastics has deteriorated over the years is because of the harder code and lower scores for men. You have to have the "home run" in gymnastics. The spectators don't get excited over 9.6s. So I'm all for the easier code now. If a coach wants to get 10.0s with easier skills and less risk of mistakes, that's his choice. But if the coach wants to continue to challenge the athletes, he can take that chance. At the national championships, you're rewarded for doing more difficult tricks if you do them well, even though it's not written in the rules. I have not seen many gymnasts in NCAA finals who were not performing more difficult skills than required. The judges do appreciate good execution of more difficult skills, and they find a way to make sure good execution of challenging skills is rewarded.

Some people win by doing less difficult skills. But it's not going to change what we do at Georgia. We're still going to do the more challenging routines. And we may get beat by teams that don't, and that's okay. It's a strategy, a choice. I think it's more exciting for the spectators now, because you have more chance for an upset in collegiate gymnastics—now that we're down to one vault, and there are a lot of ways to get a 10.0 start value. During the regular season, it's harder and harder to have an undefeated season. If you're a little off, you can get beat by a team that's not as good. So, I think the more lenient code is better for our sport.

If the NCAA had lowered the start value to 9.2, it would have helped us, but it would have hurt collegiate gymnastics. We're down to sixty-four division one programs in the country, and athletic directors are not adding women's gymnastics when they have an opportunity to add a new women's sport. We have to start looking at the longevity of the sport. To me, two of the main concerns have to be the interest of the spectator—they want the 10.0, the home run, and the closeness of competition and upsets. That's part of sports.

At Georgia, our coaches still encourage our gymnasts to perform the most challenging routines they are capable of performing safely. But we really don't have to encourage them because the Georgia gymnasts want to challenge themselves. In fact, sometimes the coaches have to hold them back.

There is no way to measure how much this incentive does for extending longevity, but it has a tremendous impact. Every gymnast wants to reach her full potential before she retires, and she knows that her senior year in college is likely to be her last year of competitive gymnastics. Because she sees that she is getting better, not going downhill, she is motivated even more strongly to perform the highest-level skills within her capability. Allowing gymnasts to pursue gymnastics routines that are exciting to them is probably a factor in extending longevity.

Unlike age-group gymnasts, who perform at meets before a few teammates, family, and friends, college gymnasts at Georgia perform before 10,000 fans who interact with them outside the gym. The enthusiasm of the fans, particularly the students, really "pumps" them.

The sense of pleasing a crowd is contagious. It builds team spirit, and the sense of belonging to a cohesive team adds to the determination, satisfaction, and enthusiasm of the gymnasts. And this feeling of being a part of something grows each year a gymnast is in college. It makes the gymnasts want to entertain, and entertaining requires performing more challenging and exciting routines.

It is heartening to see that more and more college coaches are following suit and including more difficulty in their gymnasts' routines. They have to because there are also scoring advantages in adding bonus points to a routine beyond the minimum required to reach a potential 10.0 start value. If a gymnast has to make a correction during a routine and omit a bonus point skill, she may be able to maintain a 10.0 start value if she has additional bonus points.

The final factor in extending longevity also deals with maintaining enthusiasm. College gymnasts are college students. The years they spend in college should be among the most exciting and interesting years of their lives—particularly socially. Most students live away from home for the first time. They live in a community of their peers, and they are introduced to all sorts of cultural, intellectual, and social experiences for the first time.

While highly talented gymnasts want to continue to pursue gymnastics, they would resent being pressured to spend so much time on gymnastics that they feel they are missing part of the wonderful college life. So it is important that practices and conditioning sessions be efficient in order to provide as much time as possible for the pursuit of other college activities.

These psychological factors are just as important as physical factors in extending longevity. Mental burnout can affect performance and start an endless cycle toward a premature halt to a gymnast's career.

And there is a physical benefit from reduced practice, too. The more a gymnast pounds on her body, the more likely she is to be injured and to cause possible long-term physical problems. So there is a double benefit from spending less time doing routines. A gymnast isn't likely to get injured doing aerobics or conditioning, but every time she does a landing or falls from the apparatus, her body takes a beating.

It is obvious to all of us who interact with them extensively that the GymDogs lead happy, well-rounded lives while in college. Most college gymnasts on other teams do too. Many of them meet their future husbands here. Some even get married before they graduate or complete their gymnastics careers. I don't think any college students anywhere have more fun than the GymDogs do. And I obviously have just as much fun as they do—maybe even more.

Some of the most striking statements I have heard about collegiate gymnastics came from members of the 1999 senior class. Their gymnastics performance was mentioned earlier, but psychological factors may have been at least as important as the physical ones. The class was considered the best recruiting class in history—all three U.S. gymnasts were national team members. The fourth was an alternate on the 1992 Canadian Olympic Team.

Karin Lichey and Sam Muhleman were the two freshmen who trained at the Cincinnati Gymnastics Academy (CGA) under 1996 Olympic coach Mary Lee Tracy. When Karin and Sam signed scholarship agreements with Georgia, their gymmate, Amanda Borden, also signed with Georgia, but Amanda deferred to try for the Olympic Team. Amanda made it and was chosen its captain.

Sam was the 1989 Junior Olympic Champion and could have made the Olympic Team had she not torn her Achilles Cruciate Ligament (ACL) in 1995. But even though Karin was apparently healthy, she chose college gymnastics over a shot at the Olympics. And she was considered by some the best of the Cincinnati gymnasts.

When the United States won the Olympic gold medal in women's gymnastics, Amanda and Jaycie Phelps (CGA) enjoyed all of the excitement that went along with being a part of the Magnificent Seven Tour—and the financial rewards, estimated at well over a million dollars each. In a media interview, Karin was asked to comment on her former gymmates' success. Among her comments was, "They're missing a wonderful experience in missing college gymnastics." Other GymDog team members, who might have qualified for the Olympic Team, have been quoted as saying, "I wouldn't trade my NCAA Championship ring(s) for an Olympic gold medal and all the money that came with it."

You can't imagine how these responses make me feel. I encouraged each of these young people to weigh carefully her decision about college versus the Olympics. Actually, Amanda was the only one who seriously considered trying for the Olympics, and I supported her all the way, attending the Olympic trials with her family and the Olympic finals. When the U.S. team won, Amanda came over and threw her bouquet to my daughter.

I also supported Amanda's decision, immediately after the Olympics, to forego college gymnastics in favor of participating in the professional tour, which made her ineligible for competition in college. To know that all of them, regardless of which path they took, believe that they made the right decision makes me feel that I fulfilled my responsibility in helping guide them. One reassuring result of the Magnificent Seven's professional tour is that all of them have either graduated college or are currently enrolled in college.

Mary Lee Tracy believes that college gymnastics can be a reward for dedication and hard work. This idea is reflected in the GymDogs' program. But lest you think Mary Lee doesn't emphasize training for the Olympics too, check these names of gymnasts who were training for the 2000 Olympic trials at the Cincinnati Gymnastics Academy: Dominique Moceanu, Alyssa Beckerman, Sierra Sapanur, Jenni Thompson, Brittany Smith, and Morgan White.

College gymnasts are not the only ones extending their performing careers. After dipping to an average age of 15.9 in 1992, the average age of the 1996 U.S. Olympic Team rose to 17.6, with Shannon Miller and Dominique Dawes, both aged 19. But the average age went even higher in 2000 when Amy Chow (22) and Dominique Dawes (23) made the team again, helping to make the average age 19.35—3.45 years older than the 1992 team and slightly above the 1956 average.

The average age of U.S. National All-Around Champions also tells the story of the dip and subsequent rise in age:

AVERAGE AGE	FIVE-YEAR PERIOD
18.8	1969–1972
17.4	1973–1976
15.2	1977–1981
	1982–1986
	1986–1991
	1992–1996
17.9	1997–2000 (4 years)

The gymnast whose performance I would like to see become the norm—with respect to national competition, college, and the Olympics—is Kelly Garrison. In 1980, at age thirteen, she won the national championship on the balance beam. That was too young, but she won it again in 1985 at age eighteen, and yet again in 1988 at twenty-one.

Kelly competed for the University of Oklahoma, and in 1988, her final year, she won NCAA Individual Championships on all-around, uneven bars, and balance beam. Then, immediately after college, she won a place on the 1988 U.S. Olympic Team. She was doing this when the average age of national champions and Olympians was falling.

Becky Buwick (Switzer), the highly respected and successful former women's gymnastics coach at the University of Oklahoma, coached Kelly from age ten through college, and even in the 1988 Olympics. Her story of Kelly's gymnastics career reveals how Kelly was able to achieve this unique performance. It's uncanny how Becky was learning the same things at Oklahoma that our coaches and I were learning at Georgia about longevity of performance—quite independently of each other. Here's a part of Becky's absorbing story about Kelly:

In 1987 we went to the World Championships. Kelly was twenty then, in college, and the oldest girl on the U.S. Team. The team had a horrible championship—everyone on the team from Kristi Phillips on down. Coming home on the plane we were just devastated. The one thing I had noticed more than anything was that Kelly didn't look like the rest of the competitors. She was a woman in a little girl's sport. I thought, "This is not going to work. Somehow we need to redesign her body. She can't be a little girl, but she will need to be as fit as possible. We're not going to be able to stay in this league and compete."

So that's when I talked with Coach Pete Martinelli, our own strength trainer at the University of Oklahoma. Pete really took control of Kelly's fitness training. He was very adamant about what she would eat and consume prior to competitions and during training. She got into weight training to increase muscle mass and streamline her body. Coach Martinelli devised a comprehensive program, and no one on the national scene saw Kelly for six months. It was in Athens, Georgia, in a zone meet, I believe, or USA Championships. I told her, "Don't even take your sweats off until you have to." Because she had really changed her body, and she was about to change the way women would train in her sport.

It was for the best. She was healthier. She was stronger. Her body fat content was down to around 9 percent at that time. Very lean. I think when she went to the 1988 Olympics, less than a year later, she was between 11 and 12 percent.

I think the muscle mass and lower body fat were the keys. Prior to the 1987 Worlds, her body fat was probably around 16 percent. That's still low for a woman; but not for the company that we were keeping. Something had to be done, and she made a commitment that if she was going to try for the '88 Olympics, training would need to change. We'd have to change our game plan for the better.

How's her health now? I'll put it to you this way: In summer camp, when I was still coaching, Kelly was doing double backs off beam. She was probably as good on beam at

age thirty-two, as she was ever. She's phenomenal. Her health
is very good—mental and physical health.

Becky's story of Kelly makes three points obvious: (1) Contrary
to the thinking at that time, muscle mass, nutrition, strength, and
conditioning are important keys to the performance of more mature
gymnasts. (2) Excessive training is counterproductive. (3) Coaches, in
addition to providing training, need to be deeply concerned about a
gymnast's physical and mental well-being.

Gymnasts outside the college arena are learning the keys to performance longevity. There is no more striking example than Svetlana
Boguinskaia. She was born in February of 1973 in Byelorussia, in the
Soviet Union. At the 1988 Olympics, at age fifteen, Svetlana placed
third in the all-around competition, representing the Soviet Union.
The next year she won the all-around competition at the twenty-
fifth World Gymnastics Championships with an almost perfect score of
39.900. Coincidentally, former GymDog Lori Strong competed in the
twenty-fifth World Gymnastics Championships. She was a few months
older than Svetlana. Lori's senior year at Georgia was unquestionably
her best, at age twenty-four.

At five feet four inches, Svetlana was taller than most gymnasts,
and her willowy figure made her one of the most graceful gymnasts
I've ever seen. Svetlana encountered many obstacles in her career. After
placing fifth in the 1992 Olympics all-around at age nineteen, she
decided to give up gymnastics. The Soviet Union had been broken up,
and she had difficulty finding sponsorship.

But Svetlana was not through. She loved gymnastics, and she
decided to make a comeback at the ripe old age (considered that for
gymnasts) of twenty-three. To coach her, she turned to Bela Karolyi,
who five years before had declared that her era was over. Man, did she
prove Bela wrong! Svetlana won the silver medal in all-around at the
1996 European Championships.

At twenty-six, Svetlana was touring and doing exhibitions in the
United States. She is still absolutely elegant. Svetlana gave birth to a

child in the summer of 1999. The thought of being a stay-at-home mother may have changed her priorities. Again, examining her career it appears that mental attitude had a big role in Svetlana's successful return.

It is also interesting that several other gymnasts have elected to stay out of competition and return after a year or so, to regain and perhaps exceed their previous levels of competence. Amanda Curry was a national team member in 1994 at age fifteen. Then she decided to retire from gymnastics to become a full-time, normal high school student. Amanda accomplished her goal. She was senior class president. Then, after a two-year hiatus from gymnastics, Amanda joined the GymDogs, making second team all-American on balance beam as a freshman. As a sophomore, Amanda continued to improve, making first team All-American on vault. As a junior, Amanda made first team All-American on beam and second team on vault.

Sam Muhleman, mentioned earlier, never ceases to amaze me. Out for the entire season, recovering from reconstructive knee surgery as a freshman, Sam began to participate in three events as a sophomore and got better each year. Because Georgia was loaded with quality vaulters, Sam was kept off the vault to protect her knee. But in her senior year, the vaulting lineup got skimpy. Kathleen Shrieves, who scored a 9.950 in the 1998 NCAA finals, was out for the season with an injury sustained in the first meet.

One day, about mid-season, Sam said to me, "Give me a try at vaulting, if you think I can help the team." I thought there was no way Sam could vault after not even training for vault for over three years. But I have learned to never say "never" to a gymnast who wants to contribute and fulfill her desire, unless you think what she suggests will be dangerous for her.

In the seventh meet of the season, Sam competed vault for the first time in four years and scored a 9.825 on a pike-front, a vault with a maximum value of 9.900. After staying out for a meet, Sam vaulted in three consecutive meets, scoring perfect 9.900s on each vault. Furthermore, by adding vaulting to her routines, Sam was competing in all-around, and she scored the fourth highest all-around score in the country, 39.725, in her third all-around competition. All of this at the ancient age of twenty-two.

Let me summarize my observations over the years: I'll start with the age-group gymnasts. I believe that training should be limited to no more than twenty-five hours a week for children under ten years old, and all training for serious aspiring gymnasts should be under the watchful eye of their coach.

Another suggestion is elimination of the requirement to perform all-around in age-group gymnastics. The Olympics dropped the all-around requirement for the year 2000. This could reduce training time markedly. After all, swimmers and track and field athletes don't have to perform every event. Can you picture a shot putter attempting a pole vault? And, of course, college gymnasts are not required to perform all-around either and fewer than half of them do. And teams aren't required to have two gymnasts compete in all-around at each meet as they were a few years ago.

And gymnasts should receive guidance while performing repetitions. Good coaching can improve the efficiency of time spent in the gym, and fewer repetitions mean fewer injuries.

Young gymnasts probably don't need as much physical conditioning as older ones, but they should be conditioned sufficiently to reduce injuries. Appropriate conditioning will also improve performance. So the proper mix of training of all types is critical. And, by all means, gymnasts need to eat diets suited to their physical activities.

While I think the concern expressed by some zealots about losing bone density is not founded in fact, limiting training will completely silence the activists who try to scare parents and gymnasts about bone density. And it has really hurt me over the years to see so many gymnasts come to college who have been deprived of a normal "growing up" because of overly extensive gymnastics training. Train smart, and have fun.

I advise parents and coaches to never push a child into gymnastics. If they don't enjoy it enough to be self-motivated, find something that motivates them. And coaches should use the same discipline techniques that work in other endeavors. Be strict, but be constructive and positive. It works better for every gymnast I've coached.

For the gymnasts who do well in competition and reach 9, 10, and elite levels, set college gymnastics as a goal for continued competition after high school. What better motivation can there be to keep going? We don't lose many gymnasts to the Olympics, especially since it occurs only once every four years.

Be careful in allowing young gymnasts to accept money before college. Too many young gymnasts have accepted just a few thousand dollars and become ineligible for a college scholarship worth up to a hundred thousand dollars. That's literally being penny-wise and dollar-foolish.

So are gymnasts over-the-hill at eighteen? Absolutely not. Today, barring injury, nearly every college gymnast improves right up through her senior year if she is fit and motivated. If you think I'm dreaming, read on. In 2004 a second former collegian made the U.S. Olympic Team—this one by a circuitous route. After she barely missed making the 1996 Olympic Team at age seventeen, Mohini Bhardwaj competed for UCLA from 1998 through 2001, winning two individual NCAA crowns (vault in 1999 and floor in 2001) and garnering first team All America citations. Mohini "retired" from gymnastics in 2002 following an injury. But in 2004 she decided to try for the U.S. Olympic Team again. This time, at age twenty-five, Mohini made the team. She was even chosen captain. Don't try to tell Mohini that gymnasts are over-the-hill at eighteen.

Eat On Get Out of My Gym

K elly Macy moved to Overland Park, Kansas, a suburb of Kansas City, after she had become an elite-level gymnast. She trained in Georgia and Florida during her earlier years. At that time, she was the only elite-level gymnast in Kansas and trained at Elite Gymnastics under Gerald Carley and Al Overton. Just across the river, in Blue Springs Missouri, Kelly's contemporary, Christi Henrich, was training at the Great American Gymnastics Express.

Because all athletes need to train with other athletes who can push them competitively, Kelly's coaches would take her over to train in the same gym with Christi. Christi was the only elite-level gymnast in Missouri, so it was a natural for them to train together. Kelly said that the gym in Blue Springs was "absolutely fantastic." Kelly and Christi got to be close friends, training together on weekends, performing and talking at clinics, and "hanging out" together. They both had the common goal of making the 1988 Olympic Team.

In 1986, at age fourteen, Christi finished fifth in the all-around in the national junior championships. In early 1988, Christi finished tenth in the all-around at senior nationals. She was getting close to her goal of making the 1988 Olympic Team. But she missed making the team by less than 0.2 point in the compulsories at the trials.

Not to be denied the opportunity, Christi set her sights on the 1992 Olympics. She seemed to be well on her way. She had her best year in 1989, finishing second in the all-around at the U.S. National

Championships and fourth in the World Championships. She missed the bronze medal by 0.25 point.

Despite fracturing a vertebra on a dismount in 1989 and fighting a bout with mononucleosis in the spring of 1990, Christi returned to competition in time to tie Kim Zmeskal and Erica Stokes for the silver medal on uneven bars at the 1990 U.S. National Championships. She was looking forward to the 1992 Olympics.

Kelly also qualified for the U.S. National Championship in 1988. She had made the national team as early as 1985, but injuries about the time of the championships kept her out of the running. Although she made the national team in 1989, Kelly began to see the writing on the wall. She was not likely to be on the 1992 Olympic Team. She knew that only six girls of the twenty who make the national team make the Olympic Team.

But fortunately, Kelly had set an alternative goal. She knew she wanted to attend college, so she decided to put her gymnastics talents to good use and focus on receiving an athletic scholarship. She loved gymnastics. She wanted to go to college. So what could be better?

Kelly said:

"I was excited about college at that point, after learning that I wasn't eligible for the Olympics. It was almost a relief to look at something else—a goal I knew I could reach. It was a real boost to my ego and self-esteem to be recruited by the best teams in the country—Georgia, Alabama, Utah, Arizona State, and Florida. I took trips only to Utah, Arizona State, and Georgia."

So when I offered her a scholarship to enter the University of Georgia in the fall of 1990, Kelly jumped at the chance. She hit the ground running at the beginning of fall practice.

I really expected Kelly to be good from the beginning. She was generally considered among the top-five recruits in the country. We actually rated her number two. But the consensus number one recruit was Kelly's roommate at Georgia, Hope Spivey, who was on the 1988 U.S. Olympic Team. Regardless of how Kelly and Hope were ranked before the season, it wasn't long before I was talking about them as being of equal caliber. They were our two "fabulous freshmen."

To promote our opening meet with UCLA, we decided to showcase our fabulous freshmen at the Georgia-Florida men's basketball game, which drew a sellout crowd of 10,400 fans. We put a balance beam in the middle of the floor at half time and let them go at it. They did great. Kelly said appearing before the large crowd really helped her. She was nervous at first, but after she got going, she fed off the crowd's response.

We still didn't know how Hope and Kelly would do in competition, but it didn't take long to find out. In our opening meet against UCLA, they both performed all-around. Hope took first with a 38.7 and Kelly wasn't far behind with a 38.2.

Kelly was driven, and she was intense. These characteristics would figure prominently in her behavior not too many months later.

There was a bit of premonition in a statement I pulled from the scrapbook: Kelly's statement to the *Athens Banner-Herald* newspaper after the UCLA, meet:

"I wasn't expecting to score 38.2, but I'm sure glad I did," the bubbly gymnast from Overland Park, Kansas said. "Suzanne's been telling me all fall how good I was, but I always found something to improve on. Even though I scored a 38.2, I know I can still improve, and my goal for the season is to break 39.0."

I always told Kelly she could be as good as she wanted to be. Kelly would hold onto every word I said. Kelly was definitely the most consistent member of the team. She competed in every meet like it was the national championships. Even in practice, she performed like it was a big meet.

But out of the gym Kelly was different. An article in the *Bulldog Magazine* described her this way: "Macy is California cool, freewheeling in M. C. Hammer pants and Chuck Taylor high-tops. She describes herself as 'mellow, upbeat, and obnoxious.' Macy has displayed the adaptability of a desert chameleon. As a matter of fact, she has gone a step further. More than simply adjusting to her new environment, she is said to be thriving as a collegiate gymnast at the University of Georgia."

Kelly improved more in one year than any other freshman we've ever had. Her skills improved dramatically. Kelly was the type of gymnast who blossoms in an environment where everyone is good.

Consistency became Kelly's trademark during the season. Consistency is something most of our gymnasts develop later in their college careers, but Kelly was consistent right out of the blocks. She led the team for the season in scoring average on both uneven bars and balance beam. And she achieved the goal of breaking the 39.0 all-around twice.

We had a rash of injuries during the season. That was the year Heather Stepp blew out her elbow. Hope sprained her wrist and missed several meets. And, as most freshmen do, Hope had some consistency problems during the regular season, even though she was on the 1988 Olympic Team. But Kelly stayed healthy all year. And she was an iron lady in terms of endurance. Kelly competed in the all-around in all twelve of the GymDogs' meets. By the end of the season, she was our anchor on bars and next-to-last up on beam. She just had a terrific freshman regular season.

So when the time came for our coaches to select a candidate for Freshman-of-the-Year in the Southeastern Conference, we nominated Kelly. And she won the award, which is voted on by the other coaches in the conference.

The Freshman-of-the-Year award was determined before the SEC meet. Kelly lived up to our confidence in her. On Thursday before the meet on Saturday, she accidentally put her hand through a glass window. The injury required eight stitches. Did it slow Kelly? No way! She came in second in the all-around in the SEC meet with a 39.100 and continued her upward spiral at regionals with a record-breaking 9.925 on bars. And she topped her SEC all-around score with a 39.125. Kelly was just soaring higher and higher. As mentioned earlier, she won the NCAA individual bars championship. What a freshman year!

Kelly Macy left to go home to Kansas for the summer on a high she probably never dreamed of reaching so soon. She was as lively as she could be. Her 115 pounds on her four-feet-eleven-inch frame was all muscle—just 12 percent body fat.

I would be remiss not to mention that Hope Spivey really came on strong near the end of the season. To sum it up, Hope won the Honda

Sports Award as the nation's top collegiate gymnast—as a freshman. Needless to say, I was bursting with enthusiasm to welcome Hope and Kelly back in the fall for their sophomore seasons.

Christi's story had a different outcome. In the fall of 1990, when Kelly was entering the University of Georgia, Christi was about to perform at a USA-USSR challenge meet in Oregon. Just before the meet, her coach, Al Fong, pulled her from competition when it became obvious in practice that she was too weak to perform safely.

What was going on? We'll probably never know exactly, but one of the accounts of Christi's battle with anorexia nervosa and bulimia attributes its start to a remark made by a judge in March of 1988, when Christi was in Budapest, Hungary, traveling as a member of the U.S. National Team.

Christi was described at the time as a four-feet-ten, 100-pound amalgam of muscle and iron-competitive will. Sounds a lot like Kelly at the end of her freshman year. The judge told her that she weighed too much to make a serious run at the Olympic Team. Some judges do consider that all gymnasts should be slender. Of course that's nonsense; a gymnast's weight, like that of any other person, should match bone structure and other characteristics. There is no standard weight for a given height. However, muscle mass is important, because gymnasts have to be strong to perform.

As the story goes, Christi took the remark to heart way down deep and could never get rid of the idea that she was fat—even though she wasn't.

So while Kelly was soaring to the top in collegiate gymnastics, Christi announced her "retirement" in early 1991. At the time, she attributed her physical weakness to two bouts with mononucleosis. Publicly, there was no mention of anorexia or bulimia.

Kelly didn't have the benefit of knowing just what was happening to Christi. She was looking for a way to keep her upward spiral going during the summer. She wanted to return to Georgia in the fall in even better condition than she was in when she left in the spring. Basically, her objectives for the summer were to stay in shape, get a little better, come back as a sophomore, and win another title.

I can't speak for Kelly about what goes on inside the mind of one suffering from anorexia. I believe that Kelly's story in her own words will help you understand her state of mind:

Christi Henrich and I competed against each other. We would see each other at meets. It was just a very casual, friendly relationship. We just saw each other once in a while. But when we started training over at Al Fong's gym, Christi and I got a lot closer, as far as our friendship was concerned. We saw each other pretty much every day in the summers and hung out. We were really good friends.

I was training about forty plus hours a week. It was a full-time job.

No one mentioned weight to me specifically; it was more of a general thing. They would line us up and look at us front and back. They would tell us that we needed to weigh in. They'd make gestures and suggest that maybe we need to ride the bikes a little more. Nothing was ever said about my weight in particular. It was more directed toward the entire group. I never really had a weight problem. I was always fairly thin. I never even thought much about it. When I was in high school, I may have been a little more conscious of my weight. To be honest, I was so young, and prior to coming to Georgia, my mom was preparing my food. When you're not preparing your own food, it's a lot easier to eat right.

When we would go to the Olympic training center for national training camps and like that, they would have talks on nutrition, here and there, but I don't recall it being a big issue. Not as much as it should have been.

It was a real boost to my ego and self esteem to be recruited by the best teams in the country. I always thought before coming to college that once you went to college you really didn't get better. That was the general attitude back then.

In club gymnastics they seldom checked body fat or

body density. I may have had it checked once or twice at the Olympic training center. It was more what you weighed on the scale—not body composition.

I was surprised that I progressed as much as I did during my freshman year. I think it was nice that I was surrounded by great gymnasts. That helped, because we would push each other. I always looked up to Hope, because she was the Olympian. I guess it was a little bit of a relief because there wasn't as much pressure on me. She was the star. She was in the limelight. Everyone knew about Hope. So I think I shocked a lot of people when I did as well as I did. Then, of course, winning the national title just to top it off was awesome. Even though the team didn't win the national championship, we won SECs and that was great. It was so awesome. It was an awesome experience to be involved in.

In looking back at my freshman year, I think I may have had some concerns about my weight. I grew up a lot when I went to college. I matured. I was going through the biological changes that most women go through when they are thirteen or fourteen years old. Between the time when I came to Georgia on my trip and the time I came to enter school, I had gained a little weight already. After I got here I was doing aerobics and weighing in. It was a bigger deal. It was a big part of what we were doing. It was I, myself, putting pressure on me—more than anyone else.

The body fat index was introduced to me for the first time at Georgia, because it's not what you weigh on the scales, it's your lean muscle mass which is important.

I believe I talked on the phone to Christi Henrich a couple of times during the summer of 1991 when I went home. I never "saw" her though. I never saw her or saw what she looked like.

I kind of suspected that Christi might be anoretic because when I saw her at a meet right before I left to return to

Georgia, she was very thin. She was a lot thinner than normal. She was normally more of a stocky girl. Real muscular build. She wasn't your tiny Nadia Comaneci body. She was like your Mary Lou Retton-type body. Which was not so much the style anymore—according to the coaches and judges.

My summer of 1991 was filled with pressure that I put on myself. I knew that the incoming class at Georgia with Agina, Nneka, and Andrea was considered the best recruiting class in the country. I knew that I was really going to have to push myself to stay at the level that I had attained as a freshman in order to continue to be in the lineup. I thought I could do that by trying to lose weight.

I figured that if I could lose about five or six pounds, it would be so much easier for me, and I'd be stronger. I never even considered that it could become an addictive thing. My mom was working, my dad worked—they weren't at home all day, and my sister was never home. I would really start restricting my food. I would put a limit on how many calories I wanted to eat each day. And I made sure that I was doing so much aerobic activity that I was burning everything I put in my body—and more.

So I started with an unstated goal of losing three to five pounds max. But to be honest with you, it was like a rush till I could stand on the scale and see that I had lost more weight. I lost the five pounds within a week and a half. So I said, "Wow, that was pretty easy. If I lost that much that quickly, I betcha I could lose some more."

And when I started thinking about it that way, I thought, Last week I only ate a thousand calories, so this week I'm only going to eat five hundred. And I'll increase the cardiovascular to be even lighter and lighter. The weight would just come right off. I was starving myself, really.

I was still training in the gym too. I was probably doing about four hours a day. I was training even more than I was at

Georgia. I was doing four hours a day, Monday through Friday, and then I would take the weekends off.

Keep in mind that was just in the gym. Then I would run or roller-blade or jump rope—you name it, and I did it. I lost 15 pounds—down to 100 pounds.

Emotionally, I felt great because I thought that I was strong. I was going back to Georgia in tip-top shape and make myself proud. And I was going to make Suzanne proud, and we were going to win a national championship next year, and hopefully I would repeat my bar title.

When I went into the gym at Georgia, I was feeling great. I felt like I was stronger. I didn't feel weak. But it was totally mental.

By this time I was obsessed with the scale. I would weigh myself twenty times a day. I'd weigh myself when I got up in the morning, and then I would take a glass of water, and I'd weigh myself. Then I'd go to the bathroom and then weigh myself. I'd put on clothes and weigh myself. It was just so obsessive.

When I got back to school, a way for me to not think about food was to study harder. I was doing very well academically, but I was "over studying." That was the only way I could not think about food.

Because of what I now know about anorexia, I try to think back about my attitude toward mirrors. I think that when I looked in the mirror, I saw someone who was heavy. Even when I had lost all that weight, I'd think, I'd like to lose an inch on my thighs and an inch on my butt. And I'd still be looking at the mirror and think, Yea, you've lost this weight, but if you could lose just a little bit more in your stomach, that would be awesome. I don't think I was ever satisfied.

During the summer, I really didn't notice any difference in my attitude toward my mom and dad because I wasn't around them much. I did try to cover myself up—wearing baggy clothes and this and that. I'm sure I drove them crazy talking about food and how much I weighed.

I think my mom might have begun to suspect that I was developing an eating disorder. I don't think my dad thought that I would do that.

I didn't think I had a problem. I knew that I was obsessed with food, but I knew that I was doing this because I thought it would make me a better athlete. Not one time did it cross my mind that I was hurting myself.

I never made myself vomit. My way of purging was to workout. When I ate, I would feel guilty. But instead of vomiting, I would go run.

When I got back to Georgia, they checked my body fat. My body fat was good. It was within Suzanne's percentage limits. But when I got to the gym, I discovered that I really couldn't do anything.

When I checked in, I really didn't look bad. At that point, I'd lost fifteen pounds. So the coaches didn't show any concern. But when I got to the gym, here I was the national champion and I couldn't even do a handstand on bars. That's when they started realizing that something was wrong. I think they thought perhaps I hadn't worked out much during the summer. So they were going to give me a little bit of time. But I continued to lose more weight.

Doug and Jay were the assistant coaches. I think all of the coaches may have been concerned, but it was Suzanne who approached me about it and asked, "Kelly, are you eating? I'm hearing from your roommates that you talk about food all the time, you weigh yourself all the time. And they tell me you're not eating. Is this true?" My teammates were beginning to get concerned. And when they mentioned it to me, I wouldn't listen to them. So they went to Suzanne.

She called my father. My parents were still in Kansas. When Suzanne contacted them, I think they were quite concerned that something was wrong. It really started worrying my mother and my sister. Everybody was so worried. But I was still in denial.

Suzanne went to a clinic in Florida to learn all she could about anorexia. And when she came back, I had lost more weight.

One day shortly after she returned, she pulled me aside after we had weighed in and told me that she had been in contact with my parents, and that if I didn't start eating, I wasn't going to do gymnastics anymore. My father was going to pick me up, and I was going home. She said that I could die if I continued to starve myself. I think that was a good wake-up call for me.

My first reaction was, What's she talking about? My first reaction was denial. I said, "Suzanne, I don't have a problem." And she said, "Well I'm going to make sure you don't have a problem. And this is what's going to happen. You're not going to work out. You're going to come in here and you're going to sit and watch everyone else work out. You're going to sit here and eat in the gym—a meal in front of me every day. And when your weight gets up to 105 you can start working out again. But until then, you're not going to work out."

Suzanne had me go to the University Health Center. I was meeting with a psychologist there and also a nutritionist. And I also had to go to weekly eating-disorder meetings. All of which were monitored. The monitors were supposed to tell Suzanne if I was not there. And if I wasn't there, it would go against me as far as working out. Everything was very regimented. Because I was in denial. I probably wouldn't have gone, if I hadn't been forced to go.

Suzanne wouldn't let me start training full time until I weighed 105. I got down to about 80 pounds. For every 3 pounds I gained, I could work out 15 more minutes. That started when I was down at about 80 pounds.

One thing I do want to say is that at that point when

my parents were so involved, and they were worried sick at that point, Dad had been transferred to Dayton. But my dad accepted a position to move the family to Georgia so that they could be closer to me.

During the '92 season, I competed at about 108 pounds. So Suzanne's program got me back up to near my best weight real fast. I probably weighed about 112 in '93 and 114 my senior year. My body density was acceptable all of this time. I was losing body fat and gaining muscle. I was eating a lot better. And I was doing everything I was supposed to be doing.

At the point when I started gaining more weight and I could work out, I had my days when I would slip back into it. Because it would be so traumatizing to see the scale go up. I was afraid that it wouldn't stop. I was still not completely out of it. This was through the sophomore year.

During this period, I had to actually eat in the gym and eat every meal with one of the gymnasts or one of my coaches until I was up to my weight. Even in 1993, after I was up to my weight and training full time, Suzanne would not let me move out of the athletic dormitory. Normally you can move out after your sophomore year. She required that I stay there until my senior year. That way she could check up with the dormitory monitors and make sure I was eating in the athletic dining hall.

I don't think I ever quite returned to my freshman form for certain events. I was about the same on bars and beam. But I was not back up to my freshman standards on vault and floor. The thing that helped me so much gymnastically was that there were so many good gymnasts on the team. It helped push me. I really think I was as good on bars and beam as I was my freshman year. I was a little stronger, but the other gymnasts were so strong, so it was more difficult to make the lineups.

If it wasn't for Suzanne's giving me the wake-up call, I don't really know what would have happened. All of my teammates and other coaches were just great in supporting me and helping me through this. My parents were extremely supportive, of course. They would not give me attention for my negative behavior. I could find better ways to get attention. They didn't want to acknowledge that I was doing this to myself, so they wanted to do everything they could not to recognize it.

Right after college, I gained a little weight. I grew two more inches after I was out of school. I went from four feet eleven to five feet one inch. I wanted to stop caring about my weight. I wanted to be all-the-way normal. I think in the back of my head I know that I'm never going to be all the way better. What I mean by saying that is that I know that I could always have this disease if I allowed it. It's my will and my love for myself and all my family and everybody that I can't do it. I have to go and eat that piece of pizza and not worry about how long I have to run to burn it off.

After so much attention was being given to anorexia, I was invited to tell my story on several television shows, including *Sally Jessy Raphaël*. I did the *Sports Illustrated* article, and I was on *ESPN Sports Center* focusing on the problem of eating disorders, my correlation, and my friendship with Christi. And how that really plays a vital role in making me know that that's exactly why I can't let this happen anymore, because it can kill you.

It wasn't gymnastics that made me anoretic. It was my love for the sport and my desire to excel. It was my drive to be the best and do what's required to be the best. Actually, it was probably the gymnastics environment and my desire to be allowed back in the gym which saved me.

Currently, I'm a pharmaceutical sales representative. I work for Phizer. I've been with them about seven years. I really love it. I'm able to bring my interest in health and my business background together. I call on different physicians for various and different drugs. I get to meet with well-educated people. You know, I'm a social butterfly, so it's really terrific for me.

I did gain some weight right after college. So I started working hard at eating normally and working out to stay healthy. I weigh between 108 and 110, and that's a good weight for me.

I married Brad Roberson on October 16, 1999. We have a daughter, Macy Lynn, who's about three now. Brad's my best friend and he kinda helps me on those days I'm not feeling so great. He keeps me healthy. He makes me normal—not as much of a perfectionist as I used to be.

One thing I did want to let you know is that although I look back at it as a very traumatizing experience, in a way I think it was supposed to happen to me because I had the resources and people who loved me and helped me. After that, I was able to talk about it and hopefully touch the lives of some other people who have the same problem and don't know how they're going to get through it. But since I'm so open about it, I take it as a learning experience.

If it wasn't for Suzanne, what happened to Christi could have happened to me.

Mike and Linda Macy, Kelly's parents, are more emphatic. Mike says I saved Kelly's life. Here's an excerpt from a note Mike wrote to us: "I will always remember Kelly's tenure at Georgia with laughter as well as tears. The many successes of the gymnastic team, her own gymnastic successes, the tailgate parties, her academic achievements, brought so much laughter and joy. The tears are not due to sadness, but of joy—knowing that my little girl is alive—living through that hell called OCD [Obsessive-Compulsive Disorder]. And her existence today is attributed to having a loving, supportive group. And Suzanne was the driving force!"

I was reluctant to accept the responsibility of dealing with a life-threatening illness in one of my gymnasts. I had many other responsibilities, and I was not an expert in dealing with anorexia nervosa. But her parents finally persuaded me that they thought I could help Kelly more than they could. So, even though I was scared, I realized that the Macys might be right. I had tremendous professional health and nutrition resources available at the University of Georgia. In addition, I had a team of dedicated gymnasts who loved Kelly and wanted to help. So I went to a clinic in Florida, learned as much as I could, and came back with a plan. I would harness Kelly's obsession with gymnastics to drive her to eat. I would depart from the more traditional treatments and use a tough-love approach.

I didn't have much time. I had learned that a person is considered profoundly anoretic when her weight drops down to 85 percent of her desired weight. This usually happens over several months or even years. By November of 1991, Kelly was down to less than 70 percent of what she weighed when she left Athens to go home for the summer in 1991. And she lost the weight in a matter of six months.

Kelly had been getting compliments on her weight loss from her teammates and other students, so she was in denial and difficult to convince that she had a problem. I decided to get tough: "You think you're playing games, don't you?" Kelly confidently answered, "What are you talking about? I'm doing this to be a better gymnast." I responded, "Well, you're not going to compete for Georgia. You're not going to do gymnastics here again. And you could die." I decided I didn't have much to lose. She was going to die if we couldn't turn things around—fast.

I decided to bank on her motivation to do gymnastics, so I organized the team of experts she mentioned and had her meet with them on a rigid schedule. I required her to come to the gym and watch the other girls work out. I had someone eat every meal with her and make sure she ate her prescribed diet. And I gave her a step-by-step reward. For every three pounds she gained, she could work out fifteen more minutes.

No one was more astounded than I when Kelly started gaining weight at a rate of three pounds per week, and she was back to training two hours a day within two months. Shortly after the season started, she weighed 108 pounds, and I put her on the same training schedule as the rest of the team.

In the meantime, Christi Henrich had retired from gymnastics. She went through a series of ups and downs—in and out of clinics and hospitals—for a period of three years. Her weight dropped from ninety-five pounds to a low of forty-seven pounds on July 2, 1994. And despite regaining back to sixty-one pounds by near the end of July, she died of multiple organ failure on July 26, eight days past her twenty-second birthday.

When Kelly heard of Christi's death, she was devastated. She had just completed a wonderful collegiate experience, helping her team win the 1993 NCAA National Championship and preparing to take a few more courses at Georgia to complete requirements for her bachelor's degree. "I couldn't go to the funeral," she lamented. "I wanted to remember how she was. She was such a sweet girl—she was bubbly—she was energetic. I guess I thought it could have been me. And that hit hard."

After coaching gymnastics for over thirty years, twenty in college, this is my assessment: I don't think the problem with college gymnasts is anorexia. I think it's food addiction. And the reason that these gymnasts have food addiction is because they're obsessed about what to eat and what not to eat from the time they're ten years old. And they get this obsession more from their coaches, probably, than from their parents. It carries back over to their parents, but the problem's root is probably with their coaches.

It's a constant conversation from the minute you get up until the minute you go to bed. What did you eat today? And you can ask any gymnast in any club. They grow up with that. Even with the coaches who are doing a good job, it's still a constant conversation. Hope Spivey, while training for the Olympics, couldn't get on the balance beam without being told, "You look heavier today, go weigh yourself." If she was a half pound heavier than she was the day before, she had to run laps before she could start practice. How can you look a half a pound heavier than you did yesterday?

It became not only an obsession for the athletes, but also an obsession for the coaches. And you see it everywhere. Even in the best coaches in the country, even in the coaches that would try to do it right, like Mary Lee, who are focusing on eating correctly. But still, the bottom line is a constant conversation about food. It takes on a life of its own. I doubt that there's a gymnast out there who doesn't have food addiction to some degree, and when food addiction gets to be too extreme, anorexia or bulimia can develop. So it's just a matter of being careful, evaluating at what level gymnasts have this food addiction and whether it's manageable or not.

I think that the better athlete you are, the better student you are, the better musician you are—that the people who want to be the best of the best have obsessions. They're obsessed with whatever it is they excel in. That's one of the reasons they excel. I think it's more of a problem of obsessive-compulsive behavior, and it just happens to become a food addiction or eating disorder. And when gymnastics is over, the obsessive-compulsive behavior is still there. So now it may not be an eating disorder; it may be some other obsession.

A lot of highly motivated people have obsessive-compulsive behavior. I didn't educate myself as much on anorexia as I did on obsessive-compulsive behavior. When the problem occurred with Kelly, I tried to draw the attention of her obsessions into other areas besides the food addition. Obsess on making good grades—an obsession that won't hurt you. So we would start talking more about academics: "How did you do in school? What are your grades in school?" I'd try to put those ideas in her mind, so she would start obsessing on that rather than, "What did you eat today?"

I think that coaches, without realizing it, by talking about food all the time, create a situation in which a gymnast's obsession attaches itself to food. This happens even if the coach is talking about the good things one should eat, so some kids end up being anoretic or bulimic. Even when you have nutritionists work with the gymnasts, you're feeding the theory. You're feeding the animal—more conversation about food, about what to eat and what not to eat.

Every athlete needs to be strong in order to do well. So obviously the focus needs to be on an athlete's lean muscle mass, not his or her weight. And percent body fat is related to how much lean muscle you have. The more lean muscle you have, the less body fat you have. The more lean muscle you have, the higher the metabolism. The more lean muscle mass you have, the more you can eat and not gain weight. So the emphasis should be on having a high lean muscle mass and the focus on conditioning and strengthening. I've tried to make that our focus.

I don't think we've had anyone with anorexia except for Kelly Macy. We've had people on the thin side who have been obsessive-compulsive about their eating to the point of losing more weight than they should, but not to a dangerous level that I would classify as being anoretic.

We don't have many bulimics in the traditional sense—overeating and inducing vomiting. Some gymnasts would overeat, feel guilty, and ride the bike—overeat, feel guilty, and take a midnight run. A lot of gymnasts are big on all the little games you play before you weigh yourself: not eating all day and then overeating in the evening—binging and purging—only the purge is exercise. It's exercise bulimia, and exercise bulimia is not a healthy way to live. You starve all day, pig out at night, and then go run at two in the morning because you feel guilty. When you're doing it on a regular basis—trying to exercise away your guilt and your bad feelings toward yourself—it's easy to fall into that pattern of exercise bulimia.

I've never talked much with other coaches about percentages of athletes who are anoretic or bulimic. I know that at Penn State, the girls weren't allowed to be weighed in. The administration stepped in because they had so many problems on their team that they told Steve Shephard that they couldn't weigh the girls or be involved in it at all. Some schools have taken it out of the hands of the coaches altogether and put it in the hands of the trainers. Some colleges don't want there to be any mention of weight or conversation about weight. I don't think you can coach a competitive gymnastics program and not have conversations about body composition. You have to talk about it.

But we walk a thin line. The more you feed that animal, the more it continues on—for some gymnasts, from ten years old on, it's all they've ever heard. That's a horrible situation—growing up with the obsession—horrible.

My feeling about maintaining proper body fat has changed through the years. We had years of tremendous success during which we gave the girls the information and education, in terms of eating more protein and less fat, and things took care of themselves. Julie Ballard and Kimmie Arnold in '98 and '99 are perfect examples. Their body composition went from 19 percent to 13 percent just from eating correctly—eating a low carbohydrate diet. But Kimmie, who changed her body type and changed her eating habits, was also an exercise fanatic. There's no question about it. She was on the bicycle twice a day, every day. When she went to a gymnastics meet out of town, you'd find her down on the bike in the morning. Even though she was healthy, physically healthy, and ate well, she was very obsessed about her weight. But was she bulimic in the medical sense of the word? No. Was she anoretic? No. Was it dangerous? No. Was she obsessive-compulsive? Yes.

I like to encourage the exercise, but not because one overeats. I like to encourage a change in lifestyle—that's what we talk to them about. I tell my gymnasts, "I want you to eat and exercise for a lifestyle. If you want to exercise five days a week for one hour, let's do it. But let's not exercise four times a day every day. That you cannot do for a lifetime."

I've also changed through the years my thoughts about taking advantage of self-discipline—because we have some kids now who are more in control of what they eat. They're more disciplined with what they eat. They are more disciplined with how they exercise. They maintain their lifestyle, and there doesn't need to be much conversation about weight and exercise. I've found that it's very contagious on a team. When you get a team that has four or five really good athletes, good habits take care of themselves. But if you have three or four who are overeating, then that's contagious as well.

The GymDogs have gone through years when I didn't tell the girls what to eat. I didn't control what they ate. We didn't go out to restaurants and have conversations about what they ate. But in 2003, in particular, that started to change because I felt that for the last couple of years some of our team members had not made good choices in eating patterns. It frustrates me to go to a restaurant and see fried cheese and bread being passed up and down the table and my gymnasts eating two and three pieces before they've ordered their dinner. They know better than that. But I don't want to be on them all the time about what they're eating because they're twenty-one years old. They need to take responsibility for it themselves.

I don't want to be a controlling coach who does not allow her gymnasts to order bread. I think that's what's wrong with these kids, from the time they were ten and eleven years old, instead of being taught and educated to make the right decisions, they were told, "You can't have this, you can't have that." Then they end up sneaking candy bars in their suitcases when they're growing up. They go to college and don't have a coach telling them what they can and cannot have, so they end up out of control. Different girls have different needs, so I have treated each one according to her needs.

For a period of four years, we had the team members fill out a questionnaire on food addiction. The results indicated to me that they've all got a food addiction. A few questions on the list were: "When you walk by a scale, do you feel the need and drive and desire to get on the scales to see what you weigh? Do you weigh yourself in the morning? Does your weight affect your mood and temperament throughout the day? If you weigh yourself, and you don't like what you weigh, do you take off another piece of clothing, and then get back on the same scale—and then take off another piece and another piece and another piece?" We asked the questions to every girl on the team. We learned that most gymnasts want to get on the scale when they go by. Most of them step on the scale in the morning and have their day determined by what their weight is.

An ideal percentage of body fat will vary from athlete to athlete. Chelsa Byrd reported to Georgia as a freshman at 9 percent body fat. She's healthy, strong, and successful at 9 percent; she doesn't need to be 12 percent, which is about average for the team. We try to determine a body fat goal for each gymnast based on her gymnastics ability and how she looks. If she is doing all skills, looks good, and she is 15 percent body fat, then that's fine with us. If it works for the athlete, 18 percent is fine. I used to think that everybody needed to be under 15 percent, but Gina Bañales was 18 percent. Lucy Wener was 18 percent. And Andrea Thomas was 18 percent. All were very successful athletes. Everyone's composition is different.

As far as nutritionists, we don't have a staff member called a team nutritionist; we use various ones. Currently we work through our trainer, Jennifer Cappuzzo, if we feel someone has an eating problem and her body composition isn't good. If we think a gymnast might be taking laxatives or is bulimic in some way, we don't want it to get worse. Then we require her to see a nutritionist at the University of Georgia Health Center. The gymnast makes the appointment. We want every athlete to be as strong as she was before, on her own initiative. Each gymnast selects her own nutritionist. If she doesn't like one person, she gets someone else.

The gymnasts know body composition is an important part of their success. Just like they know they have to study to make good grades. If a gymnast needs a tutor, she needs to get a tutor. If she needs a nutritionist, she needs to get the nutritionist. And actually it's worked out well. Sierra Sapunar's been seeing a nutritionist for a couple of years now because she wants to, and she likes to have the information. Having the knowledge gives her confidence. She chooses to go on her own, and I think that's the way it should be handled. For many years we had a nutritionist come to the locker room and meet with everybody, but we changed that approach.

At the University of Georgia, we have had about twenty students suffering from anorexia in all of our athletic programs combined in the last three years. None of them was a gymnast. UGA has had maybe thirty in the last five years, and none was a gymnast. One was a tennis player, a cheerleader, a volleyball player, and two were swimmers. They represented a variety of sports. Anorexia is prevalent in women in our society. Athletes are just a cross section. The percentage is not any higher among athletes than among women in general.

When a gymnast has a food addiction problem, I don't think gymnastics is the cause. The problem stems from television and magazines, and I think the problem starts when a girl is two or three years old. Kids grow up being told, "Don't eat too much of that; you'll get fat." You don't ever want to teach the negatives. You want to teach with the positives. When the child is three years old and you drive up to McDonald's, order grilled chicken, not fried chicken. Tell the child, "We don't eat fried chicken, it's not good for you," instead of, "Don't eat any more candy, you'll get fat."

To give you a little better feel for obsessive-compulsive behavior, let me tell you about Kelly's experience in a program she went into at the university that required her to eat a certain number of calories. They advised us to witness what she ate. She was completely obsessed about food. She was given a diet—small apples and other things—and I remember her saying one day, "Is this a small apple or a medium apple?" And I said, "I don't know. It's an apple." She said, "I'm supposed to eat a medium apple. This looks like a large apple. I think it's a large apple." And I said, "My goodness, it's a medium apple. Just eat it." Even then she said, "I think it's a large apple." She was so obsessive even in her conversation.

One thing that helped Kelly is that she didn't fight the support. She wanted to get well, and she wanted help. She didn't say, "Oh don't come and eat with me. I don't want you around." She enjoyed the company, and Kelly always enjoyed the attention. The support was good, but the larger her problem, the more attention she got. It was almost to the point that we weren't helping her because she was getting so much attention from all of us. It was exhausting every day. She was exhausted and she was exhausting to be around because she obsessed on every single thing she put in her mouth—to every single person in the gym. It was very hard to be around her on a regular basis, but we saw results.

No coach should have the sole responsibility of dealing with an anoretic. But even though dealing with Kelly's anorexia was exhausting, frustrating, and difficult, we kept trying because Kelly responded to us in such a positive way. The association with our team is what helped Kelly. She was motivated to gain weight because of her love for gymnastics.

Winning's _Not_ the Only Thing

A ndy Landers, coach of the UGA women's basketball team, told me once about his team philosophy: "We don't have expectations, we have intentions." I thought a lot about that, as I have always believed people only do what's expected of them. But it makes sense: expectations can feel like pressure, but intentions come from within and intentions can drive an individual or team to succeed. Every time we compete, we intend to win!

"You must always want to win," I tell my team, "but winning's _not_ the only thing."

"Winning isn't everything, it's the only thing," has been attributed thousands of times to Vince Lombardi, but _Bartlett's Familiar Quotations_ attributes it to coach Red Sanders of Vanderbilt University (in 1953). The legendary Green Bay Packers quarterback, Bart Starr, commented on Lombardi's philosophy about winning: "Winning to Lombardi was not everything, nor the only thing. He was more interested in seeing us make the effort to do our best. If we did, he knew that winning would probably take care of itself." I follow the same philosophy.

In 1997 I first published my "Fifteen Points of Pride for a Winning Program."

FIFTEEN POINTS OF PRIDE FOR A WINNING PROGRAM

(1) Recruiting: Give recruits the most objective and accurate picture possible of life as a student-athlete at UGA— no more, no less.

The decision on where to attend college is one of the most important decisions a person makes in his or her entire lifetime. It relates to much more than just what the school offers athletically and academically. Undergraduate college years are four or five of a person's most formative years. Personalities and philosophies are developed there. Lifelong friendships are formed. In many cases, one meets her future spouse at college. So it's important that the gymnastics staff and team assist a recruit in gaining a comprehensive and accurate impression of what the University of Georgia will do for her. It would be totally irresponsible to mislead a recruit about any aspect of college life at the University of Georgia in order to persuade her to come here as a gymnast.

But recruiting is a two-way street. How do we decide who we want to bring in? Obviously we want to go after the best athletes in terms of their athletic success. It's very difficult to win championships without having some of the best athletes on your team. I want to win because we have athletes who are a step above everybody else—best athletes, best routines, the strongest commitment. I don't want to win because somebody else makes a mistake. I like to win like we did in 1993 and 1998. Hands down, we were the best.

There's no rocket science about what we do in our recruiting. I think it's important for the athletes we recruit to know what our philosophy is. We make sure they understand that we believe that the happier the athlete is, the better she's going to do. So we are very flexible. In the past years, gymnasts have referred to me as Gumby because I am pretty flexible. I like to accommodate the individual needs of the girls. We always say we're a team of individuals first, and that if we meet the individual needs of the girls and work on leadership skills at the same time, then we will develop a TEAM. Instead of everyone coming in and the coaches saying, "We're a team so we are all going to do it the same way—dress the same way, etc." I don't like to be a real controlling coach when it comes to the little things; I want to give our athletes information and then allow them to make choices.

We like to get the recruits we're interested in on campus, and then our team will help her make the decision—the athlete will come because she clicks with the team, or she won't click with the team and she'll choose somewhere else. Once a recruit takes her visit to our campus, the team does the recruiting. Our athletes love the University of Georgia. They're happy here, they're satisfied, they like the way we coach, they like the policies, they like their weekends off, they like the option of having three personal days off, and they like competing every year for championship titles. When the current athletes are satisfied and successful, they sell the program naturally and honestly to the recruits.

One thing you know for sure—a current athlete is not going to lie to a recruit. Current athletes tell it like it is. If a current athlete is not happy, you can be sure that the recruit will sense that.

Visiting the recruits at their own home has changed through the years. Right now I do very little of the scouting. Jay's been here a long time. He knows what type of athletes we like. I respect his opinion. I think it's very important for the head coach to identify the strengths of all the people who work with the program and leave them alone and let them handle their end of the job. Jay's job is recruiting. I don't micro-manage the recruiting. He gives me the list of the ten or twelve gymnasts that we're going to recruit on a given year and says these are the ones. We go from there and set up contacts for the visits, but I don't get involved in the scouting part at all.

On a visit to the campus, we try to have the recruits meet either the athletic director or President Adams, and we try to have them meet someone in the athletic department who can talk to them about the support that we get financially—travel, for example—and then we have them meet with our strength coach, because that's a big part of our program. They meet with the academic people who advise them on the options for study. They also see our academic support facilities and learn how we operate to meet their academic needs. Athletes spend a lot of time in practice and traveling, so regardless of how capable they are of performing academically, the University of Georgia wants to make sure they are given additional support—beyond what non-athletes get—to reach their academic potential. The 31,000 square foot Rankin

Smith Student Athlete Academic Center was completed in 2002, and its facilities are state-of-the-art in academic support with a 230-seat study hall, 60 desktop computer stations, and many other features to help the student-athletes and the athletic department's academic staff work together to pursue academic goals. UGA spends over $125,000 on tutors for athletes. The most important thing is that the recruits leave here knowing the kind of support they have—knowing that they will have the very best.

The current gymnasts provide the recruits with all the information on the social side of being at Georgia. We give them a lot of free time during the trip. They have dinner at my house. They'll come in on a football weekend for about forty-eight hours or less. The first evening we'll all have dinner together—the whole team—and then the second day they attend the football game. After dinner, we sit in a circle, and each of the current gymnasts shares the things she likes most about the University of Georgia and the gymnastics program. For example, Marline Stephens said last year that she loved it that "Suzanne gives us a lot of personal time to do things other than gymnastics. I like being able to spend time working on sorority projects." Kinsey Rowe talked about her appreciation for the "personal days." And Sierra Sapunar mentioned she enjoys having all the aerobics and conditioning at the beginning of practice so that "when I'm finished with other drills I can leave and go to my tutors, and I don't have to wait until everyone is finished." They get across that, in general, I treat them as individuals and meet their individual needs. I'm glad when I hear them say this because it's important to me that I do respond to all of their individual needs. All gymnasts are different, and we believe that we build our team chemistry by getting to know each other and developing a mutual respect for those differences.

But, of course, the recruits want to hear what the gymnasts say when I'm not with them, and they have plenty of time to pump our gymnasts for these assessments, which may be the most influential of any. They are with our gymnasts the majority of the time.

We've had some problems with negative recruiting by other

schools in the past. Sometimes it's been really bad because we'd show up for an in-house visit at a recruit's home, and they'd ask us how we handle weight. Weight's a big issue with a lot of the athletes. We're asked whether the gymnasts are weighed in or not weighed in. Are there six o'clock workouts? Do the coaches call you elephants? We've had recruits tell us that coaches from other teams told them that we post weights on the wall or in the practice gym. Of course, these things have never been done. I don't know where some of this stuff comes from. Again, we just tell the recruits, "Ask our athletes. They'll tell you the truth. Ask any athlete anything you want to."

Of course, we explain to our gymnasts at the beginning of the year to avoid discussing other teams with the recruits. We went through a period when if someone went on medical, another school told recruits that she lost her scholarship. I don't like to be defensive, but we can pretty much defend anything anyone wants to say about us. I can go over a roster of all the gymnasts who've come to Georgia. We've never had anyone transfer. Even if for some reason a scholarship was not renewed, we've not had anyone fail to continue to stay at Georgia and graduate from school in the last fifteen years. Many have stayed here and graduated on a medical scholarship. Anna Gingrich is an example. Melinda Baimbridge was hurt before she came to Georgia and never competed, but she stayed on full scholarship as a medical hardship. We took some heat about Monica Flammer, because she made All-America her freshman year and then didn't have a scholarship after that. But we told her when she signed here that she'd be on scholarship for only one year unless she could compete two or three events. She was able to compete only one event. But we were able to get her a scholarship to stay in school and work. And she had her education paid for. And, yes, she graduated. We have always taken care of our first responsibility to our athletes, their education.

Negative recruiting—trashing other schools—is simply a no-no at Georgia. It doesn't help the recruit learn about Georgia, and it can't be reliable. Furthermore, negative recruiting almost always assures that the recruit will go somewhere else. Perhaps I shouldn't tip off the other coaches about the fallacy of negative recruiting, because several GymDogs have revealed that negative recruiting by another school helped cement their decision to come to Georgia. One even brought with her on her recruiting visit a copy of an e-mail trashing Georgia, which she received from another coach the night before she left for her trip here. She gave it to me expressing her revulsion.

Of course, a tour of the University of Georgia's magnificent campus is a part of the visit. It is one of the most beautiful places anywhere. The university is the first chartered, state-supported university in the nation, established in 1785, and nearly all of the buildings constructed over a 200-year period are still standing and maintained immaculately. Some of the older buildings have been completely renovated to make them historical showplaces.

After a meeting with the coaches to discuss gymnastics and coaching philosophy, the present gymnasts take over for the rest of the visit. Recruits visit a practice, and then they visit downtown Athens, which is known internationally as the pop music capitol of the world, having spawned many famous musical groups, including the B-52s, REM, and Widespread Panic.

So, from a gymnastics standpoint, what does the 1983-2002 decade's record mean to a young gymnast who's contemplating becoming a GymDog? It means that if she competes four years as a GymDog, her chances are this of:

Winning a Honda Award	15%
Winning Four SEC Championships	42%
Setting or Tying an Individual NCAA Scoring Record	42%
Winning Two Team National Championships	46%
Winning an Individual National Championship	46%
Winning One or More Team National Championships	88%
Making All-America	92%
Winning Three or More SEC Team Championships	100%
Being on a Team that Holds Four of Five NCAA Scoring Records	100%
Graduating from an Academically Top-Twenty University	100%

Recruiting is a two-way street. And it can be uncomfortable for both the recruit and the school. In some ways it's not unlike a sorority rush, with each side trying to size up the other, while the gymnast is trying to get an offer from every school she's interested in and each school is trying to make sure it has scholarships available for the best gymnasts they can attract. At Georgia, the team is heavily involved in recruiting. We put as much emphasis on evaluating a potential recruit's ability to work well with others as we do on evaluating her technical skills, which are much more obvious. Our current team members are key to our evaluation. We seldom make an offer to a candidate who the gymnasts on the team don't think would fit in.

(2) Student-Athletes: The physical and mental welfare of student-athletes must take priority over all other considerations.

I believe you must assure every team member that you are interested in her as a person as well as a gymnast and that you believe that she can reach the goals agreed on.

I respond in different ways when a gymnast appears to be injured. If the injury appears not to be related to the head or neck—an area where potentially serious consequences might be involved or if the injury is not a season-ending injury—I usually allow the trainers to comfort the injured gymnast and inquire later about the appropriate treatment and disposition. But if serious consequences cannot be quickly dismissed, I get to her in a hurry, as concerned as if it were my daughter—for the welfare of the gymnast, not for the impact on the team's performance.

The injured athlete is examined and diagnosed progressively by the trainer, the team physician, and a specialist, depending on the need, to make absolutely sure that the maximum possible severity of the injury is not missed. Then, in consultation with the medical staff, a rehabilitation program is developed and carried out. Of course, parents are brought into the decision-making process when appropriate.

Students have a life other than gymnastics. It is important that their worries and concerns be addressed, and that coaches play the appropriate role in deciding what is best for the gymnast. What is best for the gymnast is best for the team.

(3) Goal Setting: Set goals that extend beyond perceived limitations.

You must establish goals for the athlete that go beyond any achievements she has attained in the past. Setting goals, in itself, is motivating for the gymnast provided you lay out the intermediate steps for achieving the ultimate goals. These must all be clearly defined. Then motivation results from the melding of the desire, determination, and effort with the vision of pride and fulfillment of achieving the goals.

Every year, one of our team goals is to win the NCAA National Championship, but because that goal is far away from the beginning of the season, we set other specific team goals that may be even more challenging initially, such as our target scores for each meet and hitting 10 percent of the time in practice. In gymnastics, individual goals are just as important as team goals. They include developing new and more challenging skills and improving consistency and execution. All of our goals are precisely defined, and their achievement can be measured objectively and quantitatively. Most important, we focus on goals that we can control.

(4) Risk-Taking: Coaches owe their team members, fans, institution, and sport the training and support to perform the most satisfying, exciting, and entertaining level of gymnastics safely achievable.

This philosophy has been addressed extensively in "Over the Hill at Eighteen— Not!" Not only have the satisfaction of gymnasts and entertainment level for fans been enhanced, but the popularity and excitement of college gymnastics as a whole have been advanced by pushing the envelope.

In gymnastics, technical instruction is motivating. Gymnasts almost crave constructive criticism from skilled coaches. After all, in the past their parents paid big bucks for coaching before they came to college, so they consider skilled instruction a tangible asset. When a coach tells a gymnast why she didn't execute a skill perfectly, and then she makes the correction the coach suggests, you can see the sense of satisfaction and elation in her face when she performs flawlessly on the next try. You motivate by helping athletes achieve their goals.

(5) Academics: Accept no excuse for less than total commitment to excellent academic performance.

In reviewing postings on the Collegiate Gymnastics Forum on the Internet, it's apparent that parents of gymnasts anticipating a college career often ask for advice in helping their daughters make decisions about which college to attend.

During the past thirty years, every state legislature has increased significantly its funding of its university system. Indeed there is a great deal of competition among states and pride in their state colleges and universities. The students and parents are the beneficiaries of this competition. The bottom line is that every state-supported college with a women's gymnastics team affords excellent educational opportunities at the undergraduate level. And for those students who want an exceptional academic challenge, the honors programs at these colleges bring them up a notch higher.

But if you put weight on ratings, I will point out that four of the teams who qualified for the national championships—Michigan, UCLA, Georgia, and Florida—were listed among the top twenty in the *U.S. News and World Report*'s "Top Public National Universities for 2001." Stanford, which also qualified for the national championships, is listed among the top twenty privately supported universities. I separate the two listings because of the strong bias in favor of private institutions reflected in the evaluations. Georgia ranked fourth in *Kiplinger*'s "Top Ten Schools that offer Academic Excellence and Academic Value" and fifth in *U.S. News'* "Great Schools at Great Prices" for the year 2003.

Once a gymnast begins college, it is important that she excel academically as well as athletically. A section in the chapter "Putting It Together" addresses the UGA Athletic Association's academic achievement program. There are no professional careers in gymnastics performance, so gymnastics competition cannot be considered a step toward a career, except as a coach. Therefore, the pursuit of a meaningful college degree is more important than gymnastics performance, but the two are not mutually exclusive. In fact, they are probably synergistic. With our team, academic and gymnastics excellence seem to go hand-in-hand.

(6) Fitness: Strength and conditioning are the keys to good performance and longevity in gymnastics. Learn what works and apply it, always giving the gymnast's well being top priority.

We try to make sure that each gymnast fully appreciates the measurable benefits of our strength and conditioning program. One of the changes females undergo about the age they come to college and leave club gymnastics is that they get heavier—they begin to look like mature women. They can't propel themselves high enough into the air and stay long enough to do the flips and twists they need to do in challenging routines unless they get a lot stronger than they were previously and have a great deal more stamina. The only way to achieve the physical attributes necessary to be a collegiate gymnast is to undergo appropriate weight and aerobic training. We make sure we demonstrate to each gymnast that she can do better gymnastics as a result of undergoing this extensive training, but we make it as entertaining and interesting as we can.

(7) Longevity: In a well-managed collegiate program, gymnasts can and should improve their skills and performance each year they are in school, even former Olympians.

The chapter "Over-the-Hill at Eighteen—Not!" is devoted to this philosophy.

(8) Discipline to Perform: Self-discipline to pursue tenaciously one's full potential is the most important success factor in athletic and other accomplishments.

I like to think that the word "self" is an understood modifier of discipline, because if someone else is controlling your activities, you're not exercising discipline, you're merely following instructions. A great deal of gymnastics training and academic pursuit depends on an individual's discipline to perform arduous activities on his or her own initiative—for example: the rigorous repetitions involved in rehabilitation from injury and the seemingly endless study required for academic excellence.

(9) Discipline to Conform: Discipline is the training that makes punishment unnecessary.

College coaches must understand the nature of college students in getting them to conform to rules. College kids think conformity "sucks"—in their words. However, they are clever and innovative. If you can define objectives without directing team members, in detail, how to achieve those objectives, they are likely to come up with better approaches than the ones you might devise. So I much prefer general guidelines to hard and fast rules, but the guidelines must have well-understood boundaries. And a gymnast must understand that if she goes beyond those boundaries, there will be appropriate adverse consequences.

I emphasize "using good judgement," and when I say a gymnast uses good judgement it means that I am happy with the decision she makes. The gymnasts have to do some analysis to determine for themselves what constitutes good judgement. And, after all, that's what they'll have to do when they're out on their own.

I know that even in the best programs, an athlete's behavior sometimes requires corrective action. The corrective action must be carefully thought out before it is implemented. It must have a positive result. It should not reflect a coach's anger, even though we all get angry with athletes at times. You must be predictable, consistent, and direct. Don't play games. Don't be sarcastic. It is essential that an athlete undergoing corrective action—you notice I don't say "being disciplined"—understands that she was told of the guidelines or rules she violated before she violated them. She must know, given the same circumstances, that anyone else with a similar past record would receive the same treatment. The treatment must not be embarrassing or demeaning, and the objective of improvement must be clearly appreciated by the one undergoing the action and the other team members.

I work to make every aspect of our program positive. Making athletes feel that discipline is positive isn't easy. But it can and should be done. When discipline truly achieves its goal, the athlete feels good about it, you feel good about it, the other coaches feel good about it, and the teammates feel good about it.

(10) Integrity: Honesty is the essential foundation of all successful endeavors in athletics and all other aspects of life.

One of the areas most discussed in terms of a coach's honesty in dealing with college athletes is the allocation of scholarships. A four -or five-year college education can cost up to $200,000. While much of it is paid for by the state in state-supported institutions (and thereby not reflected in tuition), the cost is still there. In college athletic programs, athletes who receive scholarships paying virtually all expenses train and perform along with those who "walked on"—with their parents picking up the tab. The coach decides who gets scholarships and who walks on.

NCAA scholarships are for one year only, renewable in July of each year. When we sign a gymnast to a scholarship, we make sure she understands this, and we review this with her when she reports to school. But, even being fully aware of the condition of offer—it's written in their gymnastics notebooks—every gymnast who receives a scholarship offer assumes that she will remain on scholarship all four performing years and maybe even one additional year, if it is needed to complete her education. The vast majority of scholarships remain intact for four or five years. But occasionally scholarships are not renewed. The most common reason for not renewing a scholarship at Georgia is for medical reasons, in which case the athlete is awarded a medical scholarship for the remaining time to complete her education. The medical scholarship is not counted by the NCAA against the limit of twelve scholarships per team for women's gymnastics. Some gymnasts are given a medical scholarship during their first year of college and never compete—remaining on scholarship for four years. But you can be sure that every gymnast on medical scholarship had rather be competing, and they contribute enthusiastically to the team by working as managers, assisting in promotions, and in other team-related activities—doing everything they can to earn their keep.

Coaches sometimes have to deny renewal of a scholarship as

a means of motivating an athlete who is not performing up to her potential for emotional reasons. In *Six Psychological Factors for Success* by Stephen Brennan and Bill Donaldson, many of the twenty-five coaches interviewed mentioned not renewing a scholarship as a potential disciplinary tool, but it was always the last resort.

Each year athletes have to earn scholarships, and in the vast majority of cases, returning athletes on scholarships do earn an additional year. In two cases at Georgia in which gymnasts on scholarships simply did not maintain the expected level of performance, after all we could do failed to help them, we elected not to renew their scholarships and release them to attend another school, hoping that the change in environment would help restore their performance to a level previously demonstrated. In both cases, the gymnasts elected to remain at Georgia and asked to be allowed to compete as walk-ons. And in both cases, the scholarships were re-awarded after one year as walk-ons. This corrective action proved to be beneficial for all concerned. Both gymnasts regained enthusiastic and positive attitudes and competitive skills, and both graduated. They have both expressed gratitude for the "tough-love" lesson.

(11) Fairness: Never compromise fairness to yourself, your team, or your opponents. Be fair not only to the letter of the rules but also in the true spirit of sportsmanship.

While there may be obvious differences in athletic abilities among our gymnasts, they are all respected for what they are as people, not athletes. If you visit one of our practices, you can't tell the walk-ons from the top gymnasts in the country. They all receive the same attention from the coaches and support staff and the same respect from their teammates. It is vital to our team chemistry that everyone on the team be involved in the competitions, so unlike a lot of schools, all our gymnasts travel to away meets with the team.

Unfortunately, some coaches feel so much pressure to qualify for postseason competition that they select meet judges who will be biased in their favor. What sort of message does it send to gymnasts when a coach attempts to manipulate scoring or other non-competition-related activities (such as encouraging intimidation by fans) in order to win?

(12) Community: Contributing more than a fair share to the communities of UGA, Athens, and Georgia is essential to being a Georgia GymDog.

Participating in car washes to raise money, assisting Habitat for Humanity, and similar activities are contributions to the community, and we do them, but these are things any student can do. Finding an activity that takes advantage of unique characteristics of athletes can be more meaningful. Young girls consider college gymnasts celebrities. Interaction between gymnasts and young girls, especially troubled or underprivileged young girls, can have a profound positive influence on the youngsters. The GymDogs participate in the Athens-Clarke County Mentoring program, in which they are paired with young girls who need help in developing self-esteem or who need to know that someone who is highly regarded takes a special interest in them.

The program is rewarding to both parties in the pair, providing opportunities to interact with young girls in a manner not normally available to gymnasts who have been so busy training prior to college.

Each year we seek unique opportunities for the GymDogs to contribute to the community. In 2003, an unfortunate and challenging occurrence with a first-year alumna, Talya Vexler, provided her, and us, an opportunity to turn twenty-three-year-old Talya's positive attitude and courage in dealing with breast cancer (a one-in-one-hundred thousand occurrence for a twenty-three year old) into a positive fundraising program for the Athens Regional Medical Center's Breast Health Center. At the beginning of the 2004 season, fans were asked to pledge an amount of their own choosing to the center for each score of 9.9 or higher by a GymDog during the 2004 season in Talya's honor. The program was a huge success.

(13) Image: Coaches and gymnasts are role models for thousands of youngsters. Always keep this responsibility in mind and live up to it.

Being a positive role model is essential in the mentoring program, and because of their popularity, college gymnasts are almost constantly under the microscope of public scrutiny. Accepting the responsibility for setting proper examples is a maturing experience.

And how can coaches gain the respect of their team members if they don't act responsibly themselves? Being fair to team members and demonstrating good sportsmanship in competition help develop lasting admirable characteristics among the gymnasts. When former athletes are asked to name the most influential people in their lives, nearly all of them include coaches on their lists. The coach has a responsibility far beyond that of teaching and improving gymnastics techniques.

(14) Not Winning: Always do your best, hold your head high, and graciously congratulate a victorious opponent.

I don't like to use the words "loss" or "failure" because nothing is a total failure. It's a "partial success." So how do you deal with the disappointment of not fully attaining your goal? Let me relate the experience we had at the 1997 NCAA National Championship, which we entered as the overwhelming favorite.

During the season we attained the highest regular season average in the history of NCAA women's gymnastics—over a point higher than the second place team. We scored the highest score of any team in the preliminary rounds. But on the first event in the Super Six, the balance beam, three GymDogs fell from the apparatus, counting two falls and digging a hole that would be impossible to climb out of, unless all of the major contenders counted at least one fall.

So what do you do in a situation like this? First, you have to erase the past from your mind by concentrating on the future. You can't do anything about the past. Then you have to concentrate on every skill, every routine, and every event, in that order. And we did it! We won each of the other three events. That is as good as we could have done. But, unfortunately for us, no other team counted even one fall, and we came in third, 0.55 points behind the champion, UCLA.

And how do you deal with the loss? First, put yourself in the place of the winner. How would you like to be treated if you won? Remember the Golden Rule. Would you like the other team to demonstrate sour grapes? So I told the team in 1997 that as soon as it was evident who won, they should take off running as fast as they could toward the winning team's place on the floor and congratulate them enthusiastically. We gave the meet away, but we didn't give away our class and good sportsmanship. We could at least win the sportsmanship contest, which is important. As soon as it was determined who won the national championship, I took off across the floor first, with the team right behind me, to congratulate UCLA.

Then we had to face our fans. They had arranged a victory party for us. They felt terrible. They had supported us all season. We needed to support them. So I told the team to go into the victory party with the biggest smiles they could put on their faces, just as big as if we had won. "Let the fans know that you appreciate their support and that you are proud of what you achieved during the season and the way you came back and won three of the four events. That will pick them up." And it did. Just as important, it lifted our team's spirits too. Holding your head high after disappointment is difficult, but it's a surefire way to lift your spirits.

(15) Winning: You must always want to win. And winning comes as a result of fulfilling the objectives above.

One of my most ardent beliefs is that "Winning is *not* everything." You recruit right, you set goals, you train right, you stress academics, you teach good technique, you teach good sportsmanship, you teach fairness, you teach integrity, but you don't teach winning. Winning comes as a consequence of doing all of the other things listed in the points of pride well. Of course you must want to win. You must intend to win. And if you do all of the things you are supposed to do well all of the time, you will win most of the time.

Remember, gymnastics is a sport involving the body/mind concept—physical training seeking beauty, strength, and efficiency in movement combined with the psychological attributes of high self-esteem, physical courage, determination/perseverance, expressiveness, reliance, and self-confidence. Master being a good gymnast and you are a winner.

Two Hundred to Ten Thousand

When Liz Murphey, the women's athletic director at Georgia, took me to see the coliseum (now Stegeman Coliseum) on my interview trip in 1983, the cavernous structure was illuminated only by the light that filtered through the pedestrian passageways to the lobby. As I looked up at the waffle-embossed concrete ceiling far above the floor, scanned the 10,000 empty seats, and sized up the spacious floor, I recognized immediately that the structure was tailor-made for gymnastics meets with huge crowds. I could picture 10,000 screaming GymDog fans. The coliseum, then, was one of many factors that played a role in my decision to accept the position as Georgia's head coach.

My first promotional activity after I arrived was the teams' (men's and women's) first "Georgia Gymnastics Jamboree" held in the coliseum in November of 1983. The purpose of the jamboree was to promote the sport of gymnastics statewide and for the public to become familiar with UGA's teams. Olympians Tim Daggett and Kathy Johnson performed, bringing their recently gained popularity to the event. The fans might not be interested in Georgia gymnastics, or might not even know that much about it, but they would come to see the Olympians. The Jamboree was strategically scheduled the night before the Georgia-Georgia Tech football game in Athens. A lot of fans come in for the football game the night before and look for something to do.

In addition to the Olympians—and, of course, our own teams' representatives—the meet featured exhibitions by the state of Georgia's best club gymnasts and 200 other young gymnasts from across North Georgia. Perhaps the contrast in skill levels helped fans recognize the skill levels of the GymDogs. Our teams' skills were even more challenging than those of Tim and Kathy, whose routines were watered down.

The Jamboree was a show, so it was lights and costumes and entertainment. In addition to selected top gymnasts, we invited gym clubs from around the state, knowing that if a club came with fifty kids, then all their parents would come. We got people here by putting their kids in our show. It was a tactic that worked—over 4,000 attended.

With 4,000 at the 1983 Jamboree, things were looking good for attendance during the 1984 competitive season. Then came reality. Fewer than 200 fans attended my first meet with Alabama. That was a long way from what I had envisioned—one-fiftieth to be precise. But I was undaunted. I remained just as certain that we would someday fill that coliseum for competitions as I was that our team would someday win a national championship. We just had to figure out how to do it.

In the initial years, the early eighties, we really focused our attention on winning. We put all our energy into recruiting and getting the talent that you obviously need to have a winning team. It's difficult to sell a team with a losing record! We felt that before we could really focus heavily on attendance and spectator growth, we had to have a quality product—something people wanted to pay to come and see. After we won our first national championship in 1987, we started to focus more on the attendance.

But I didn't wait for the national championship to interact with the media. The newspaper sports reporters and other staff, all the way up to the publisher, cringed when they saw me coming into the press building for the local newspaper. They knew I was coming to point out the lack of press coverage for a recent meet or to ask for their help in promoting an event. And I would keep coming until I got what I wanted. They tabbed me, "the woman who wouldn't take 'no' for an answer." The athletic association had a sports information staff, but it just wasn't aggressive about women's gymnastics back then.

Shortly after I arrived in Athens and went to my first football game, with over 80,000 fans tailgating and screaming with enthusiasm at the game, I became totally aware that "Georgia is a football school." To try to say any other sport is as important would be suicide. When you're dealing with run-away enthusiasm that's been going on for a hundred years, you find some way to jump on its back and ride that enthusiasm. That's what I did and still do. When I make a speech to a Bulldog club or a civic club out of town, I make sure I know the latest information about Georgia football and spend a good portion of my speech providing information about the football program. This isn't hard to do because I'm one of Georgia football's biggest fans. Then I ease into gymnastics, trying to get sympathy by telling the crowd, "Years ago, the men over at Butts-Mehre were so entrenched in men's sports they thought harass was two words." (Butts-Mehre is the Athletic Administration building.)

I tell them I can do something for them that our football coach can't. I can refund their money if they are unsatisfied after they attend one of our meets. This always gets a good laugh. I've never had to refund a penny. (This sales approach must be attributed to Sarah Patterson at Alabama, who has been a terrific promoter for gymnastics at the University of Alabama and who was working hard to accomplish the same objectives I was.)

I distribute wallet-sized gymnastics schedule cards everywhere I go. In my talk at a Rotary meeting in Gainesville, Georgia, in 1988, I said, "I noticed you took all the cards I left on the registration table. Those two leotard-clad girls in the picture aren't models—they're both national individual champion college gymnasts; and you may not have noticed, but there's a gymnastics schedule on the other side."

I also let the press travel with the team to important out-of-town meets in order to get better coverage. I knew that the media would have to be impressed with the demeanor of the team and the well-organized, but low-key, loose-reined management on a trip. It's impossible to spend much time with the GymDogs "around the clock" without getting hooked on them.

But the print media wasn't the only way we needed to promote if we were going to fill that coliseum. After we won the 1987 NCAA Championship, I asked the team if they wanted people up there in the stands and they said, "Yes." So I told them they would have to help.

"At the beginning it was really rough," said Lucy Wener, a former U.S. Olympian and three-time national uneven bars champion. "We'd put flyers on cars, give them to our professors, and put them on buildings. Suzanne would come into practice with thousands of flyers, and we put them everywhere. Then we'd stand in the tunnel before the meet and peek out. We would be so excited if there was a section that was almost full."

Help also meant stuffing envelopes to mail to faculty members. It meant going to men's basketball games and passing out gymnastics schedule cards at half time, going to merchants and asking them to display the GymDogs' schedule posters in their windows, and going to restaurants and retail stores and asking them to display "tents" on tables.

Of course we established a one- and two-week gymnastics camp for gymnasts age six to eighteen and for all levels through elite. We now draw an average of 400 young gymnasts every year (turning many away), without advertising, and they and their parents remain interested in the program.

One of our most successful promotional activities during the early years was performing at half time at the men's basketball games. I think literally hundreds of fans—faculty, students, and the general public— have told me that's what attracted them to their first meet. We stopped after our attendance exceeded the basketball attendance.

Another part of promotion I tried to instill in the gymnasts early on is making sure they're accessible to the public, knowing that if they get to know people and meet them on a personal basis, squat down and talk to the children eye to eye, the crowd will be more apt to come back. There are so many athletes in so many sports—college football, college basketball—who are not accessible to the public. They go from the field to the locker room, from the locker room to the interview room, back to the tunnel, and to the car. In the early years, we stayed out on the floor at the end of competition. The audience could come down on the floor, and we'd sign autographs; we were always making ourselves accessible. Now, we only have one poster signing a year, but it lasts for over three hours.

Along with just being accessible came being friendly, likable, or even charming. Elite gymnasts are used to training forty hours a week throughout middle school and high school. They have led sheltered lives and aren't always comfortable interacting with strangers. So I had to become a "socializing instructor." When the gymnasts passed out schedule cards at basketball games or went to merchants, they were to wear their warm-ups that identified them as GymDogs. They were to travel in pairs, which provided reinforcement and comfort to the gymnasts—two people, rather than one, lends an impression of "team." They were to smile and look people in the eye. I instructed them to introduce themselves. When a gymnast says, "Hello, I'm Lucy Wener," there is one chance in ten the person may have read about her. That really helps. And people usually introduce themselves to people who start the exchange. At banquets and get-togethers, the girls are not allowed to "huddle up" with each other or there will be a hill to run on Monday morning. I teach, then encourage, then insist on total interaction with the fans.

Most sportswriters don't know much about gymnastics. They are almost all male, and they have played football, basketball, and baseball. When they write about gymnastics, except for covering meets, they usually write personal interest stories. So we adapt and steer them to our more articulate gymnasts or to those whose story is so compelling they don't have to be articulate. After reading these stories, people will like a particular gymnast so much they may come to a meet just because she did a good job selling the program.

"Networking" is a term I use often. If you can just get the spectators there that first time, they're likely to come back. And sooner or later they'll each bring a friend. Then the friend will begin coming on his or her own. And then he or she will bring a friend. That's literally exponential growth. And our meets quickly became a who's who night out that started at the top. I personally visited deans and heads of departments to invite them to our meets. The girls on the team focused on getting their professors to attend, and free T-shirts and give-aways got the students there. Before we knew it, when fans came to a meet, they saw lots of familiar faces. GymDog meets became the place to go and be seen.

It didn't take me long to learn that you need all the help you can get in promoting a woman's sport in college. Fortunately, I found plenty. There were the folks who contributed money, some gave a hundred thousand dollars each to endow scholarships. So far we have over two million dollars in contributions. There are others who contributed time and talent. We have lots of smart folks who love to write, organize, sell—whatever—to exercise their talent while contributing to our program. And the more I call on them, the more they seem to like it.

Sponsors pay for our billboards. There are about fifteen of them in Athens and a few in surrounding towns. In addition to home-meet schedules, they usually have a picture of a gymnast in an action shot and are designed to attract attention.

The sponsors help finance other promotional materials—ticket brochures, schedule cards, and calendars. The gymnastics program's calendar is the envy of all the other sports programs. It has become the most popular calendar in Athens. A picture of a gymnast is paired with each month. University of Georgia athletic events for all teams are noted in the block for the appropriate date, with the gymnastics activities in red ink. Judging from the number of sponsors, they must fight over the space, but advertisements consume less than 20 percent of each page. Merchants and fans eagerly anticipate their release each December.

I got the idea of having meet sponsors from Ernestine Weaver. When I first came to Georgia, the number one team in the SEC was the University of Florida. Ernestine Weaver, who was the coach at the time, was a mentor as much as a rival. I emulated her; I thought she was wonderful. The University of Florida was the first program that had sponsors at each meet. They had SunTrust Day, and Coca-Cola Day, and other sponsors. We do the same thing now at Georgia. It has been such a success that we have had almost the same six sponsors for the last ten years.

Most coaches don't take time to get concerned about publications and the design of brochures because they think that's what the promotions people get paid for. But when I visited recruit Marie Robbins, who eventually signed with Alabama in 1987, and saw all of the impressive media guides from other schools displayed beside Georgia's skimpy one, I was incensed. The sports information office had set aside $600 for the GymDogs media guide. So I called on our supporters for $7,000 for the next year's guide. I think I woke up the sports information folks.

Besides media guides, I am heavily involved in deciding what the ticket brochures, posters, stationery, and every other piece of printed material related to the GymDogs should look like. For years I worked directly with Kirk Smith, owner of an artistic, graphic design, and advertising company, in developing the most effective materials possible. Kirk is one of those enthusiastic supporters who are so important to the team. He's certainly near the top of the list in terms of dedicated GymDog fans, so his designs are zealously inspired. His design for the national championship materials in 1995 was so good the NCAA adopted it to replace the standard one they had used for years. And LSU patterned their 1996 materials after his designs also. Copying is a two-way street. When I saw the Tennessee women's basketball ticket brochure, I called Kirk and said, "I want something like this for our brochure next season." Both brochures consolidate all the ways to contribute and purchase tickets into one package. Kirk gave me what I asked for.

Since 1987, the Georgia gymnastics team has focused its promotional plan on a different theme, used as a slogan, each year. I wanted to make a statement about our team and set the stage for each season through our slogan. In 1987, our theme of "Take It to the Top!" was decided upon because we had been ninth, seventh, and fourth in the nation in 1984, '85, and '86 respectively, so winning the national title was the next natural progression. Our team traveled forty-five minutes from Athens to find a hot air balloon which could be used as our poster background. People asked me, "What if you don't win, saying take it to the top is a little presumptuous, don't you think?" I never thought about "What if we don't," I only thought about, "How can we win it all?" To me, the theme is the beginning of the picture. The rest, as you know, is history, and the annual mission of our program continues to be defined by our team theme.

Traditional rivalries always stimulate interest and attendance. UGA's rivalry with Alabama is the strongest rivalry in college gymnastics and one of the biggest rivalries in college sports, period, especially women's sports. That rivalry started because of the winning records—we won our first national championship in 1987, then the next year they won, then we won in '89, they won in '91, we won in '93, and they won in '96. We each had three wins, and then we won in '98 and '99, and they won in 2002, so we've got six wins to their four. In the early years, it was definitely real close, back and forth, but in the late 90s Georgia was definitely dominating. We won twelve out of fifteen SEC Championships, so I don't think that the rivalry continued based so much on the records as on the tradition.

Our booster club is named The Ten-0 Club and that is a great name. So great that UCLA recently named its booster club after ours. I call it "the greatest booster club in the universe." The club was organized shortly after I got here, and it has grown tremendously since, with approximately 600 members now. Unlike so many booster clubs, many memberships include both husband and wife, and even children. The Ten-0 Club helps with the preparation for home meets, arranges block hotel accommodations at special rates at away meets, sells GymDogs' paraphernalia, and sponsors preseason and post-meet parties, tailgate parties, and the end-of-the-season recognition banquet. The Ten-0 Club produces a great newsletter, which we mail to members of the UGA Athletic Board and to the University System of Georgia Board of Regents. The GymDogs are the only team at Georgia who send our media guides to the board of regents. The Ten-0 Club also augments the GymDogs budget by purchasing items on my "want list" that fall below the athletic association budget line.

I love the young kids who come to the meets, and there is a tremendous focus on them. They are thrilled by the entertainment aspect of the meets. The Ten-0 Club sponsors a "GymKids" club, and we have a special practice to entertain them and serve pizza and soft drinks. At two meets per year, the GymKids are given lightwands and they form two lines about 200-feet long. The GymDogs enter the floor between the lines, amid flashing lights and fireworks. Nearly everyone I know who has a kid in the club says that standing in that line with the GymDogs marching through is the highlight of the year for the child. These kids are important, because if they come to a meet, they have to bring their parents. Each GymKid brings one or two adults, and probably a sibling or two. And then they grow up and continue to attend—a different twist to networking.

Up until a few years ago, the coaches took one day a week away from practice to take the team to elementary and middle schools to entertain the school kids. Practice gets mundane, so we look for ways to break it up. Doug and Scott—and then Doug and Jay—would load the beam on a truck and drive out to the schools. This experience is good for the kids and good for the GymDogs because it gives us some much-needed exposure. We went to most of the elementary schools around Athens, and we went to all three of the middle schools. In addition to performing routines and giving autographs, the gymnasts field questions from the pupils, and Chris Rodis used to chat with the students about staying away from drugs. This may have been our biggest promotional activity in the early days.

It's particularly important to promote the attendance of university students at the meets because they add excitement and provide the true college atmosphere. The *Red and Black,* the campus newspaper, provides wonderful coverage. And many who get hooked during the four years they are here as students come back as alumni.

I write a myriad of notes and formal letters to people to thank them, to congratulate them—almost any reason to get their attention. I write formal congratulatory letters to new deans, department heads, and other people in important appointments at the university. When appropriate, I'm not shy about writing, whether it's to a faculty member, a congressman, the governor, or the University System of Georgia Chancellor. Somehow I figure out a way to relate what they do to contribute to—sometimes to benefit from—the gymnastics program. It's just human nature to appreciate a letter from a person you think would be too busy to write. And if you appreciate the letter, there's a chance you'll want to go to a gymnastics meet just to show your appreciation. I was euphoric when Georgia signed the top five on the GymDogs' recruiting list for the 2000 season. I had to thank someone. So I wrote the president of the university telling him how much we appreciated his role in making the University of Georgia the prestigious academic institution that it is, because it helped us wrestle away from Stanford a couple of gymnasts who assign a high priority to a school's academic reputation.

A coach wants the academic higher-ups to remember his or her name. Thirty-four colleges and universities make up the University System of Georgia, and there are about one hundred athletic coaches in the system. The chancellor, who heads the entire system, may remember the names of the head football coaches at Georgia and Georgia Tech. He probably doesn't know the names of many other coaches. Except for one. He absolutely for certain knows the name Suzanne Yoculan. I've made sure of that by writing and inviting him to the meets. And he comes from Atlanta once or twice a year.

Early in my career, I was learning to seize the moment when an opportunity for increased visibility came along. *Athens Magazine* described such an incident when Georgia won the 1989 national championship in Athens:

As the announcement that the GymDogs had won the championship blared from the P.A. system, the spotlight suddenly shifted from the circle of UGA gymnasts to their coach, Suzanne Yoculan, who flung her arms toward the ceiling in triumph. Yoculan then made her way across the coliseum floor to celebrate her team's victory with UGA President Charles

Knapp, whom she spotted in the first row of the reserved section.

Get the picture now: a dignified university president being embraced by an attractive young lady in a red leather miniskirt. But as she wrapped her arms around President Knapp, Yoculan wasn't just celebrating her team's victory; she was also playing to the CBS-TV cameras. "When I got to President Knapp, he said something like, 'What's this all about?'" Yoculan recalled recently. "Well, it was a total TV ploy. I saw the cameras and I thought, 'Good move, Suzanne, get President Knapp in the picture.'"

The CBS tape-delayed telecast focused on the celebration, just like I had hoped.

A more lasting influence resulted from the CBS coverage. That was the first time the media had noticed my attire—but not the last. By the time we won the 1993 national championship in Corvallis, Oregon, my high heels and short skirts had become a trademark.

The GymDogs had rewritten the record books in four events, setting a team score of 198.00 out of a possible 200. The team's accomplishments were the main focus of attention, as they should be, but my heels and hemline were also a part of the story.

For my first five years at Georgia, nobody ever noticed what I wore to meets, and I never thought about it. Then things changed at that 1989 event. Even the *International Gymnast* magazine reported that the Georgia coach wore a red leather miniskirt. But there was a positive side. I realized very quickly that the more outlandish I was, or the team was, the more was written in the newspaper. People say I'm flamboyant. And the more emotion the team showed—anything that was different from the norm—the more ink we got. And we needed the ink if we were going to build attendance.

After the media began focusing its attention on my clothing, my behavior, and my leadership style, I reluctantly accepted that promoting me became a major means of promoting the program. In fact, I had begun to attract the media's attention to the point that most newspaper articles about the team carried *my* picture. When a journalist came from out of town to do an article on the team, it invariably became an article on me. TV cameras at the meets stayed on me at about a four-to-one ratio, relative to the other head coach. Invitations to be a public speaker increased, and I was selected as honorary chairman for all sorts of charity races and other contests. I simply had become well-known, primarily because our team was winning, but also because I was flamboyant, and I nearly always provided memorable quotations in extemporaneous conversation. I did not want the attention, but the more I got, the more the team benefited.

I even made an arrangement with an automobile dealer to do his commercials if he would support our program by sponsoring a meet and our team poster. I posed beside a Jacuzzi in exchange for a company's advertising on a GymDog's poster promotion. A carpet store posed me sprawled on a rug in my living room in a velour pants suit, barefoot, for a full-page color ad in *Athens Magazine*. This is not the typical demeanor of an athletic coach. But if it increases exposure of our program and isn't inappropriate for a college coach, I'll do it. And when I do radio interviews and spots on the Atlanta TV stations, there's no dead mike or camera time. The reporter only has to ask me a question and hold the recorder mike for several minutes before asking another. I like to talk—sometimes too much.

For a while, magazines, both local and national, focused on me more than on the team. In February 1990, *Athens Magazine* did an article titled, "How Do You Solve a Problem Like Suzanne?" I posed for a full-page color photograph, sitting on a dark carpet in red and silver western boots (with a "Georgia G" on them), black leotards, and a red sweater—in a tucked position. The background was the bare left legs of four gymnasts standing in line, like dancers.

Atlanta Magazine's Melissa Bienvenu did an article titled, "Coach Yock-A-Lot and the Electric Rock 'n' Rollin' Red-And-Black Hot Squad." Unfortunately, it contained little about the team—just me. But if an article's readers come to our meets, they'll soon discover the wonderful world of college gymnastics and forget about me. *International Gymnast* did a full-length piece on me in December of 1998. It was supposed to be about the team, but even *International Gymnast* focused on the coach, not the team. In March of 2000, Steve Hummer, one of the *Atlanta Journal-Constitution*'s senior sports writers, spent about a week hanging around me and the GymDogs. His article contained over two pages of pictures, with a half-page teaser on the front section of the sports page and a picture teaser on top of the main front page. He was impressed with what he saw and learned, and the editors must have liked what he wrote. Our attendance flourished.

Several years ago I selected Alan Tibbetts, local radio announcer, to be our master of ceremonies and announcer at the meets. Alan has a magnificent voice; he does taped-radio commercials for several stations. At the gymnastics meets, he wears a tuxedo and comes to the center of the floor exercise mat for his introductory remarks—like the ring announcer at a circus, with lights out and the spotlight on him. Then colored spotlights from all sides are focused on the big ball with multi-faceted mirrors that hangs near the top of the coliseum and sends out polka dots of light while the visiting gymnasts are introduced. And finally comes the grand entrance of the GymDogs, with fireworks (both visual and audible) added.

Some criticize the show biz atmosphere—mostly chauvinistic sports writers who love to pan anything that isn't football or men's basketball. But the young kids absolutely love it, and they comprise a big percentage of the fans. In reality, the GymDogs' entrance is no more show biz than the Georgia Bulldogs' football team entrance into Sanford Stadium, following cheerleaders and Uga—the world's most celebrated college mascot—through a passage bordered by the 400-piece Red Coat band, blaring "Glory, Glory, to Ole Georgia." At selected meets, Uga comes up from his Savannah home to usher out the GymDogs, thanks to Sonny and Cecelia Seiler's love for the team. Perhaps the major function of the pizazz at the beginning is to get the crowd into the meet, and it serves this function effectively.

Playing cheerleader comes natural for me, and sometimes I lead the fans in cheers with more enthusiasm than even the UGA cheer-leaders show. At the Florida meet in 1999, I was particularly into the celebration after the floor exercise, waving my fist in a swirling motion, screaming, and even doing a "jitterbug" with the team.

I received this e-mail after one meet: "Congratulations on a great meet. There were many thrilling moments. But the most harrowing one was when you dashed over to congratulate Jenni Beathard after her bars routine and hurdled the bars guy wire at the three-foot level, in your high heels and tight skirt, without altering the rhythm of your gait."

So there I was in 1993 with the top program in the country. Average attendance had gone from 200 in 1984 to 3,000 in 1989 and to 6,000 by 1993. Gymnastics in Athens, Georgia, had become a pro-duction with me in the forefront. It was never my plan or desire to be in the media or worry about what I wore. But here we were, building attention and support for the team because of our success, our hard work, and my flash! But we were not there yet. There were still 4,000 empty seats in the coliseum.

In 1994, we opened our season against LSU on January 28 to a crowd of over 9,500. We felt a change in the air, a madness to get season tickets—anticipation of the beginning of gymnastics season even during football season. And then it happened. On March 12, 1994, Georgia gymnastics had our first selout crowd for the Georgia vs. Alabama meet—10, 217 in attendance. This was the largest attendance ever at a women's sporting event in the state of Georgia. The record held until the U.S. women's soccer team played at Sanford Stadium for the gold medal during the 1996 Olympics.

Establishment of the first renewable season ticket program for a gymnastics team—it allows fans to retain their same seats from year to year for a modest contribution—is an example of committed vol-unteers working together to make something happen. When Bill Donaldson joined the Ten-O Club board of directors, one of his first suggestions was that we establish such a program. There were many ups and downs between the time I finally agreed to try it and the first sales. But each time there was an apparent set back, someone stepped forward with an answer.

When the chairman of the Georgia Student Education Fund, the program for renewable season tickets for football, wanted no part of combining football and gymnastics, Coach Dooley came up with the brilliant idea of establishing a separate program for gymnastics, which was tabbed the Gymnastics Endowment Fund (GEF). I was concerned about the effect the program would have on families bringing young children. I didn't want to hamper the tradition of a family atmosphere. I agreed that retaining a low ticket cost for children of non-contributors would probably take care of that concern. When we met with Senior Associate Athletic Director John Shafer, I expressed my concern that we might lose too many fans if they had to contribute money to buy season tickets. At the time, about 600 season tickets were sold annually.

After we sent out the brochures announcing the renewable season ticket program, the ticket office got a few letters from irate recipients and sent them over to me. I sent personal letters to each complainer, and nearly all of them became contributors to the GEF. By the deadline for responding, $40,000 had been collected—more renewable season tickets than regular season tickets the year before. People actually bought 800 renewable season tickets at $75 each ($50 for the contribution and $25 for the seat) compared to 600 non-renewable ones at $25 per seat the year before. For the 2003 season, over 1,800 renewable season tickets were sold, with a total of over 5,000 season tickets, including students and faculty.

Associate Athletic Director for Development Kit Trensch has done a magnificent job of managing the GEF. She established a hospitality room in the coliseum where contributors can visit before each meet—chatting as they would at a tailgate. Periodically, contributors are recognized from the coliseum floor—each time contributions reach $150,000 for a new scholarship. And a special reception is held, after a home meet, once a year for contributors. Kit has made being a contributor a status symbol. It's sort of like having two booster clubs,

Ten-0 Club members and GEF contributors. Of course, there is a substantial degree of overlap with people contributing to both.

Karlene Lawrence is listed in the gymnastics media guide as the
Publications and Systems Coordinator. But if there is anything that
Karlene doesn't do with regard to publications and computer systems—
and anything else she can help anyone with—I haven't found it. And she
does everything to perfection. She started a first in college gymnastics—a
project to do live posting of GymDogs' scores on the Internet. Now
nearly every major team has followed suit. Posting gymnastics scores on
the Internet is inexpensive and extremely appreciated by fans of the participating teams as well as other fans who want to follow the meets. Over
50,000 hits are recorded for some meets. Surely the TV folks will soon
recognize the potential for live telecasts of dual meets.

By 1998, attendance and revenues were growing—average attendance was just under 10,000, the capacity for Stegeman Coliseum. But I
wanted to sell out the coliseum before the season each year. I've grown
tired of hearing that gymnastics is not a "revenue-producing sport," and
that we're dependent, like all other sports, on football for our major
financial support. It's important to note that although we're not self-
sustaining, we are revenue producing. It's been obvious to me for a long
time that it's virtually impossible for us to be totally self-sustaining. First,
our ticket prices for meets average $5, and with the seating capacity
and only six home meets, our total revenue from ticket sales can never
exceed $300,000. (Contributions to the Gymnastics Endowment Fund
of $100,000 per year are not considered income.)

It's obvious that television is the key to increased support and
contributions. Just ten years ago, the Utah and Georgia gymnastics
teams were number one and two in the country in average attendance
per event for all women's sports. But in the last five years, Tennessee
and Connecticut women's basketball have skyrocketed around us, and
attendance for other women's basketball programs has grown significantly too. This is because many NCAA women's basketball games are
telecast live nationally every week, and gymnastics meets continue to
be telecast by tape delay and they are mostly televised regionally.

I met with Assistant Athletic Director for Promotions and Marketing Avery McLean to suggest that we have our home meets telecast live in the Atlanta market. He suggested, instead, a weekly *Suzanne Yoculan Show*, like many football coaches around the country have. I was pumped. That was a super idea.

I talked with Andy Landers about the two of us getting coaches' shows, and Andy went back with me to ask Avery about funding a coach's show for women's basketball as well as the gymnastics coach's show. At the time many women's college basketball coaches had shows, but Andy didn't, even though he'd taken his team to the final four several times. Andy and I felt that the university should help find advertisers for the show and that the promotions office should sell the ads or at least assist us. Avery did arrange for me to meet with the producer of UGA's football coaching show, but no money or assistance was made available to us.

Andy was discouraged. He didn't feel that he had the time or that he should be the one to pursue this. Of course, I felt the same way about my program, but I didn't want to cut off my nose to spite my face. I was closer to getting a show than I'd ever been before. I only had about two weeks before preliminary taping began. So I went for it. And somehow, someway, in less than two weeks, I raised the initial $40,000 to air the show. No one turned me down for additional advertising spots after I got the initial funding—which, by the way, came from Poland Spring, who was seeking ways to expand its participation in Olympic Sports. Poland Spring was already involved in international tennis and had contacted Georgia Crown, its distributor, about putting money into gymnastics at another school. Don Leebern, Georgia Crown's CEO, suggested Georgia as the recipient, instead, and the rest is history. Poland Spring came on board in a very supportive way, and we had the first collegiate gymnastics coaching show in the country.

The Suzanne Yoculan GymDog Show is different from most coaches' shows. I was encouraged by Steve Graham, the producer, to do the show alone using no sidekick to pilot me through the ordeal, as most coaches do. I had been at Georgia almost twenty years, and Steve wanted me to focus on the athletes from our team, as well as the visitors

In its first year *The GymDog Show* was carried by about eight or nine stations in Georgia. Apparently, viewers loved it. In 2000, the show's coverage mushroomed. It was aired literally all over the South, and not at midnight like some coache's shows. *The GymDog Show* aired during prime time.

With all this exposure, particularly in Atlanta, we certainly hoped that the 9,951 seats in Stegeman Coliseum would be filled for every meet. But in 2000, winter storms hurt attendance at what are normally two of the most popular meets, LSU and Alabama, and we filled Stegeman only once. In 2001, however, the weather was more cooperative and average attendance was 9,854 (over 99 percent capacity). We turned away hundreds of fans at the four meets that were complete sellouts, and we had a first—fans were actually scalping tickets before the Alabama meet.

Even if every seat available for the general public is sold as a renewable season ticket, the revenues won't nearly match the gymnastics annual budget. There are only two other sources of revenue that haven't been fully tapped: TV revenues and corporate contributions designated exclusively for gymnastics.

I don't want to seek corporate sponsorship to the point that sponsors take over the program. Nearly every Georgia home meet is telecast now, by Fox, ESPN, or College Sports Southeast, and the national championships are telecast by CBS. But all of these are tape-delay telecasts. Georgia has telecast one or two dual meets live on Media One, and it worked well. According to the Sports Marketing Group of Dallas, Texas, women's gymnastics ties with major league baseball as the third most popular spectator sport on U.S. television. That is, when gymnastics is available. Good gymnastics usually isn't— not live. And college gymnastics is the most exciting and entertaining gymnastics of all.

The format of dual meets is ideal for live telecasting right now. No events are simultaneous. We alternate between the two teams' performances on vaulting and bars first, and then beam and floor next. Action is almost continuous for each of the four rotations, with three minute touch warm-ups in between. The ideal time for commercials is during the warm-ups.

I asked Greg Marsden about his experience with live telecasts at Utah. He's way ahead of us on this, and his assessment should be the best available. Here's what he had to say:

> We usually have two live broadcasts each year. They are done in real time.
>
> Do I think that live TV is better? I know that I will watch live events that I would never watch a taped delay of. Live TV makes it seem like a bigger deal. Being in the moment is always preferable. Die-hard gymnastics fans will watch either; the difference is in capturing the nontraditional gymnastics viewer.
>
> I have always been an advocate of this. Our ratings here of our live broadcasts are similar to what our men's basketball gets.

The Sports Marketing Group's survey would have predicted what Greg's real life experience demonstrated. And take a look at the impact of live telecasts on the attendance of women's college basketball. In 1994, the top-two teams in the country in average attendance (including all women's sports) were Utah and Georgia gymnastics:

RANK	SCHOOL	SPORT	ATTENDANCE AVERAGE
1	**Utah**	**Gymnastics**	**10,511**
2	**Georgia**	**Gymnastics**	**8,638**
3	Ohio State	Basketball	8,411
4	SW Missouri	Basketball	8,191
5	Texas	Basketball	7,614
6	Texas Tech	Basketball	6,931
7	Tennessee	Basketball	6,542
9	Connecticut	Basketball	6,243

But look at attendance for the 1999 season, after national TV began telecasting women's college basketball live.

1	Tennessee	Basketball	16,565
2	Connecticut	Basketball	10,863
3	**Utah**	**Gymnastics**	**10,568**
4	Purdue	Basketball	9,681
5	**Georgia**	**Gymnastics**	**9,506**
6	**Alabama**	**Gymnastics**	**9,139**

With the national telecasts airing, the top basketball teams surpassed the top gymnastics teams in attendance. There are 304 Division I college women's basketball teams with an average attendance of 1,427 compared to 70 Division I college women's gymnastics teams with an average attendance of 1,264 fans. Fan interest seems to be pretty close for the two sports generally.

One of my next projects is to convince a national TV network to establish a live weekly program (same time each week during the gymnastics season), pitting not one, but two, college gymnastics teams ranked in the top ten as opponents. That would ensure nothing but top quality individual performances. Then, on the night six different regional meets take place all over the country, telecast a slightly-delayed (like the golf tournaments) program, going from region to region. This would be the build-up for the three-day NCAA Championships, telecast with a similar five-to-ten-minute delay. If Greg Marsden's assessment and the Sports Marketing Group's analysis are right, college gymnastics would draw a tremendous audience and television revenues and attendance would go up all over the country.

My job's not finished. There are a lot of people in this country who still don't know how exciting college gymnastics is, and we still haven't become financially self-sufficient at Georgia.

Stay tuned!

Chemistry

Every athletics coach will tell you team chemistry is powerful. Good chemistry can help you win. Bad chemistry will kill you! But what is team chemistry, and how do you achieve it?

In tennis doubles, the timing and strategies between the two partners are essential. In football, the coordination and communication among the members of the offensive line are critical. In baseball, the double play is another perfect example of working together. These are examples of teamwork, not chemistry. In gymnastics, there is no physical interaction between gymnasts. Each individual does her own routine, untouched by anyone else. No ball is passed, no one blocks out a member of the other team.

I define teamwork as "a group of individuals who are either leading or following, but are all moving in the same direction." There is no teamwork without leadership. That's teamwork, but you also hear the phrase over and over again: "This team has good (or bad) chemistry."

Team chemistry grows out of having responsibility to one another. Feeling that if you fall off the beam, even though you're up there alone, it doesn't affect only you, it affects everybody. This attitude makes you a much better athlete. Even though gymnastics is considered an individual sport, it really isn't because you need team chemistry to win. When you have a team whose members don't care about the performance of another, the team lacks chemistry and won't overachieve. When one person falls, it is chemistry that makes the others want to compensate.

I believe team chemistry develops through respect—respect of the coaches for the athletes, of the athletes for each other, of the athletes for the coaches. There is total understanding and respect, not only for the things you like about one another, but also for the things you dislike. Differences in one another are accepted and understood. It's difficult for you to have respect for a boss you don't know or one you never come in contact with. The same is true with a team. You develop respect for someone by seeing how he or she handles frustrating and difficult times.

But team chemistry involves more than that. If you walk into our practice gym, you can't distinguish the scholarship athletes from the walk-ons on the basis of the amount of attention the coaches give them or the amount of support they receive from the other gymnasts. That's one reason gymnasts elect to come to Georgia without a scholarship, turning down scholarship offers from other schools. They know they will receive some of the best coaching in gymnastics. And this equal treatment carries over to the accessibility of coaches and support staff outside the gym. While there may be obvious differences in athletic abilities among the gymnasts, they are all respected as people, not only as athletes.

Bill Russell, the great former basketball player for the Boston Celtics and a tremendous leader, defines chemistry this way: "Chemistry is what makes the sum of the combined parts greater than the sum of the individual parts." In other words, strength is added when gymnasts' talents are combined to form a team—together their talents exceed beyond what each individual can contribute performing alone as an individual.

Is developing team chemistry challenging in college gymnastics? Is it ever! First of all, you're dealing with people of tremendous diversity. If you want an example of diversity in higher education, just take a look at the GymDogs. The gymnasts have come from all over the United States (including Puerto Rico) and Canada. Over the years Caucasians, African Americans, Asians, and Hispanics—Catholics, Protestants, Jews—country girls and city girls—have been on the team. Some come from affluent families, and some parents have struggled financially to pay for gymnastics training. Some join sororities and others don't. They major in everything from pre-med to journalism to sports management. Their personalities and hobbies vary as much as their floor music.

For the most part, college gymnasts have competed as individuals prior to coming here, so you would expect them to be self-centered and not really concerned with their teammates. Most of the freshmen have been sheltered, practicing gymnastics thirty to forty hours a week for six to ten years. By the time an athlete becomes a senior, she has become socially independent, and the sophomores and juniors are somewhere in between. At times, the best gymnasts are seniors, and at other times the freshmen have been the more prolific contributors. Some are intellectual and others have simple interests. And perhaps the biggest challenge comes from the fact that they are women.

The support staff is also a part of the chemistry—particularly those who work with the gymnasts almost daily, such as the sports medicine trainers, the strength coach, or the academic achievement advisor. Gymnasts come from as many different training regimens as they do gyms, and they bring with them their own ideas about what treatments for injuries work for them. They are not always the treatments the GymDog trainers think are best. The trainer has to be skillful in how she communicates about changing the gymnasts' routines if that is necessary. She has to read their attitudes and empathize.

However, the biggest part of team chemistry develops outside the gym. One of the things the girls talked about in 2003 when I had the end-of-the-year meeting with the six rising seniors was the fact that because of our use of chartered flights, we didn't stay overnight in hotels. Cory Fritzinger pointed out that we didn't have all of that time together sitting up late at night, with the girls coming into my room and talking and watching movies like we had in previous years. That was missing because we flew in for a meet and left right after the competition. Travel to competitions and time away together provide a great opportunity for team-building. I noticed when the University of Arkansas started their gymnastics program that coaches Renee and

Mark Cook planned lots of activity in the hotel for their team. We often see the Arkansas Razorbacks having a scavenger hunt or running through a hotel in some sort of costume. Renee and Mark obviously understand the importance of team chemistry.

It's hard to get to know each other in the gym because the teammates are focused on practice and on their individual skills. But early in the year, conditioning and strength workouts bring athletes together. The girls talk a lot to each other while they are conditioning. They are running and conditioning and, at times, complaining together, but always encouraging one another. Athletes become united when they are struggling together. Our conditioning program is developed around team-building activities.

In the years when we had the best team chemistry, the team liked to be together. In addition to the activities that were planned and mandatory, the gymnasts arranged many social activities that they all participated in. They spent so much time together that respect was inevitable. They knew each other!

It may seem strange, but minor conflict builds team chemistry because it lets the gymnasts see the different attitudes among them. It's in activities outside of the gym that gymnasts usually have conflicts. When Karin Lichey's doing a beam routine, Sam Muhleman's doing a bars routine, and Stacy Galloway's doing floor, there's no conflict, so there's no team chemistry being built. But when they're hiking on the trail and Karin wants to be in front, and she's irritated because somebody got ahead of her, there's a conflict because she wanted to be first. That's when we develop team chemistry. By the end of the hike, we were all laughing about it and we all gained a mutual respect for Karin and her drive to succeed.

Often in practice we have team intrasquads on different events. If one person misses her routine, everyone has to go again. It can be very frustrating, especially for freshmen. I remember one incident when Lucy Wener was a sophomore and Corrinne Wright was a freshman. During a bar intrasquad, Corrinne was missing her routine over and over because she merely didn't feel like doing it. It wasn't that she couldn't hit the routine, she just didn't want to. Lucy was repeating her routine over and over as well, but she was hitting hers. After the fourth time, Lucy said, "I have hit my routine 9.95 every time and I don't want to have to go anymore." And I said, "All six of you have to hit. Go Again." Then Lucy said, "Well I don't think it's fair; I shouldn't have to go again. I hit my routines. Corrinne, get it together." They were getting on each other, getting mad, and at the same time, team chemistry was being developed. It is up to us as coaches to create situations during training that are filled with pressure and accountability. It is during these frustrating times that chemistry can develop. It's a process, not just something that occurs.

Team chemistry cannot develop without leadership, so where did the leadership come from when the chemistry was good? And when the chemistry was bad, where did we fall short in terms of leadership? I contend that everyone on the team must be a leader or a follower. There cannot be any obstructers. Leadership can come from different individuals on different days or in different situations. Leadership can come from freshmen or seniors, all-arounders or individuals. Leadership can come from the coaches. Through good leadership, respect develops and ultimately team chemistry.

So how was the chemistry on the 1997 team? We seemed to have it and then lose it. The GymDogs swept through the regular season undefeated, with a bad performance at LSU ending in a tie. The only other close meet was a 0.175-point win over Alabama in Tuscaloosa. Any win over Alabama in Tuscaloosa is significant. The GymDogs broke the conference meet scoring record in winning the SEC Championship, and then I gave them a well-deserved extended break from practice before regionals. Was it a mistake? I don't think so. But the GymDogs had six falls at regionals, four committed by juniors and seniors. Go figure. We came in second to Florida and had to sweat out making nationals until the scores from the other regionals were in. Because only the winners in each regional meet were assured of a berth, all other teams qualified on an at-large basis, depending on their scores. Even with six falls, Georgia had the sixth highest score in the country (including the regional champions), so our "sweating" wasn't necessary.

It looked like the GymDogs had fully shaken off the "bad showing" at regionals in the first round of the national championships, scoring the highest score of any of the twelve teams. But then disaster struck in the Super Six. Starting on beam, our team had three falls, counting two. We didn't display much confidence on the beam. But what kind of chemistry does it take to come back after disaster and blow the other teams away on the other three apparatus? That's what the GymDogs did. Even so, UCLA and Arizona State didn't falter on any apparatus and UCLA won by a small margin because Georgia had already lost it on beam. The GymDogs could have won with just one less fall. We returned the favor UCLA gave us in 1989. Individually, GymDogs garnered three national championships, and two runners-up slots.

So what happened? Was the leadership just not there? Was it some other aspect of chemistry? Leslie Angeles and Lisa Kurc, two of the three seniors, were not the assertive leader types, but they were not obstructers either. Our third senior, Leah Brown, demonstrated tremendous leadership and focus throughout the season.

Three individual championships, two runners-up, and three events at the NCAA's, but no team championship. The individual performances exceeded the team performance—not the other way around, which would be indicative of good chemistry. For the NCAA Championships, at least, that would indicate bad chemistry. But we had one bad event and three exceptionally good ones. In this case, I do not believe the loss had anything to do with chemistry or leadership. We had it. The point is you can still lose even with great chemistry, but you will never win without it.

So, we've never had a team that won a national championship that did not have good team chemistry. There may have been more chemistry in the 1999 team, both good and bad, than in any other team I've coached. The team started out great, went through many crises, and ended with an undefeated season and a second consecutive national championship. Because the 1997 team was the strongest in the nation, the 1998 team went undefeated, and the most talented senior class in NCAA history was returning—all healthy for the first time since they matriculated. The GymDogs were picked unanimously in the 1999 preseason coaches' poll to repeat as national champions. Early indications signaled that we would breeze through the season. After the preseason intrasquad meet, I suggested that there was enough talent for us to split the team into two teams and both could make the Super Six.

Before the ink could dry on the impressive scores put up at the intrasquad meet, catastrophe struck. Sam Muhleman, a senior who was looking forward to her best year, suddenly decided she wanted to leave the team.

The problem was more complex than just getting her to agree to come back. Two of the girls didn't want her back, her roommates— Jenni and Stacy. They had an argument that somehow related to Sam and her fiancé. The details aren't important because the whole thing was irrational. They were seniors, our team leaders, and they acted like a bunch of—well—like a bunch of college girls.

I had meetings with them separately. I didn't dare try to get them together. They were livid. The whole team was gossiping about it. I absolutely hate conflict resolution, but I had to resolve this problem— and quick. There just seemed to be no resolution except for Sam to leave the team, and I knew she didn't really want to. She'd been injured with one thing or another throughout her gymnastics career, and for the first time she was healthy and really looking forward to competing for individual championships in three events. She was one of the most talented gymnasts in NCAA history, and she'd never been able to realize her potential. I couldn't let this happen to her. But I was at my wit's end.

I met with Doug and Jay extensively. Ultimately I decided to write a letter to arrive at the gymnasts' homes near the end of the team's Christmas break. We hoped that a letter assuring them that they would not be coming back to an unpleasant situation would be welcomed. The letter follows:

Dear _____,

From time to time, incidents regarding team member
conduct occur that I believe I should review with you. We all
need to keep communications open from me to you and from
you to me. So I am writing to provide my position on what
occurred last week.

First, I want to tell you all how much I appreciate the
work you are putting in this year and the excellent attitude
you are displaying in the gym. You comprise one of the most
talented teams we've had at Georgia (which means one of the
most talented in women's college gymnastics), and you are
fully capable of winning the second part of our first back-to-
back championships. But talent and hard work, alone, do not
win championships. Teamwork, leadership, cooperation, and
mutual respect are essential elements for championship teams.

While I see nothing but strong evidence that your
teamwork and dedication, while in the gym, will fully meet
the requirements for success this year, we have experienced
personal relationships outside the gym that could threaten our
wonderful team relationships. I know that you want to deal
with these potential problems just as much as I, so I am asking
your understanding and full cooperation throughout the
season. Let me add that we probably have fewer such problems
than any other team. I am intensely thankful for that.

Attached is a copy of my "Fifteen Points of Pride for a
Winning Program." As I review it, I see it largely as an "in-
gym" document. But four items—Student Athletes, Discipline
to Conform, Integrity, and Fairness—do relate to outside-the-
gym activities as well.

In addressing those items, I should point out that while
I expect you to fully exhibit a "big team-little me" attitude, I
must assign the physical and mental welfare of each of you as
an individual my highest priority.

Honesty is the essential foundation of all successful endeavors. I appreciate so much your display of openness and honesty this past week. Although I don't like to be spoken to harshly, if harsh language helps us communicate better, it is certainly better than not communicating adequately. And anyone who says that always being honest is not challenging may not be honest in his or her assessment. So thank you for your honesty.

Fairness is even more difficult than being honest because it involves conflicting priorities and judgements that are far from black and white. Fair treatment of each individual is an integral part of fair treatment of the team. Fairness involves being consistent, but being consistent in arriving at fair treatment does not always result in identical treatment for different individuals engaged in similar activities. In evaluating appropriate responses to problems, I must take into account the circumstances under which the problem developed, the prior behavior of the individual(s) involved, and the impact of any decision I make on the present and future welfare of the person(s) involved. And I wholeheartedly believe that what's good for the individual, even if it involves dismissal from the team, is best for the team in the long run.

I am reluctant to even comment on your personal relationships outside the gym, because I feel that you need to be mature to the point that you can handle such things yourself. I do want to always be available for consultation, however, whenever you think I can help and by all means when you perceive a potential serious problem. Because, looking at problems from the outside, I usually see more than one side to a problem, I will seldom assign blame or be judgmental. I will, however, make suggestions and ask questions designed to stimulate consideration on your part.

I can offer no better general advice than to follow the Golden Rule. Be considerate, try to see the other viewpoint, turn the other cheek at least once, and critically examine your own conduct. Above all, try to think of how you will feel about your decisions five to ten years from now. If you do this, then I'm sure you have the good character and maturity to resolve your problems, even though the resolution may result in changes in behavior or changes in relationships.

Finally, please forgive me for being a little sentimental. As you remain a part of Georgia gymnastics, I get to know each of you better, and invariably admire each of you more the longer you are here. By the time you are seniors, I truly love each of you. All you have to do to confirm this is look at those humongous tears rolling down my cheeks on Senior Night. They're not crocodile tears, and I'm not crying just because we're losing your gymnastics skills.

So let's get it together, keep it together, and make this the best year ever in Georgia gymnastics. And call on me whenever you think I can help. Helping you is not only part of my job, it's what makes my job the best in the world.

My sincere wishes for a wonderful holiday season.

Love,
Suzanne

Did the letter help? As it turned out, Sam missed only one practice, but because she missed a practice, she was suspended from competition in the first meet at Washington. But she participated two days later at UCLA.

Next, the injury bug began to bite. At Washington, Kathleen Shrieves tore an ACL, which required surgery and knocked her out of competition well beyond the season. Then a little later Danielle Maurone joined the "ACL Club." Stacey, Sam, and Brooke Andersen were already rehabilitated members of the club, so they could offer encouragement. But all of that depth I described at the time of the preseason intrasquad meet was beginning to diminish. Kathleen's injury was particularly hard on the vaulting lineup. Slowly the team was beginning to see that hardships could be ahead. They began gelling emotionally. It was obvious in the gym and at the meets that the chemistry was turning from bad to good, fast. Stacey, who earlier wanted Sam off the team, became Sam's biggest cheerleader. All four seniors were putting up big scores.

If the chemistry was bad, it certainly wasn't reflected in scores. The GymDogs were ripping right along through Washington, UCLA, Alabama (in Athens), and Florida before they had a less-than stellar performance at LSU. Through three rotations, Georgia held a slim 0.100 lead with LSU ending on floor and Georgia ending on the dreaded beam. It is tough to outscore your opponents on floor when you're on beam, and the slim 0.100 point lead was not likely to hold up. The thirty-nine-meet winning streak seemed almost certain to end in Baton Rouge. It got worse—while LSU was putting up a 49.200 on the floor, the GymDogs' second gymnast up on beam fell, meaning that the last four would not only have to hit, they would have to hit big. They did, with Sam, Jenni, and Stacey, who were at each other's throats just seven weeks earlier, all contributing to the beam score. The 49.375 score on beam gave Georgia a 196.100 to LSU's 195.825. The GymDogs had certainly come through, after digging themselves a whopping hole.

I decided it was time to get the team into an "in your face" mode before facing Alabama in Tuscaloosa. I knew the Tide and their boisterous fans were sick of Georgia's ten consecutive wins over Alabama, and our team would need to be focused and confident. I had T-shirts prepared with the message, "We will defend what is ours, Georgia GymDogs, National Champions." Of course, the T-shirts would only be donned if the GymDogs won, and the team didn't know we had them printed.

The 14,079 Tide fans were intimidating, but to no avail. The GymDogs hit twenty-three consecutive routines. I can't recall the GymDogs' losing a meet when they didn't have to count a bad routine. The meet was "over," with only Jenni Beathard's beam routine left.

I was so relieved that before Jenni's routine I had the gymnasts don the T-shirts—really sticking it to the Alabama fans. Did the distraction contribute to Jenni's fall (which was insignificant as far as the outcome of the meet)? Maybe, but I don't think Jenni cared. The frustrated Alabama fans broke into a spontaneous—then quickly subdued— cheer when Jenni fell. Not a very sportsmanlike thing to do, normally. But I think they knew the meet was over, and they were signaling that, bitter as it was, they admired the near-perfect performance by the GymDogs and our gutsy move in putting on the T-shirts. And the fall gave them something to cheer about—finally. Jenni turned to face the Alabama fans, smiled broadly, waved her hand, and remounted the beam. She totally won them over. The subdued cheers turned into louder, unabashed cheers of admiration for Jenni's attitude. Great fans! Great girl! Georgia 197.300/Alabama 196.350.

Arnold Balk, who the team honored at the recognition banquet after the 1998 season as the "fan of the year," had planned to drive to the February 19 Michigan meet in Ann Arbor by himself. He didn't show up. Just before the meet, I was informed that Arnold had been found dead in his home, the victim of a heart attack. I didn't tell the team until after the meet. Because he had no immediate family, Doug McAvinn handled most of the arrangements for the funeral of this "gymnastics family member." Arnold was a member of the large First Baptist Church in Athens, teaching a Sunday school class there, so his funeral was well attended. He also had been quite a women's soccer fan, even though the sport was only a few years old at Georgia. The entire soccer team went to his service; and, of course, the gymnastics team was there. Arnold's funeral consisted of a sermon by Minister Jon Appleton; a eulogy by Bill Barker, the soccer coach; and eulogies by gymnast alumna, Julie Ballard and senior gymnasts, Jenni, Karin, and Sam. The gymnasts' eulogies—each distinctly different, reflecting the personalities of the eulogists—moved every member of the congrega- tion. The young women certainly demonstrated a lot of class, compas- sion, and strength—only Sam was unable to hold back her tears.

Tragedy brings people together. Although the gymnastics team had already begun to bond together after the rocky beginning, Arnold's death and funeral was the catalyst for an even tighter bond. The fragmentation of the seniors that was so ominous at the beginning of the season miraculously seemed a thing of the past.

Stacey was finally having a good year. She was one of the most heralded gymnasts to come out of Canada. She was recovering from a seriously injured knee when she came to Georgia, but she was confident almost to the point of being brash. Gymnastics was Stacey's life, and she didn't fit into the team concept immediately. She was still hampered by the long-term recovery from surgery her freshman year. In her sophomore year, she began contributing on three events, but a second ACL injury in the opening meet of her junior year forced her into another year-long rehabilitation. Finally, healthy again, Stacey was a big contributor on beam and floor as a senior. The tremendously talented bars team bumped her off the lineup for the event that was her strong suit in Canada. But a more important transition had taken place—Stacey's misfortunes had changed her outlook. She was beginning to be the consummate team player. Her lofty individual goals had given way to team goals.

And then came Senior Night. Each senior's family came to the floor to take the spotlight with their gymnast. Both of Sam Muhleman's parents and her sister, who was a cheerleader at Georgia, were with Sam. Jenni Beathard's parents and brother were there. Licheys came from all over for Karin—sister GymDog Kristi, both parents, two sets of grandparents, Aunt Debbie, etc. But Stacey Galloway was joined only by her mother, Linda, who was a single working mom and didn't get to many meets at Georgia. And there was something that must have touched everyone's emotions about their obvious closeness when just the two were in the spotlight. This set the stage for what may be the most significant perfect 10 ever scored at Georgia. Yes, Stacey, in her final routine in Athens, scored a well-deserved 10 on floor—her first. I think her floor performance motivated her to go through four post-season meets feeling as proud as she deserved to be. More important, the other seniors were almost as happy for Stacey as Linda was—an example of how a positive experience can help chemistry. The bond beween the four seniors was even stronger than before their break-up at the beginning of the season, and they had become the leaders everyone hoped they would be. The chemistry on the 1999 team was, without question, alive and well.

The GymDogs did not need any more tragedy-related bonding. But there was more to come. As expected, Sam was having a spectac-ular year. She was ranked fourth nationally on floor, eleventh on bars, and fifteenth on beam, despite being the leadoff gymnast on beam. And because she was now doing vault, she was getting all-around scores for the first time at Georgia—she posted a meet-high 39.650 against Michigan in Ann Arbor. That's in national championship range.

The GymDogs were going into the SEC championship meet in Tuscaloosa looking to extend a second straight perfect record. During a practice session on Friday night, before the Saturday meet, Sam fell on her neck doing a vaulting routine. The pain was excruciating. The trainers immobilized her neck and rushed her to the University of Alabama Hospital. I was devastated—not for what losing Sam would do to the team, but out of concern for Sam's health. Less than a year earlier Sang Lan, the Chinese gymnast, had been paralyzed for life resulting from a neck injury while vaulting. Sang Lan's tragic accident played heavily on my mind. Although all of the preliminary examina-tions were encouraging—maybe it was just a sprain—the full extent of the injury would not be determined until Sam returned to Athens for a more extensive examination. But, at least, she would be able to leave the hospital safely, wearing just a plastic neck stabilizer, and she could be on the sidelines at the meet.

I was bushed the next morning. As I began to feel some relief that Sam would likely be okay physically, my attention turned to different obligations. We had to find some way to ease Sam's mental anguish from seeing her most promising and final year go up in smoke. And I had to rally the team to perform up to its potential in a highly com-petitive meet. Georgia and Alabama were ranked one and two in the nation, with Alabama's RQS only 0.550 points below Georgia's. The

GymDogs had been distracted by their concern for Sam. And the meet was in Alabama's own gym with their highly partisan and vocal fans.

I decided to tell the team that even though we would lose a half point by having Sam out of the lineup physically, she was going to contribute a full point by becoming our biggest cheerleader. The idea was so absurd it might be effective. Suggesting that Sam, the least rah-rah member of the team, would be a dynamic cheerleader broke up the team with laughter, taking their minds off Sam's misfortune. And giving Sam a challenge to do something she had never done before would hopefully give her the sense of contributing that she needed.

I couldn't believe Sam at the meet. She was down on the floor with the team and was wearing a plastic neck brace and her warm-ups. She was yelling and clapping her hands as much as her neck support would allow. In the *Gymnastics Insider* the next week, David Allen Johnson wrote, "Sam's presence as a cheerleader seemed to fire the GymDogs." Apparently she took her new assignment seriously. Oh, the score?—Georgia 197.475, Alabama 196.775, Florida 195.875.

Back in Athens, Sam's injury was diagnosed as a fractured C-3 vertebrae. She would have no residual impairment, but she would have to wear the neck support for several weeks, ending her career, as was expected. Sam's loss was felt most on the beam. Because of her reliability, she had been the leadoff gymnast on beam for three years. She was replaced in the beam lineup by Talya Vexler, a freshman who had also shown uncommon consistency. Talya was an alternate on vaulting as well as becoming a starter in the beam lineup.

The night before regionals, in Logan, Utah, Talya sprained her knee while vaulting, taking her out for regionals and the championships. The GymDogs were no longer the odds-on favorite to win. We could not afford many mistakes. And who would replace Talya? Another freshman, Emily Chell, was recruited as a vaulting specialist. She had not developed as hoped on vault, and she was certainly not counted on to compete beam in the NCAA regionals. But she answered the call, with a respectable 9.775, replacing a 9.275 by one of the "old reliables," who fell. It was her first college routine in any meet. Emily's routine was watered down to just enough for a 10.0 start value. But, hey, she hit it! Even with all the injuries, the GymDogs had the highest regional score in the country, making us the number-one seeded team going into nationals.

The GymDogs arrived for nationals in Salt Lake City a physically beaten-up, tired group of gymnasts. We proudly wore our new T-shirts, which read, "A wounded dog is a dangerous dog." We had CHEMISTRY! We continued our perfect record, scoring the highest of any team in either qualifying round. And on Friday night, in the Super Six, we had two falls and two other low scores, but we had just enough left to nose out Michigan 196.850 to 196.550, completing back-to-back perfect seasons. Emily Chell hit two more beam routines, scoring a 9.850 in the preliminaries to make second-team All American.

Several GymDogs qualified for the individual championships held on Saturday night, but there were no individual titles this year—even though two GymDogs were defending champions and one was a champion-to-be in 2000. We left it all on the floor in Friday's team championship. Stacey made All-America for the first time, during her last chance to compete for it. On Saturday, she competed for the individual beam championship and had an excellent routine, but as she dismounted she was too tired to fight for the landing and took a big step backward. She knew that the step was probably all that was between her and at least a tie for the individual national championship. As it turned out, it was. But I could read her face as she smiled and waved. There was no disappointment. She had finally become a total team player. The team national championship was all that mattered. Stacey was totally content with her college career. Back to Bill Russell's definition: this time the sum of the combined parts was greater than the sum of the individual parts. A team championship—no individual championships. Was the difference chemistry?

Now if you ask me what team chemistry is, I have an answer: "The GymDogs' 1999 season." Throughout the season we faced one problem after another. Conflicts, arguments, injuries, lineup frustrations, and the pressure to win back-to-back titles brought us together. We got to know each other, respect developed, so good chemistry was inevitable.

Putting It All Together

If you look back at my first year, I almost ran the gymnastics program single-handedly. My only assistant coach was in graduate school and had previously coached men. I shared a secretary with about ten other coaches of nonrevenue-producing sports. Travel was in one van, sometimes in two, except for trips such as the NCAA Championships in Salt Lake City. Today we travel with ten to fourteen gymnasts and more support people than gymnasts—frequently on chartered planes.

Part of the austere situation in the early days was due to a lack of support in terms of staff. And part of it, also, was because I wanted to do everything myself. Our team didn't ask for a lot of help. For example, we did the promotions. Fourteen people—the gymnasts—can do a lot more than one staff member. We all put our heads together and lined up every Sunday afternoon and put labels on thousands of flyers to send to the faculty throughout the campus. And we were one of the first sports to have an annual team poster—particularly, one with a theme.

One of the most important factors in the success of a program is consistency of the staff. Without that it's very difficult to win championships and build on the foundation you've established year in and year out. Fortunately for me, one of the best parts of our program has been that Doug McAvinn—our number one assistant coach—joined me in my third year and has been with me since then. Having Doug with me all this time has been one of the key factors in our success. Through the years, our second assistant coach has sometimes changed. When we won our first national title in 1987, Carl Leland was coach along with Doug. The 1989 championship was won with Scott Bull as assistant coach. Delene Darst was an assistant coach in 1991 and 1992. Jay Clark was coaching during the 1993 and 1999 championship years, and Steve Ballard stepped in to assist Doug and me in 1997 and 1998. But through all these changes, Doug remained a constant. He and I can sit in our separate offices and don't even have to talk about things that much because he knows exactly what he needs to do and I know exactly what I need to do. We can meet together once a week about the direction of the girls and the team. He has his strengths and I have mine, and this relationship has made the coaching part of the job extremely easy and very rewarding.

Doug is the best technician in the country; there's no question about it. He can teach any athlete anything, if she has the athleticism and desire. He does a lot of video taping and analyzing and instructing from the tapes. He can tell a gymnast specifically what she needs to do with her body and what her body is not doing—keeping her from having the desired results. He's very versatile, and he has a personality that blends very well with mine.

Doug is extremely focused on small details, while I look at the big picture. The roof could be falling in over the vaulting runway, and he'd still have the girls going down the runway. He would notice only the vault. One time I watched Lori Strong cry the whole time she was vaulting. She'd do a vault and walk back to the end of the runway and she'd be crying. I watched her vault and wipe her eyes and vault and it went on and on. So I finally walked over to Doug and said, "What's wrong with Lori?" And Doug answered, "I don't know. Is there something wrong with Lori?" He is just so focused on the skill itself, whereas I like to coach all the events because I see everything. It's hard for me to stick to one event. So together, Doug and I compliment one another.

I've taken advantage of his strengths. There are days when he comes over and works on beam dismounts, days that he works on tumbling, or days he will help Jay on the uneven bars.

Jay Clark, our second assistant coach, joined us in 1990 and has been with us ever since—except for the 1997 and 1998 seasons.

Jay is the best recruiter in the country, no question about it. Any recruit who gets a visit from Jay is just sold—he bleeds red and black. He is absolutely sincere about his love for the university and his belief that this is the best place in the country. His success in recruiting comes from his passion for the University of Georgia. All athletes need to go school where they want to get an education, and where they're going to be happy. Jay's the perfect person to sell them on UGA, not just the gymnastics program, but the university as a whole. As he says, "It's easy to sell what you know and believe in." I feel very comfortable that we'll have him here always because I can't see Jay recruiting for any other school.

Doug spent a lot of time teaching Jay conceptual gymnastics and the foundations and how to spot. Then he worked in our summer camp, and he learned more and more. To his credit, he took it upon himself to teach in the Ten-0 Club children's program. Jay began learning basic gymnastics and how to coach youngsters and teach cartwheels and other beginning skills. Then he wanted to own his own gym and was able to take over Classic City Gymnastics Academy. He took two years off from college coaching just to coach club kids full time and see what that was like. Now he is a much better college coach because he's taught all levels of gymnastics.

Jay has also become a great technical coach, and he has good feel for composition and what skills are good for what girls. He has good insight into planning for the future. For example, if he teaches a gymnast this skill this year, we can progress to the next skill in that sequence next year—we can build on it. But I think more important, Jay's an emotional coach. He has a sense of humor that brings the girls close to him. Through the years, he's become a confidant to them. Sometimes he knows more about what's going on with them outside the gym than I do.

We all coach all the events, from time to time. We all coach floor, for example, taking turns spotting, etc., depending on the day. We have coaches meetings every Monday where all of us are involved in composition and review the progress and plan for each girl on each event. We team coach everything.

According to the NCAA rules, each institution can only have three full-time coaches and one volunteer coach. As I mentioned earlier, I believe the longevity of our current full-time coaches (Jay, Doug, and me) is a contributing factor to our consistency in being a top program in the country. Contrary to that, yet just as important to our success, have been the contributions through the years from our ever changing volunteer coaches. Although these individuals have had different personalities with different strengths, they have all brought to our program fresh ideas, insight, energy, and enthusiasm.

Our first volunteer coach was a graduate student and gymnastics judge, Raul Arocho. Raul loved gymnastics and stepped into the position for one year as he completed pharmacy school at UGA. Raul was positive and fun, and we all still swear that the vertical jump he demonstrated when a GymDog performed a good routine was higher than any basketball player, even thought Raul was only five feet six inches tall.

Delene Darst was a UGA volunteer coach for a short time before being employed as a full-time coach on our staff in 1991 and 1992. She was as committed to her volunteer position as she was when she was paid, never missing a day of practice or a meet. Delene was an accomplished coach and brevet judge, so she brought with her expert knowledge on the rules as well as expectations for composition and execution, which our team needed. Most people only knew Delene as a tough, low-scoring judge, but we knew her as a loving and sensitive coach and friend. I wish so much that Delene had been coaching when we won our title in 1993 because a big reason for our success has to be attributed to her contributions leading up to that championship season.

Agina Simpkins was a member of our 1993 championship team and a very successful competitor. She was second in the nation in the all-around three years in a row and an individual national champion on the uneven bars. As a gymnast, Agina was always late and she is the reason we began our current three-strikes-and-you're-up-the-hill rule.

I remember Agina being late for practice on consecutive days because of "a flat tire." Agina never had her own car. As a volunteer coach, Agina was helpful and inspiring . . . when she didn't have a "flat tire."

Kim Tagtmayer was the antithesis of Agina. She was always early, always organized, and very effective. When Kim left Athens, she went to coach under the legendary Mary Lee Tracy at the Cincinnati Gymnastics Academy.

When I think of Lori Strong, I just think of class. Lori was mature for her age. And she was an excellent coach. Lori was so disciplined and great for fine tuning of the routines—great for choreography. Lori is a detail person and a detail coach.

Jackie Estes was a relatively young person and she was interested in working in or owning a gym. Being an alumnae, competing for Georgia before I came, she really loved being part of the program. She was someone the girls could go cry to and complain about me. More than a coach, she was a real good friend to them.

Our present volunteer coach, Julie Ballard Clark, is the best young coach I've ever worked with. Having been a GymDog from 1995 through 1998, she's seen our program change and grow through the years and seen the type of work it takes to keep a program at the top. She has a keen perception about skill selection and composition and what to change and when to change it. She pushes the girls to the next level, and she doesn't put up with excuses. I feel like I can miss practice when Julie is there—but I don't. Julie has been our volunteer coach for over five years now, and I don't want anyone else. So much for change. I'll take consistency in the staff any day.

If you ask the CEO of a big company—or of a little one for that matter—which employee he or she would be most lost without, the CEO is likely to respond without batting an eye, "My secretary, of course. I'd have to shut down if she left." Nowadays, people have come up with all sorts of politically correct names, such as office manager or administrative assistant, but for me it doesn't matter what you call her; Lisa Mobley is absolutely indispensable. She's been with us over fifteen years, and she knows everything that is to be known about college gymnastics in general and the GymDogs specifically. She can deal with almost anything I need her to, except coaching, and she has the best temperament of any person I know. Everyone loves her and admires her and, unfortunately, imposes on her to do all sorts of things they should be doing themselves. For the past several years, Donna Hallman has assisted Lisa in our vastly over-crowded and over-worked administrative office. She runs Lisa a tight race for her wonderful temperament, which is so important in interactions with all the folks who call or visit our office.

Another integral part of our staff is our trainer. For many years, our trainer was a graduate assistant, and one of the most frustrating things for me was that we didn't have all full-time people involved in our sport. Every year we were getting a new student assistant and a new graduate assistant, and I had to spend so much time educating them about how we do things. I found that it was just easier to do it myself.

From a trainer's standpoint, it was an extremely difficult job because in the sport of gymnastics, your trainer and your strength coach are two of your key people. During the years when we had student or graduate assistant trainers, the coaches taped ankles ourselves. Sometimes we didn't have a trainer travel with us, and we had to do much of his or her work. Now we not only have a head trainer for gymnastics only, but two student trainers, including one who travels with the full-time trainer to every out-of-town competition. We have a doctor and a massage therapist who travel with us to every competition as well. Boy, have things changed.

Many of the GymDogs were national competitors. They're used to having things their way. They're very demanding. They're babied. When gymnasts are on the USA National Team, Dr. Larry Nassar is at their finger tips. They have massage therapists, acupuncturists, chiropractors—anything and everything they need or want. They have it all—one-on-one coaches. Then these girls get to college and they have to adjust to the new procedures. The trainer has to make sure they make these adjustments without letting the process affect their performance or positive attitude. Some of our best trainers through the years include A. J. Champion, Jane Becker, Jen Healy, Lisy Irby, and Caryn Demorest. Kelly Ward was our trainer during 1994 and eventually married GymDog Caroline Harris (member of the 1998 and 1999 championship team). Kelly is now a physician's assistant with the local orthopedic group and is our "team doc."

The most important relationship I have, besides the relationship with my coaches, is with our trainer. The trainer and I have to click. There's a fine line between "they need to sit out a practice" or "they can do a little bit of one or two events" or "a little bit of all things today and none tomorrow." Or the trainer may say they can't do anything. I hope we can keep the trainer we have now, Jenn (Jennifer Cappuzzo), forever. For one thing, she has a gymnastics background. We've never had a former gymnast as a trainer before. I used to think that wasn't important; a trainer just needed a background working with high-level athletes, no matter what sport. A high-level team can't have a trainer who took care of volleyball and soccer at Centre College. We have to have a trainer like Anna Ferguson, who took care of basketball at Nebraska—where there is competition and pressure to win. One of the things about high-level gymnasts is that they are so frustrated when they're injured. The pressure they put on themselves to get back out there and compete is so intense. You have to understand this and include it in your relationship with them.

I realize that Jenn, who actually competed in gymnastics herself, has an uncanny feel for what needs to be done. Jenn has the right personality too. She's consistent, she's not moody, she doesn't have her own personal barometer, she's mature, and she knows what she wants to do with her own life. She's got it all together. She's the perfect person for us.

Doug is the coach who focuses more on strength and conditioning. Of course, at the beginning, the coaches ran the strength and conditioning program without any support. We did the research to learn the proper physical strengths for gymnastics, and we told the strength and conditioning coaches what we wanted to accomplish. We had to be more instructive because you might get a strength coach with a football background who would just want to bulk the girls up.

Doug oversaw these areas for years. As the strength coaches changed
at the University of Georgia, we'd have different ones assigned to us
from the athletic association. Some were better than others. Then we
got Eric Fears.

Eric has been with us since 1996. He has been named a Master
Strength and Conditioning Coach, the highest honor bestowed by the
National Collegiate Strength and Conditioning Coaches Association.
As far as Eric's and the Gymdogs' relationship was concerned, he was
considered an equal coach. We now had a strength coach who is also a
motivator. He attends every meet and is down on the floor, home and
away. He's part of our circle. He meets with our coaches on a regular
basis. But we don't just talk about who's going to do how many reps.
At times, we talk to Coach Fears about a particular motivational ploy
which we want him to implement prior to a big meet.

It's great to have an expert of his caliber who's been with us so long.
We don't have to oversee his work. We know the discipline he requires
of the girls. We know that he's doing the proper conditioning and we
know he knows what's going on in the gym so that he can coordinate
that with what he's doing. Here's Eric's assessment of strength and conditioning in gymnastics:

When the girls come in to college, they are strong and
lean. I've come up with a circuit program designed to build
some additional strength and to maintain the strength levels.
If you don't do any strength training during the season, your
body wears down, and your muscles tend to get a little weaker
because of the demand of the sport. If your strength levels
deteriorate, you become more susceptible to injury. Hopefully
we can minimize the chance of injuries, especially nagging
pulls and shoulder soreness, through our strength program.
And with the conditioning part, we keep their wind level up
while they are performing.

Gymnasts use nearly every muscle in their bodies over the
course of the four events. Consider dismounts from the beam,

running toward the springboard on the vault with your lower body, and pushing off the horse with your upper body. The floor exercise definitely uses every muscle in the body. And bars requires tremendous strength in the shoulders.

And you have to be fresh. You must be careful not to cause more fatigue. You have to tailor the program to gymnasts to be fresher, stronger, maintain quickness, and stay healthier.

You mustn't overbuild muscles. My program during the season is designed to maintain the strength that you've gained in the off-season. In the off-season, you have to be careful because you don't want to get too big and too strong to the point that you lose flexibility. That would take away from gymnastics. I don't want to put extra muscle weight on the gymnast that she may not need. It is detrimental to performing the skills. They have to maintain their flight time—hang time in the air.

We do all of our aerobics and strength and conditioning prior to practice because years ago that's what the Russians did. They did all their conditioning first to get the body warmed up and to get the muscles going. We realized it was also a great incentive for our gymnasts. In the fall we have individual workouts and allow our gymnasts to leave when they finish their workout. If a gymnast is only doing one or two events, she can leave because she's already done her conditioning for the day or her aerobics for the day. Whereas if you had conditioning at the end, at 4:00 or 4:30, then the gymnasts who were done earlier would have to sit around and wait. I'm a big proponent of time-lost motion, of making good use of your time. The girls hear me say that a million times. I don't see any reason for them to have to sit around.

After formal practice starts, each gymnast is assigned to a starting event. The gymnasts go to their events on their own. They have their workout and then they rotate to their other events. Some people only do a couple of events. Some people are highly efficient, like Sam

Muhleman. She would come in and have her five bar routines done
before anybody else had their handgrips on. She'd have her five beam
routines done in ten minutes because she never fell, and she'd be ready
to leave practice. Of course, coaches would oversee all of the routines.
We'd practice from 1:45 p.m. 'till 4:45, and some of them would be
finished with their workout at 3:45. And they were gone.

The team physician is hired by Ron Courson of the athletic association, and the University of Georgia makes sure that he or she is
readily available to the gymnasts—that's the most important thing.
Rather than having the gymnasts go to the health services building
and wait, there is a team physician at the coliseum in the mornings
who can handle anything from the flu to a sore throat. And then one
day a week, he's here to address orthopedic needs. The team physician
interacts mostly with the trainer and the trainer communicates with
me. A physician or physician's assistant always travels with us.

Rick Lewis, a nutritionist, interacts with us in conducting research
on bone density. Dr. Lewis provides us with a nutritionist who can
work one-on-one with particular athletes as needed. Rick is a great
resource in making sure that the gymnasts are well-informed about
nutrition and body composition.

Beth Mignano has been the gymnastics team's massage therapist
for seven years. Beth is available to our gymnasts during the week and
before and after competition, both home and away.

I always tell the people who work with us in promotions, "If you
have an idea and don't think we have the funds to implement it, don't
let that stop you from presenting it to me." I can help them get the
funds if I think their idea is worth doing. Kelley Barks was the best
promotions person we've had in terms of bringing new ideas to me.
Kelley always had a new idea and always followed through.

Our first sports psychologist, starting back in 1995, was Stan
Beecham. Dr. Beecham worked closely with our 1996 and 1997 teams
on imagery training and he taught us a great deal about the importance
of team chemistry. But Stan left before the 1998 season, when Julie
Ballard and Kim Arnold were seniors. So without a sports psycholo-

gist in 1998 and 1999, Julie, Kim, and I worked to continue the performance enhancement training that Stan taught us. Kim never did a beam routine without performing visualization first (she never missed a routine either) and Kim and Julie led all the team meetings. So even though Stan Beechum was not on staff during the championship years of '98 and '99, his teachings were with us. I have always believed that a team must remain focused on the "Big Picture" because it is too easy to get hung-up on the short-term problems which can distract you from the "Big Picture." Stan was great at validating and supporting my beliefs.

Craig White has been our sports psychologist since 2000. Sometimes he meets with the team as a whole, and sometimes it's important for a gymnast to work with him directly on more personal issues. I make sure that the girls communicate with me; we handle that through biweekly meetings. I meet with each girl individually and make sure that they have what they need. We address any problems they have—personal, roommate-wise, or academic. The sports psychologist mainly meets with the girls as a group so they have an opportunity to "vent" without the coach there. I rarely know what goes on in these meetings. The sports psychologist does a lot of counseling with seniors. It's very important for seniors to have a lot of direction. Their whole lives have revolved around gymnastics. Their gymnastics careers are coming to an end, so it's critical to anticipate some of the emotions and some of the pressures they put on themselves. The psychologist also helps with injured athletes. Being injured, especially being out for a long time, such as surgery requires, imposes a difficult period on the gymnasts' lives.

But it's important for the sports psychologist, like all the other support staff, to recognize that they are just that—support staff. They are supporting what we, the other coaches and I, have established in terms of philosophy, beliefs, policies, and rules. I've never had a problem with any of the support staff being contradictory. And that speaks highly of the quality of the people we've had here.

One of the things that has been wonderful at the University of Georgia is that everyone who has been involved in our gymnastics program has been very passionate about the sport. They love the sport of gymnastics and they love the people involved, so they want to go the extra mile and take the initiative and help any way that they can.

And then there's security. Do we really need a security person? Probably not. I don't know of another team that has a security representative. But Wayne Dill does hundreds of other things, like making sure we get to places on time. He takes care of all the travel arrangements. Could an assistant coach do that? Sure, but having someone who can focus on arrangements almost eliminates travel-related problems. He's staved off over-zealous fans after away meets on occasion. And on trips he runs lots of very essential errands that help things go more smoothly. The gymnasts on our team can focus on competition because we have Mr. Dill, and he takes care of all our problems.

Academic counselors are essential. Susan Lahey is back with us. Some of the great ones in the past have been Becky Galvin and Ludlow Lawson. You can't be an effective academic counselor unless you care about people, and ours have all had a passion for the gymnasts and the sport. We haven't had any who haven't been good, and you can attribute that to our associate and assistant athletic directors over the years—Lee Haley, John Shafer, Damon Evans, and Glada Horvat, who hire the counselors. Susan is particularly good at taking advantage of educational opportunities when we travel. For example, the first time she was with us when we went to Salt Lake City, she made sure the girls heard the Morman Tabernacle Choir. The counselors make academic achievement something the girls are proud of by meeting with them as a group and complementing them individually about their achievements—relative to their abilities.

We seldom rank high on the GPA rankings among other schools. But I find it hard, almost unfair, to compare the GPA at one school to those at another school. The girls at Stanford, for example, are not less intelligent than the girls at a college with open admission standards. It may be harder to get a 4.0 there than it is at some other schools. And it depends on what major a student is pursuing. Last year, Kinsey Rowe was the only mathematics major in the country to make Academic

All-American. If a school has an entering freshman average SAT of 900 versus a school like Georgia where it's 1250, the expectations of the school are going to be different. On our team, we have a full range of students.

Certainly I'd love to have everyone be like Kinsey Rowe and Kelsey Ericksen, whose SAT's were over 1400 and who are in the honors program and make 4.0. But look at Sierra Sapunar, with a 950 SAT. She's a workaholic when it comes to academics and she has a 4.0 in a tough curriculum. What I'm proud of is that they all graduate, and they all make the most of their abilities. What I like to look at is the University of Georgia's predicted GPA of athletes entering school, based on their previous performance and test scores, versus what they actually have when they graduate. And all of our gymnasts graduate with GPAs higher than their predicted GPAs. For example, Sandy Rowlette had a 1.3 predicted GPA upon entering Georgia. She graduated with a 3.3. That to me is more important than our team GPA. And, among our graduates, we have our share of physicians and lawyers and post-graduate degrees—as many as other teams. Our team members overachieve. We're only going to win national championships with overachievers. And our gymnasts need to be overachieving in the classroom as well.

When I first began coaching, I did the choreography. I love dance. I felt like I wasn't keeping up with the latest trends in choreography, so I contacted my friend, Russell Warfield, who I knew from Woodward Camp back in the early eighties. He was a gymnast at Ball State and is now a professional dancer and choreographer on Broadway. As a matter of fact, he was just on Broadway in *The Producers,* and he was in the original cast of *Cats.* He started coming down one week each year in the fall in about 1988 and to this day is still choreographing the GymDogs' routines. Now, due to NCAA rules, the gymnasts themselves make the arrangements for Russell to work on their routines, and they pay him for his services. Russell is still passionate about gymnastics, and he's still involved both in artistic and rhythmic programs, when he can work it in. He's the best. And by the way, all of our

NCAA Floor Exercise Champions, seven titles in all, had floor routines choreographed by Russell.

There has been the usual turnover in sports information specialists. Usually, each one has to learn gymnastics from the ground up. But each one seems to build on the progress that previous ones have made. Tyler Sabo is our current sports information specialist. The beginning of my twentieth year at Georgia was in 2003, and I wanted the media guide to reflect the history and accomplishments of the team in a special way. Tyler did a great job of integrating the history into appropriate places. With the turnover in so many of our non-athletic assignments, I try to link volunteers who have institutional memory with the new folks on the job. It usually works out well, but the volunteers have to be respectful of the responsibilities of the person I ask them to work with.

Speaking of volunteers, we'd never be at the level we are without them. Even now, with all the money and support and the increased budget, we couldn't do without the Ten-0 Club and other volunteers, because they are passionate. It's not a job to them. They want to do anything they can to help. Among them are writers, organizers, fund-raisers, designers, meet assistants, you name it.

I could go on and on, listing folks who contribute their time to our program, some paid and some volunteers. It's certainly different from the early years. One of the consequences of building a nationally recognized program with thousands of fans is that the support grows—maybe even faster than other parts of the program. So my job changes. I have to stay focused on the "Big Picture," which is winning the national title and, as you can see, there are many people who have to fit into this "Big Picture." The athletes, the coaches, and the support staff are the details of the picture, and they all have to have a place, a purpose, and a connection. I have to put it all together.

On the Plateau

The six consecutive years at the top of the end-of-the-regular season RQSs (Regional Qualifying Scores)—from 1994 through 1999—signaled that the GymDogs were on a plateau at the top of the women's college gymnastics structure.

College women's gymnastics, in general, took tremendous strides during the 1990s. Let's continue to take a look, year-by-year, in the context of the GymDogs' seasons.

1994

Graduation in 1993 took Jennifer Carbone, Sandy Rowlette, and Heather Stepp, who garnered fourteen All-America citations and three individual national championships among them. They occupied eight of the twenty-four team's slots in the 1993 Super Six competition. But the freshmen who replaced them tallied twenty-one All-America citations and three individual national championships before they left. National team member Leslie Angeles was considered among the top-two or top-three recruits in the country; Leah Brown, also a national team member, wasn't far behind; and Lisa Kirk added solid depth. The GymDogs also returned six All-Americans: Andrea Dewey, Nneka Logan, Kelly Macy, Agina Simpkins, Hope Spivey, and Lori Strong. So you can't cry too much about the loss to graduation. In fact, the coaches' preseason poll ranked the GymDogs first, and we were considered the odds-on favorite to repeat as national champions.

Besides the returning talent, there was another reason to expect the GymDogs to prosper in 1994. The code of points was changed to make it more difficult to put together routines with 10.0 start values. Some gymnasts on other teams, whose routines previously were rated at 10.0, would now have start values of 9.9 or 9.8. Ken Short was predicting that average individual scores for bars, beam, and floor routines—vault scoring was not changed—would fall by 2 or 3 tenths of a point. That could drop meet scores by 3 points or more. Ken later revised his assessment, but he wasn't far off in the beginning. At the time, I didn't think the rules went far enough. Under the new rules, all of our gymnasts would still have 10.0 start values on all routines; some would have bonus points to spare. Quite a few gymnasts on other teams struggled to arrive at 10.0 start values. The GymDogs' past practice of throwing more difficult routines was paying off. At the end of the 1994 regular season, the difference between the GymDogs' RQS and that of Alabama (second-highest) was a whopping 1.806 points. To put this in perspective, the difference between Alabama's 194.819 and ninth highest UCLA's 193.150 was only 1.669 points. So, in terms of average scores during the season, it was Georgia and then the rest.

The GymDogs' superior scoring power was reflected in the season won/loss record. We went 10 and 0 through the regular season. The closest contest was a 195.275 to 194.000 over Alabama at Alabama. The average margin of victory during the season was 3.408 points. In the postseason, the GymDogs won the SEC Championship meet by 1.525 points and the NCAA Regionals by 4.275 points. The forty-eight consecutive wins, from the beginning of the 1993 season through the 1994 SEC Championships, included eight wins over Alabama. If you add to that the 4 and 0 record against Alabama in 1992, that's twelve consecutive victories over the team that was the other half of "college gymnastics' biggest rivalry." The reputation of the rivalry was in jeopardy.

The ease with which victories were coming could pose a problem of fighting excessive complacency. Were the GymDogs invincible? I think it's fair to say that if we hit our routines—not counting a fall—no other team had demonstrated the capability to score higher. Only Alabama had a season-high score higher than

Georgia's lowest score during their last seven meets; the closest Alabama had been able to come in head-to-head competition was the 1.275 difference at the dual meet in Tuscaloosa.

Between the final regular season meet and the SEC meet, I had been through a highly stressful salary negotiation, and I was the target of harsh criticism from some single-minded staff in the Athletic Department. I'm afraid I began to vent my frustration.

The first "venting" came in a press conference after the SEC meet, when a young reporter—representing the campus newspaper—asked the totally meaningless question, "Would you say now that you are the team to beat?" I didn't waste a lot of time on diplomatically explaining what the questioner should already know. I simply retorted, "We're unbeatable." And I was right, provided the GymDogs don't count a fall, as I've already explained. I could have responded, "Well, if you examine our record and our RQS this year and compare them to those of all the other teams in the country, you'd have to conclude that we are not likely to get beaten unless we count at least one—and probably two—more falls than any opponent." But I didn't. The reporter didn't know diddly about gymnastics.

Our performance at regionals tended to reinforce my assessment of the team's strength. Even though the GymDogs counted a fall on floor, our 196.775—4.275 points above second-place Florida's 192.500—made me think my "unbeatable" statement wasn't so far fetched.

Additional reinforcement comes from the final RQS values:

TEAM	RQS
Georgia	196.625
Alabama	194.819
Utah	194.781
Michigan	194.712
LSU	194.681

The 1.806 difference between our RQS and that of second-place Alabama's, compared to the 0.138 spread from second to fifth, says a lot.

The counted fall at regionals allowed fall-less Alabama, in another region, to score 0.225 points above the GymDogs. So seeded second to Alabama, at nationals in Salt Lake City, the GymDogs won the afternoon session on Thursday with a sloppy 195.050. We fell four times, counting two, and our scores across the board were significantly lower than we had attained since the second meet of the season, when the teams just aren't nearly up to postseason form. Alabama counted no falls in the evening session and won with a score of 196.300. Even Utah, performing at home, fell three times on the beam, but their 194.925 was good enough for second place in the session. UCLA, BYU (Brigham Young University), and Florida rounded out the Super Six.

As the GymDogs left the motel in Park City after a pep rally in the lobby with the 200 fans who had made the trip, Leah Brown closed the heavy sliding door to one of the vans on Agina Simpkins' finger. Was this an omen? The finger was quickly iced and did not appear to affect Agina's performance on the first three events—she averaged 9.869. But the GymDogs continued to be lethargic, scoring 0.2 to 0.3 (as a team) below our season averages on vaulting and floor. For some reason, the judges were generous on bars, and all teams scored high, but the spread on bars among Georgia, Utah, and Alabama was less than a tenth of a point. Despite our sloppy performance, the GymDogs were headed into the final rotation on beam with a score of 147.775, leading Utah, finishing on floor, by 0.625 points. If we hit our routines on beam, our beam score would likely be about 49.0. Utah could not score 49.625 on floor—necessary to pass Georgia with a 49.00 on beam. Alabama was already finished, just 48.575 points ahead of Georgia. No sweat. Just don't have more than one fall.

Even with the GymDogs' sloppy performance through the first three rotations, it looked like we would still stumble into the championship, propelled by sheer talent and the benefit of the years of throwing difficult routines before the code was changed. But then the full impact of the dehydration hit—resulting from staying four thousand feet up the mountain at Park City and commuting daily. As we were about to go into the three-minute touch warm-up on the beam, Agina fell to the floor grasping her leg in severe pain. Rather than continuing our warm-ups, the gymnasts gathered around her as the trainer tried to determine the problem. I lost my cool. I was giving my attention to Agina's problem. Doug was checking with the judges about our options. The gymnasts did not complete their touch warm-ups. The judges could not hold up the meet indefinitely. The trainer carried Agina to the locker room in his arms, and she hobbled back a few minutes later. She had suffered severe cramps, usually associated with dehydration. I elected to allow Agina to remain in the lineup, although I could have—and in retrospect probably should have—substituted Kelly Macy, a senior and a pretty consistent beam worker.

Did I say, "No way?" It happened. Three falls on the beam, counting two. Agina and two others fell. The three who did not fall averaged 9.85. Two more scores like that would have given the GymDogs a 49.250, clearly out of reach. The GymDogs scored a 48.075 on beam for a meet score of 195.850, Utah edged Alabama 196.400 to 196.350. The GymDogs were third, taking our only two losses of the season in the Super Six.

Aside from the cramps, Agina had a fabulous championship experience. She came within 0.050 point of tying Kentucky's incredible Jenny Hansen for the All-Around title. Hope Spivey scored the only perfect 10.0 of the championships in winning the floor exercise. On the uneven bars, Lori Strong tied Utah's Sandy Woolsey and Michigan's Beth Wymer, who tied for the second year in succession. Jenny Hansen took both beam and vaulting. Five GymDogs garnered twelve All-America citations: Hope (floor), Lori (bars, floor*), Leah (all-around, floor*), Leslie (all-around*, floor*), and Agina (all-around, vault, bars*, beam*, floor*). (* denotes second team.)

The tighter scoring rules took their toll in the number of 10.0s scored for the three days of competition. Hope's lone 10 was compared to twelve the previous year.

1995

But there was plenty of reason for optimism about 1995. Multi-talented Scott Bull returned from UCLA as the volunteer coach, while

heading the Athens-Clarke Gymnastics Academy program. The loss of
Hope Spivey and Kelly Macy took only four slots from the 1994 Super
Six lineup. Even that loss was tempered by the arrival of two-time
national team member Kim Arnold—widely considered the number
one college recruit in the country—and Julie Ballard, who had elected
to forego elite-level competition in order to remain in her hometown
gym. She burned up the level 10 gymnastics, qualifying for the level
10 nationals for four years. During their college careers, they garnered
three individual national championships and sixteen All-America
citations between them. So expectations for the 1995 team were high.
The preseason coach's poll again put the GymDogs at the top of the
heap, this time with a unanimous vote.

It didn't take long for the GymDogs to learn that, despite having tremendous talent, the three seniors were not the leaders needed for a successful season. In fact, they were the team's major disciplinary problems.
If I were looking for an example of how poor chemistry could decimate
a team, Georgia's 1995 season would be hard to beat. After breezing
through three easy victories, the GymDogs went to Provo, Utah, for a
three-way meet with BYU and Utah—without seniors Nneka Logan
and Agina Simpkins, who were suspended from the team for the meet.
Their absence, coupled with more falls than hit routines on the first
event (bars), additional counted falls on beam, and a sub-par floor routine,
resulted in a 2-point loss to Utah. The other teams around the country
appeared to have made the necessary adjustments to the more challenging
code of points introduced in 1994, as the scoring gaps in Georgia's next
three wins averaged only 1.03 points—with the largest margin a home
victory over Alabama, 196.200/194.825, despite a counted fall by the
GymDogs on the uneven bars.

What happened in the gym at the Alabama meet wasn't as
memorable as what happened away from the gym. The ESPN tape-
delayed telecast played up the rivalry between the teams and the
coaches. Both coaches were interviewed on camera, separately. The
interviewers' questions were not telecast, just the coaches' responses.
At one point, I said, "I respect Sarah, but I don't particularly care for

her." Then, in a post-meet press conference, I commented on Sarah's complaining that the uneven bars at Georgia were narrower than the ones in her gym. Both widths were legal by NCAA rules at the time. So I said, "Losers make excuses; winners make adjustments." For those statements, SEC Commissioner Roy Kramer reprimanded me for violating the SEC Code of Ethics, which prohibits a coach from publicly criticizing another institution, its coach, or its players.

When the GymDogs traveled to Alabama for the second of our traditional annual home-and-home meets, the press built up the meet by creating me as a villain. The Birmingham paper said, "Yoculan calls Patterson a 'loser'." It worked. A record number of 12,021 highly partisan fans attended the meet, booing loudly when I was introduced. Coach Patterson asked them to show good sportsmanship, but only after the crowd had booed. It was the most flagrant exhibition of poor crowd behavior I have witnessed at a gymnastics meet.

I was asked to make a statement about booing at gymnastics meets for the Ten-0 Club newsletter, *Ten-0 Talk*, February 1996: "It was painful to us last year when our team and I were booed by an untypical, small, but highly vocal representation of fans at an away meet. It was also painful to our loyal fans and our families in the stands. However, it would be even more painful to us if our fans booed our visitors." That's when I first published my "Fans' Code of Conduct."

In the meet, the GymDogs counted falls on both bars and beam. Alabama, meanwhile, scored a season-high 197.200 to Georgia's 195.225. The team that was supposed to be invincible had now lost two meets, both by about 2 points.

The up-and-down season continued for Georgia as we scheduled a six-team meet at home on March 12 to serve as a "dress rehearsal" for hosting the NCAA National Championships in April. Everything worked smoothly, including the GymDogs' performance—we scored a season-high 197.625, 1.150 points over second-place UCLA'S 196.475. Too bad it was a dress rehearsal. The 197.625 would have easily won the team championship the following month, and Lori Strong's

all-around performance of 39.775 would have been just 0.025 under
Jenny Hansen's championship score.

The "up-and-down" characterization of the GymDogs' season was
extended into the SEC Championships at Gainesville, Florida. It was
time for the down cycle, and the GymDogs obliged. We committed
three falls on beam, counting two, and still managed a third-place score,
well within a fall of the championship. Alabama won, but many felt
LSU would have won had there not been flagrantly biased judging
on vaulting. At the SEC coaches meeting after the season, I had little
trouble getting the other coaches to agree to have four judges at future
Southeastern Conference Championship meets. Had there been four
in 1995, LSU probably would have won their first SEC title.

Even with the erratic season, the GymDogs remained on top of
the final RQS values:

TEAM	RQS
Georgia	196.725
Utah	196.469
Alabama	196.337
Michigan	196.262
LSU	195.850

At regionals, it was time for the up-cycle. The GymDogs hit
twenty-three routines, scoring the highest regional score in the nation.
In winning their regions, Alabama and Utah also hit twenty-three
routines to come in second and third nationally.

The up-and-down cycle got out of phase at the national championships in Athens, as the GymDogs had our "up meet" in the preliminary session instead of the finals. In hitting twenty-three routines
in the afternoon session, the GymDogs scored a session-high 196.825.
UCLA's winning score for the evening session was 196.375, as they
also hit twenty-three routines.

The roof caved in at the championship meet on Friday night. The
GymDogs fell four times, counting two falls, to come in fifth, 0.575

point behind winner Utah, who counted no falls. In fact, Utah hit 24 routines. The Utes won this championship because of their consistency. Take away counted falls and Georgia (2), Alabama (1) and UCLA (1) would all have scored higher than the champions. It was becoming clearer each year that a team who counts a fall in the Super Six is not likely to win the championship.

A lot of non-gymnastics-related lessons could be learned from the 1995 season. There were many distractions: the lack of leadership, disciplinary problems, perhaps too much social activity, an automobile accident, and a scary fall from bars at practice, all during the national championships at Athens. But that is part of athletic competition. Utah put together a perfect performance when it counted most and repeated as national champion, their ninth NCAA Championship.

In the individual competition, Michigan's Beth Wymer won the uneven bars for the third consecutive year, edging out Lori Strong 9.950 to 9.925. Beth and Lori were all that kept Kentucky's Jenny Hansen from sweeping the individual championships, as she took first place on vaulting, floor, beam, and all-around. Leslie Angeles and UCLA'S Stella Umeh tied Jenny on floor.

Six GymDogs garnered seventeen All-America citations: Agina (all-around, vault, beam, floor), Lori (all-around, vault*, bars, beam), Leah (all-around*, vault, beam*, floor), Julie (all-around*, vault*), Kim (vault*, floor), and Leslie (floor). (*denotes second team)

As frustrating as the 1995 season was, trying to reconcile so much strength and so many bad meets, the GymDogs just couldn't be too sad. We lost three seniors, who had accumulated an individual national championship and twenty-one All-America citations. But in their senior year, one was suspended from the team in mid-season, and the two remaining occupied only six of the slots in the Super Six lineup. Perhaps more important, they also were rid of some out-of-the-gym problems that may have cost more than the seniors' athletic achievements had contributed. And a super recruiting class would arrive in September.

1996

In the fall of 1995, thanks to the outstanding recruiting of Jay Clark, we signed the best recruiting class in the history of college gymnastics. Stacey Galloway, an alternate on the 1992 Canadian Olympic Team, who finished twenty-first at the 1993 and 1994 World Championships, committed first. Then Amanda Borden, Karin Lichey, and Sam Muhleman from Cincinnati Gymnastics signed.

As if Stacey and the three CGA kids were not enough, there was even more icing on the recruiting cake. We had invited Jenni Beathard, another outstanding national team member, for a visit because she was such an outstanding gymnast and she deserved the trip. But we hadn't pursued her, even though everyone here was crazy about her, because she lived just a stone's throw from the University of Florida, where her brother was already in school. I thought she was a lock for Florida. When I learned through a UGA professor that Jenni's father had called him saying his daughter was totally thrilled about her trip to Athens, I got on the phone, then I got on the plane, and I got a commitment from Jenni. Just like bad luck, when good fortune rains, it pours.

As it turned out, Amanda deferred to the next year so she could compete for a spot on the 1996 Olympic Team, but that still left the GymDogs with the best recruiting class in women's college gymnastics history up until that time.

Apparently, the other college coaches didn't buy into Georgia's talented team. After picking them as a shoo-in for the two previous seasons and seeing them fall in the Super Six, the coaches ranked—in order—Alabama, Utah, Michigan, and UCLA all ahead of Georgia in the coaches' poll. *College Sports Magazine* ranked Georgia first, leaving the other four below them in the same order as in the coaches' poll. Ken Short couldn't believe what the coaches did: "It's hard to think what the coaches who ranked the Georgia team this low could have been thinking. . . . This team is as rich in talent as any in the history of the NCAA. . . . This team has the potential to win as convincingly as the '93 Georgia team." You will see at the end of the season that the coaches were right in putting Alabama first.

It didn't take Karin Lichey long to make some waves in college before she even entered school. Although she was not interested in trying for the 1996 Olympics, Karin wasn't afraid of international competition. Freshman Karin and sophomore Julie Ballard tried out for the World University Games, and they were among five gymnasts from the USA to compete in Fukuoka, Japan, against gymnasts from the rest of the world who would represent their countries in the 1996 Olympics. Our own Doug McAvinn was one of the coaches. Karin came in second in the all-around, higher than any U.S. gymnast had placed before.

Kim Tagtmayer, who had coached at the Athens-Clarke Gymnastics Academy for four years, replaced Scott Bull as volunteer coach. She focused primarily on beam. Kristi Bluett, an Athens native, transferred from the University of Florida and Katie O'Neill, a level-10 national competitor from the Atlanta School of Gymnastics, joined the fabulous four in the freshman class. Actually, the fabulous four didn't have the immediate impact that was hoped for because of nagging injuries. Stacey and Sam were recovering from knee surgery, Jenni was bothered with bone spurs in both ankles, and Karin suffered from a stress fracture in her back the last half of the season. But after a sluggish start, winning with less than satisfying scores at Florida, the Sunshine Fest in Nassau, and LSU at home, the GymDogs ripped off five consecutive scores over 197.

Without question, the highlight of the year—maybe the century— came at the Kentucky meet, when Karin scored the only perfect 40.00 in the all-around ever scored in gymnastics at any level.

The following week, number-two-ranked Alabama hit twenty-three routines in posting a school record of 197.550 before a record crowd of 13,563 screaming fans in Tuscaloosa. The GymDogs counted a fall on floor and had several form breaks and touches on bars and floor, but we would not have defeated the Tide, even without the problems. Our losing score was 196.675.

An event more disturbing than the loss to Alabama occurred while the team was in Tuscaloosa. *Sports Illustrated* sent reporter Dana Gelin down to cover the meet and do an article on Karin's perfect 40.00. Dana interviewed Karin and me, and then she decided to get

Sarah Patterson's reaction. Sarah had not seen the Kentucky meet. Sarah made a perfectly reasonable statement: "When I heard Karin had gotten a 40.00, I thought three things. She had to be in a great zone, the atmosphere had to be just right, and the judges had to be in the right frame of mind." There is really nothing wrong with Sarah's statement. Although "right frame of mind" is ambiguous, it didn't necessarily mean that Sarah was questioning the judging. There is enough uncertainty in gymnastics judging that judges can over score or under score without being purposely biased. So their frame of mind could have prevented them from awarding two 10s on each event.

But that third thought was all Gelin needed to write a highly cynical column, implying that the 40.00 might not have been deserved. Of course, Dana Gelin was not at the Georgia-Kentucky meet. If she wanted to interview a coach other than me, she should have interviewed Leah Little, the Kentucky coach, who witnessed the event. The Georgia-Kentucky meet was heavily covered by the press, some of whom were knowledgeable about gymnastics. None of them questioned the judging. And no one has ever questioned the judging at that meet. More important, the judges at the 1998 NCAA Southeast Region meet were assigned by USAG and the NCAA, and scores at NCAA Regional and National meets are the only ones considered official for NCAA records. Karin's 39.875 at that meet still stands as the record NCAA all-around score. Gelin did her readers a disservice.

Karin's record wasn't the only record the team broke in 1996. In her journey to the perfect 40.00 in the Kentucky meet, Karin helped set a team record 49.775 on the uneven bars. Lori Strong joined Karin with a 10.00. Jenni Beathard (9.950), Leslie Angeles (9.925), and Leah Brown (9.900) finished out the scoring. Just three weeks before, the team set a team vaulting record of 49.925 at Auburn. At least one of the two judges awarded each of the five vaulters a 10.00. It is little wonder that a new record was set.

The season-high scores for the top-five vaulters in the nation belonged to GymDogs in the February 21 national rankings. When I looked at the season-high scores for individual gymnasts, it was obvious that the GymDogs dominated every event, although not to the extent they dominated the vaulting. Ken Short's assessment of the depth of talent at the beginning of the season appeared to have been confirmed.

The GymDogs won our last two regular season meets against Michigan and Michigan State and headed for the rubber match with Alabama at the SEC Championships. Here's how *Gymnastics Insider* described it:

> At Lexington, Kentucky, the Southeastern Conference Championship was decided during one of the most dramatic moments in the 16-year history of the meet. It occurred in the fourth rotation. Number one, nationally, Georgia and number two Alabama had separated themselves from the pack and were virtually even at 98.625 and 98.600 after each team had completed two events. Georgia had completed vaulting and bars (ranked number one nationally on both), and Alabama had completed beam and floor (ranked number one nationally on both). Who would perform better on its "weaker" events? Georgia was in the dreaded position of competing on the beam while host-team Kentucky was on floor, stimulating a highly vocal crowd of 3,478.
>
> Georgia also had to remove from their lineup freshman sensation, Karin Lichey, who aggravated a previously injured back while warming up. The second gymnast up on beam fell. Leah Brown, up fourth, had to compose herself, following an uncharacteristic fall on bars. This was the moment! This was the meet! A fall from Leah and Alabama wins. Leah knocked out a 9.850, and Kim Arnold and Lori Strong, neither of whom had fallen all season, wrapped up the apparatus and the meet. Alabama's fall-less 196.950, just 0.100 off the previous all-time SEC meet record would not be good enough to stay with Georgia. The Bulldogs went on to set new meet records

on beam (49.325) and floor (49.300) to go along with their
new meet-record team score, 197.450.

The 1996 end-of-regular season RQS values:

TEAM	RQS
Georgia	197.400
Alabama	196.894
Utah	195.931
Michigan	195.919
Florida	195.731

The regionals signaled that Alabama had arrived. Although the
GymDogs won the Southeast Region handily with a 196.950—
second highest regional score in the country—Alabama hit twenty-
four routines in the Central Region to set a new NCAA postseason
mark of 198.075.

In the preliminary rounds at the NCAA Championships in
Tuscaloosa, Georgia won the afternoon session with a 196.400. We
tallied one fall each on bars and beam, but did not count a fall. Alabama,
in the evening session, counted two falls and was still able to score
196.325. Adjust that score for counted falls and you have 197.625. If
Alabama stays in the "zone" it's been in since the SECs for one more
performance, any other team can forget winning the championship.

And Alabama did stay in the zone. Each team of the top-four
finishers had two falls, but Georgia was the only one who managed to
have them both in the same event—uneven bars. The GymDogs also
had a couple of sloppy floor routines. Alabama won the NCAA
Championships, before a howling home crowd, with a new NCAA
Championships record of 198.025, 0.025 higher than Georgia's 1993
score. UCLA was in second place with 197.475. Georgia and Utah
tied for third.

No one gave Alabama this championship. They won it—going away.
After the meet, I acknowledged to the press: "I would like to congratulate the University of Alabama because they were the superior team

tonight, and even if we hadn't made the mistakes we made, Alabama still would have won. That was very obvious." I didn't have the benefit of all the scores when I said that. That's how dominant Alabama was.

Perhaps the most significant aspect of the individual championships was that Kentucky's Jenny Hansen, after winning the all-around three consecutive years—part of a total of eight individual championships in three years—did not win an individual championship. Even without additional championships in 1996, Jenny stands head and shoulders above all other NCAA gymnasts until now, and her position at the top of the heap is not in jeopardy.

Alabama gymnasts won three individual crowns: Meredith Willard won the all-around, Stephanie Woods won bars, and Kim Kelly tied Arizona's Heidi Hornbeek on floor. Utah's Summer Reid won beam, and Leah Brown won vaulting.

Six GymDogs received ten All-America citations: Leah (all-around*, beam, vault), Lori (all-around, beam, floor), Kim (vault), Jenni (bars), Leslie (bars*), and Karin (beam). (*denotes second team)

A coaching change for the 1997 season would see Jay leave the team to start his own gym, Classic City Gymnastics. Steve Ballard, Julie's brother, who had been in graduate school at Georgia after playing football at Tulane, replaced Jay. He concentrated on coaching bars and coordinating recruiting. Agina Simpkins, from the GymDog class of 1995, replaced Kim Tagtmyer as volunteer coach, concentrating on beam.

1997

When the U.S. Olympic Team won the gold medal, the money waved before the "Magnificent Seven" to join a professional tour and to endorse products was too enticing to turn down, even though accepting the money meant losing eligibility for college. So Amanda Borden, who had signed with Georgia, Amy Chow (Stanford), and Kerri Strug (UCLA) were all lost to the professional ranks. That left Georgia with only three freshmen, Brooke Andersen and Caroline Harris, who filled the scholarship Amanda had left open, and Courtney Whittle, a level-9 gymnast from Dalton, Georgia. Brooke was Georgia's top elite gymnast, and Caroline was a level-10 national team member. The GymDogs lost only one gymnast to graduation. But what a gymnast! Lori Strong was an individual national champion on bars, won twelve All-America citations (at least one in each event), and scored a 39.625 all-around—the highest in the meet—in her final collegiate appearance at the Super Six. She may have been even more valuable as a leader.

What could go a long way toward making up for the loss of Lori was the improved health of the rising sophomore class. And they did contribute more, but the team leaders in the final posting of RQSs were senior Leah Brown and junior Kim Arnold. The coaches' poll proved to be prophetic again as they chose UCLA as the top team. Georgia was third, behind Alabama, who was decimated by injuries at the end of the season and did not make the Super Six for the first time since the format was established. RQSs demonstrate the strength of the 1997 GymDogs: At the end of the season, we led in team RQSs for three of the four events, were second on the fourth, and—of course—the team RQS by almost a point.

TEAM	RQS
Georgia	197.722
Utah	196.847
Michigan	196.565
Alabama	196.555
Arizona State	196.030

At the SEC Championships, the GymDogs posted a new SEC and NCAA record team score. Seeing so many GymDogs receiving individual awards—we took first, second, and third in each event and first and second in the all-around—prompted a "best-of-the-rest" computation for the championship meet. What would the score have been had Georgia competed against the rest of the entire conference competing as one team? The rest of the conference was not a bunch of patsies; among them were the fourth-, fifth-, tenth-, and twenty-third-ranked teams in the nation. The GymDogs' score was 198.375. The "Best of the Rest" scored 197.375.

Scores posted by Florida and Kentucky were their best of the season, and LSU posted one of its best, as none of these teams counted a fall. There were four judges on each event.

Some of the story of the 1997 NCAA Championships bears recounting. After hitting twenty-three routines to take the top score in either session of the preliminaries, the GymDogs had three falls on the opening event, beam, in the Super Six to blow the meet before it got started. The falls were all committed by "supersophs," two of whom were ranked seventh and ninth nationally in the last individual rankings before the NCAAs. Go figure.

The final results:

UCLA	197.150
Arizona State	196.850
Georgia	196.600

The individual championships looked more like what Georgia was capable of scoring. Kim Arnold won the all-around, Jenni Beathard won bars, and Leah Brown won the floor exercise. Florida's Susan Hines won vault, and Elizabeth Reid (Arizona State) tied Summer Reid (Utah) for the beam championship. The GymDogs also had two runners-up and one third-place finisher. Kim Arnold finished second on floor exercise, and Leah Brown was second on vault and third on all-around.

Six GymDogs captured fourteen All-America citations: Leah (all-around, vault, bars, floor), Kim (all-around, vault, beam, floor), Jenni (bars, beam★), Sam Muhleman (beam, floor★), Leslie Angeles (floor), and Lisa Kurc (vault). (★denotes second team)

It had been four years since the 1993 season, when the GymDogs won our last national championship. Statistics each year had indicated that we were the strongest team in the nation during each of these years, yet we had failed to win a national championship. In 1994, 1995, and 1997, we simply gave the championship away at the Super Six. Fans were beginning to speculate that the GymDogs choked at the big meets. An untimely cramping in 1994, all sorts of distractions in 1995, one bad event in 1997—all reasons, if not excuses, for a poor meet at the wrong time. But good teams are supposed to overcome adversity, even if it comes suddenly. It seems that Georgia was the only team, since UCLA in 1989, to "give away" a national championship, and we did it three times.

On the other hand, the best teams don't always win, especially when you are up against five of the best six teams in the country. In a dual meet, the other team has to hit if you miss in order to upset you. There is a pretty good chance that the other team won't be perfect. But when you are going up against five of the best six all at once, only one of the five has to hit. The odds are not all that much in your favor. Look at the odds in the Kentucky Derby. Usually the favorite pays two or three dollars for a dollar bet, meaning that the bookies give him only one chance in three or four to win, even though he's the favorite. And I believe it's been about fifteen years since the favorite actually won the Kentucky Derby. Perhaps what brought to attention Georgia's third-place (three of them) and fifth-place finishes was that Georgia is the only team who could fall below championship expectations. We were always expected to win. Nevertheless, I had had more than enough of being a bridesmaid. Maybe 1998 would be different.

1998

Coaches at other schools had begun to lose faith in the GymDogs' ability to hit at the Super Six. Even though the fall-adjusted score for 1997 indicated that the GymDogs would have left the other teams in our chalk dust had they not fallen three times on beam, the coaches picked UCLA to repeat and Georgia to come in second in the preseason coaches' poll.

If a volunteer coach ever had a major impact on a team, it was new volunteer coach Lori Strong. She brought a major positive influence to the beam lineup for the 1998 season. Lori provided the same total control and quiet leadership as a coach that she displayed as a gymnast.

The graduation losses were pretty substantial. Leah Brown, Leslie Angeles, and Lisa Kurc had amassed three national individual championships and twenty-one All-America citations among them. They vacated nine slots in the 1997 Super Six lineup. But, believe it or not, we were optimistic with good reason. Three national team members and a dynamic elite-level vaulting and floor specialist were coming in the freshman class. Amanda Curry, Kristi Lichey, Suzanne Sears, and Kathleen Shrieves comprised the second-best recruiting class in GymDog history. Kelli Prestigiacomo rounded out the recruiting class. And the best class members were only juniors. Add to that seniors Kim Arnold and Julie Ballard.

The rules for judging college meets were altered for the 1998 season, making it somewhat more difficult to attain high scores. As usual, I didn't think the changes were sufficient to allow judges to make the distinctions among performance because too many gymnasts were still able to assemble routines with 10.00 start values. The biggest impact would likely come in vaulting, where the pike front vault was devalued from a 10.00 to a 9.90. Gymnasts would now have to add a twist to the pike front—making it a pike half—to attain a 10.00 start value on vaulting. Few teams had more than one or two 10.00 value vaults at the beginning of the season, and Georgia was well into the season before five gymnasts were performing 10.00 vaults. But, all in all, the more difficult the code of points, the better advantage the GymDogs have, because they push the envelope in throwing high skills.

True to our well-deserved reputation, the GymDogs began the season with consecutive meetings with the toughest competition we could schedule. We started with UCLA (ranked one in the coaches' poll) and followed with Alabama (six) at Tuscaloosa, Florida (eight) in Gainesville, and Michigan (four). Only Alabama was able to come within a point, as Georgia won 196.550–195.650. The rest of the schedule wasn't much easier, but the opponents had no chance because the GymDogs didn't really have a bad meet. Our lowest score, after the first meet of the season, was 196.325, which was posted during a meet when we were resting the "heavy hitters."

Of course, the GymDogs' team RQSs were atop each of the four events at the end of the season. The team RQSs:

TEAM	RQS
Georgia	196.881
Michigan	195.912
Alabama	195.880
Utah	195.575
Florida	195.531

The GymDogs breezed through the SEC Championship meet and Southeast Regional Championship meet, shattering Alabama's NCAA scoring record with a 198.575, posting the highest score in any region and being seeded first in the NCAA Championship meet. The NCAA Championships were held at Pauley Pavilion on defending champion UCLA's campus. In the first session of NCAA Championships, the GymDogs continued our scoring rampage with a 197.825, 0.900 point better than UCLA's winning score in the other session.

In the Super Six, UCLA, the only team who seemed to be capable of challenging the GymDogs, blew themselves out of contention, counting two falls on their first event, beam. The scores: Georgia, 197.725; Florida, 196.350; and Alabama, 196.300. The supporters from the Southeastern Conference teams began chanting, "SEC, one, two, three." Talk about tough schedules: for the entire season, the undefeated GymDogs had beaten number-two Florida four times and number-three Alabama five times.

Kim Arnold won the all-around championship for the second consecutive year, edging out teammate Karin Lichey 39.725 to 39.700. Larissa Fontaine (Stanford) and Susan Hines (Florida) tied for vaulting. Heidi Moneymaker (UCLA) won bars, and Betsy Hamm (Florida) tied Kim Arnold and Jenni Beathard on beam. Stella Umeh (UCLA) and Karin Lichey tied for the floor exercise championship.

Nine GymDogs won twenty All-America citations: Kim Arnold and Karin Lichey (everything), Jenni Beathard (bars, beam), Sam Muhleman (bars, beam, floor), Kristi Lichey (beam), Kathleen Shrieves (bars★), Julie Ballard (floor), Suzanne Sears (floor), and Amanda Curry (beam★). Five gymnasts made All-America on bars and floor, and six—including a score that was thrown out—made All America on beam. (★denotes second team)

I won the NCAA Coach-of-the-Year Award and Doug won the very first NCAA Assistant Coach-of-the-Year Award.

Two major coaching changes took place during the summer. Jay Clark returned, replacing Steve Ballard, and Lori Strong left. There was more to this change than just coaching turn-over. Steve and Lori became Mr. and Mrs. Steve Ballard and moved to Raleigh, North Carolina in the summer of 1999. Also, just a week after Lori and Steve's marriage, Julie Ballard married Jay Clark. How much fun—to have two gymnasts become sisters-in-law.

It would be hard to replicate Lori's coaching on beam, but if it could be done, Jackie Estes could do it. A member of the 1979 GymDogs, for twenty years Jackie had been involved in every aspect of gymnastics—administration and coaching. She was also active in the UGA Atlanta Alumni Club. Jackie continued to bring the calm to the team Lori had brought, which balanced my flamboyance.

1999

The graduation of two-time NCAA All-Around Champion Kim Arnold and All-American Julie Ballard would be substantial going into the 1999 season. They filled seven slots on the Super Six team, and they accumulated a combined three individual national championships and sixteen All-America citations. The incoming freshman class did not offer promise of immediate replacements. Talya Vexler just missed making the national team in 1997, but she had surgery at the beginning of the season and would be limited to beam during her freshman year. Eileen Diaz, a 1996 Puerto Rican Olympian, was only expected to help early on bars. Emily Chell was considered a vaulting specialist, and Danielle Maurone was a level-10 floor specialist. Although all four were potential all-around candidates, during their freshman year combined, they were not likely to fill more than four positions in the lineup.

But we still had tremendous optimism because all four of the seniors were healthy for the first time, and the rising sophomore class was coming into its own. The coaches cast thirty-two of the thirty-nine first-place votes for the GymDogs, showing their usual tendency to give significant weight to the reigning champions. It was a dramatic up-and-down season. The bottom line is that, despite all the problems the team encountered during the season, we went undefeated all the way through the NCAA Championships for the second consecutive year, adding a third undefeated laurel to our bouquet.

Final RQS values:

TEAM	RQS
Georgia	197.444
Alabama	197.088
Utah	197.075
Michigan	196.700
LSU	196.156

A new regional format provided six regions with six teams each, instead of five with seven teams. The major change was that, except for regional meet hosts, the top-twelve teams were assigned to regions on the basis of their Regional Qualifying Scores, with the top teams being matched with the bottom teams, decreasing the likelihood that a top-ranked team would be upset in regionals. The concept was sound, provided judging throughout the country and throughout the season was uniform. But it wasn't, and a major controversy resulted concerning assignment of the ranked teams to the regions. As it turned out, the twelve teams qualifying for nationals were remarkably close to the top twelve in the RQS rankings.

For the first time since the Super Six was established, Utah failed to make it, in its own arena. This left UCLA and Georgia as the only teams who have qualified for the Super Six every year. The scores for Super Six—the championship—were:

Georgia	196.850
Michigan	196.550
Alabama	195.950
UCLA	195.850

No GymDog won an individual national championship. We left it all on the floor in winning the national championship on Friday night. Utah's brilliant Theresa Kulikowski edged out Karin Lichey by 0.100 point for the all-around title. Heidi Moneymaker (UCLA) won vaulting; Angie Leonard (Utah) bars; Kulikowski, freshman sensation Andree Pickens (Alabama), and Kiralee Hayashi (UCLA) tied for beam; and individual qualifier Marny Oestrang (Bowling Green) won the floor exercise.

Eight GymDogs earned seventeen All-America citations. Karin Lichey (everything), Kristi Lichey (all-around, vault*, bars, beam), Jenni Beathard (all-around*, bars, beam), Amanda Curry (vault, beam*), Stacey Galloway (beam), Brooke Andersen (vault*), Suzanne Sears (vault*), and Emily Chell (beam*). (*denotes second team)

It's great to have the strongest senior class in the history of college gymnastics. But wow! What a blow when you lose them! We lost Sam Muhleman to a season-ending neck injury at the SEC Championships. The senior class, minus the services of Sam—who would have increased the number by a net of three—occupied ten slots in the Super Six. Remember Sam's season-ending neck injury at the SEC Championships. Including Sam, the seniors accumulated three individual national championships and twenty-three All-America citations during their careers—despite that, on average, they competed only about two full seasons each because of injuries.

2000

For the 2000 season, the GymDogs would have to rely heavily on the incoming freshmen if we were to get back to the Super Six. Would we fall off the plateau? Anna Gingrich and Breanne Rutherford had great credentials; both were on the U.S. National Team. Monica Flammer was the national champion on beam in 1995, but she was coming off a three-year "retirement" after failing to make the 1996 Olympic Team, and her recovery to previous performance level was not assured. Cassie Bair was a flashy level-10 performer from Georgia. There was certainly potential there, but relying on freshmen is risky. The senior class that just graduated didn't have a stellar freshman year. The other coaches and I were realistically looking at the first year the team may not make the Super Six.

Assessment of the team's chances changed dramatically after the pre-season intrasquad exhibition for the fans. The two seniors, who filled only two slots on the 1999 Super Six team, reached their peak. Talya Vexler, a rising sophomore who was hampered by injuries and didn't compete in the previous season's Super Six, was healthy. And the four juniors were healthy, with Kathleen Shrieves returning. Unfortunately, the freshmen were not knocking the lights out; they were coming slowly and suffering from injury and conditioning problems. But the upperclassmen, with little help from the freshmen, provided the basis for optimism. I announced after the exhibition that I thought the GymDogs could not only make the Super Six, we might have a chance at a "threepeat" for the national championship.

The other team coaches must have heard me. They awarded Georgia about half of the first-place ballots to name them number one in the coaches' poll—showing their respect in the Georgia coaches' ability to fashion another championship team, even with the severe losses to graduation.

My assessment was that Georgia gymnasts had been in a class by themselves for seven years, and now we were moving down into the pack. But we still would be among the top five. We just wouldn't be above the rest. I think this change is what made fans somewhat pessimistic at the beginning of the season. Their point of reference was the GymDogs in a lofty position, out by themselves, and now we were just one of the best.

The first meet of the season was the result of one of my promotional schemes. After Georgia, Florida, and Alabama came in one, two, and three in the 1998 national championships, I suggested that the Southeastern Conference sponsor an "SEC Challenge," pitting the top-three SEC teams against the top-three teams in the nation, outside the SEC. The conference officials liked the idea, but because of sponsorships we called it the Super Six Challenge. It took a year to get the challenge into place, but on January 8, 2000, Georgia hosted Alabama, UCLA, Michigan, Nebraska, and Florida (replacing Arizona State from the 1999 Super Six). I think most teams found it difficult to get gymnasts ready for such a major meet so early in the season, but we had traditionally scheduled a top-five team as an opener every year.

Alabama seemed to be a little better prepared than the other teams. In winning, with a score of 195.750, the Tide counted only one fall, as Georgia, Michigan, Florida, and Nebraska counted two each. UCLA counted five falls, as only one gymnast was able to stay on the beam, and her score was 9.525, giving UCLA a beam score of 46.275. What a contrast this UCLA performance would turn out to be with those of their last four meets of 2000.

The national rankings reflected the parity of the teams. Four teams, Georgia, Alabama, Utah, and Michigan, were ranked number one at one time or another during the season. The GymDogs' only losses were to Alabama during the regular season—the Super Six Challenge loss and the dual meet at Tuscaloosa.

Before the season, the Georgia fans had predicted that the GymDog freshmen would have to step forward, but they didn't. In no meet did they contribute more than four routines, almost always filling three slots on the beam. That the team had no more falls on the beam than it had with three freshmen participating is a tribute to Jackie Estes' hard work. The coaches used twelve or thirteen gymnasts in nearly every meet, digging deep to find contributions from freshmen and walk-ons that would perhaps add one or two tenths of a point to an apparatus score. We didn't hit twenty-four routines in a meet all season. A reporter for the *Mobile Register* managed to extract one of my in-your-face statements before the third meeting with Alabama. Here's part of his article:

> The Crimson Tide inflicted the only loss of the season on the defending national champion GymDogs in the season opening Super Six Challenge in Athens. Georgia returned the favor in a high octane dual meet win in Athens on January 28 after Yoculan promised a GymDog win.

"All of our competitions have been close," Yoculan said. "Just because we've won eight of the last nine SEC titles, even though we had beaten them eleven straight times before they beat us, every single time you could feel the heat of the moment, the heat of the competition. Neither Sarah nor I wants that to die out."

The loss at Alabama was the result of a sloppy meet, with four falls, counting one and a 9.65 score, while Alabama hit twenty-four routines and won 196.500 to 195.850. The Alabama meet, the eighth meet of the season, was Georgia's worst performance since the second meet. Georgia was now one and two with Alabama. Alabama was winning by hitting its routines, while the GymDogs were not.

And Alabama continued its solid performance at the SEC Championships. The GymDogs did not give the SEC Championship to Alabama. Alabama won it, hitting twenty-four routines. The GymDogs had two falls, but did not count one, and tied with LSU for second place. It was only the second time since 1990 that we did not win the SEC Championship.

Meanwhile, UCLA was coming out of the doldrums. After the Super Six Challenge, they had one more frustrating meet. Utah was still undefeated, all-time, in their own arena—I mean undefeated in dual meet competition since the beginning of gymnastics there, twenty-five years ago. When UCLA visited Utah, it certainly appeared as if Utah's undefeated streak might be over. UCLA started out miserably, falling three times on bars. But the Utes returned the favor, counting a fall and a low score on bars. At the end of two rotations, UCLA was leading 97.625 to 97.575. But the Bruins fell twice on the beam, and Utah escaped again 196.350 to 195.150. UCLA was still suffering from inconsistency. Then they turned it around, counting one fall in their last regular season meet, none in the Pac-10 Championships, and one in the Region 1 Championships.

For the first time in seven years, the GymDogs did not finish the season with the highest RQS:

TEAM	RQS
Michigan	197.225
UCLA	197.015
Georgia	196.965
Utah	196.705
Nebraska	196.675
Alabama	196.670

Notice a spread of only 0.555 between number one and number six. Also, it is interesting that the top-six finishers in RQSs were the six teams that would later make the Super Six, adding validity to the RQSs.

The GymDogs won the regional meet at Logan, Utah, with an unspectacular score of 196.725, counting a fall on beam. This was not a year for the GymDogs to be dominant. Our regional score was fourth best in the nation behind (in order of high score) Alabama, UCLA, and Nebraska.

The NCAA Championships were hosted by Boise State University at Boise, Idaho. On Thursday, Georgia won the afternoon session and UCLA "entered a zone," hitting twenty-four routines to win the evening session. In the Super Six, only 0.800 point separated the flawless Bruins from fifth-place Alabama. UCLA hit forty-eight for forty-eight in Boise and deserved its second NCAA Championship, because they had to hit. No one gave them any slack. One counted fall and they are fourth. Their score: 197.300. Utah edged the GymDogs for second, 196.875 to 196.800. Nebraska, Alabama, and Michigan finished fourth, fifth, and sixth. Only Michigan counted a fall, and adjusting for the fall would not have changed their position.

Considering where we coaches thought the GymDogs might wind up, before the season started, third place was satisfying to Georgia, particularly since some heroics were involved. Here's how Ken Short described it in *Gymnastics Insider*.

> The most gutsy performance of this nationals occurred in the last rotation. Georgia All-American Amanda Curry

pulled a calf muscle warming up for vault. She had trouble just running down the vault runway in the three-minute touch warm-up. Coach Yoculan pulled her from the lineup. That left Georgia with only five vaulters. So when Georgia's first vaulter scored only a 9.7, Amanda begged her coach, pleading "I can do better than a 9.7. Let me vault." After Georgia's fifth vaulter, Kristi Lichey, finished her first vault with a mark of 9.95, Coach Yoculan told Kristi to take as much time as she could before her second attempt so the coaches could run some numbers and see where they stood. Kristi improved her score to 10.00 on her second vault—the only perfect score of the championships. But the numbers told Coach Yoculan that a good vault by Amanda Curry could be the difference between third and fourth place and possibly even gain them a second-place finish. Coach Yoculan allowed Amanda to vault. Curry's 9.8 raised the GymDogs from a fourth-place finish to a third-place finish at 196.800 points.

After the meet, Coach Yoculan stated, "This third-place trophy will sit right in the middle of our five first-place trophies, because this team has worked harder than any other I've coached. They have turned 9.8s into 9.85s, and they have turned 9.85s into 9.90s . . . I am so proud of them because they really exemplify what Georgia is all about. Don't count us out. We don't give up."

UCLA Head Coach Valorie Kondos Field was philosophical about the win: "Last time we won this we had to have someone else make mistakes. It's much harder to do when it's yours to take. It's great to know we went out and hit twenty-four routines last night and then hit twenty-four of twenty-four tonight."

Greg Marsden was elated with his team's performance in coming in second: "It was our peak performance." Utah, whose trademark is consistency, had struggled during the season, but they didn't have a fall in the Super Six.

UCLA also brought home two individual national championships: Mohini Bhardwaj won bars, and Lena Desteva won beam. Nebraska's Heather Brink won the all-around and vault, and GymDog Suzanne Sears won floor.

Reflecting the number of gymnasts participating for Georgia, eight GymDogs brought home fifteen All-America citations: Kristi Lichey (all-around, vault, beam, floor), Suzanne Sears (vault, floor), Talya Vexler (beam, floor), Amanda Curry (beam, vault*), Brooke Andersen (vault*, floor*), Kathleen Shrieves (bars), Monica Flammer (vault), Eileen Diaz (bars*). (*denotes second team)

An apparent change in philosophy at UCLA—focusing more on regular-season meets instead of just the NCAA Championship meet—had placed them among the top five in final RQS values and improved their won/loss record relative to prior years. This record reflects a team's ability to avoid having a bad meet against a strong opponent:

TEAM	WON	LOST	TIED	WIN PERCENTAGE
UCLA	39	6	0	.867
Georgia	30	5	1	.847
Utah	24	5	0	.828
Alabama	28	9	0	.757
Nebraska	28	9	0	.757
Michigan	30	12	0	.714

These records measure performance for the entire season, right through the Super Six. Any examination of won/loss records must be accompanied by some evaluation of the competition, if the record is a measure of the team's ability to "avoid a bad meet against a strong opponent." Lining up a bunch of patsies would clobber an NCAA football or basketball team's chances of postseason opportunities; but in gymnastics, no consideration is given to won/loss records. In terms of strength of competition, UCLA doesn't look so good. Considering only the regular season meets—teams have no control over postseason schedules—UCLA faced thirteen teams who were not ranked in the top twenty nationally at the end of the year. These wins are essentially "gimmies." UCLA faced only ten teams who were in the top twenty and lost to six of them. Contrast this with Alabama, who faced only five teams not ranked in the top twenty, and Georgia, who faced only two, both mandated SEC opponents. In fact, the GymDogs faced teams that ended up in the 2000 Super Six eight times during the regular season. No schedule is too tough for my taste. If I were a bantamweight boxer, I'd probably want to fight the world's heavyweight champion.

Here are the season records against the top-twenty teams:

TEAM	WON	LOST	WIN PERCENTAGE
Georgia	14	2	.875
Alabama	10	2	.833
UCLA	4	6	.400

Could the toughness of schedules influence attendance? Alabama and Georgia averaged 9,510 and 8,857 fans per meet, second and third in the nation. UCLA averaged 1,507, twelfth in the nation. College gymnastics is an intercollegiate competitive sport. Fans like to see good gymnastics, and they like to see good gymnastics by all participating teams. They like to win, but they especially like to beat good teams. The regular season should reflect the competitive nature of the entire program. It's not just an exhibition or training session for the NCAA Championships.

Between the 2000 and 2001 seasons, Jackie Clifton retired as volunteer coach after a stellar two-year hitch. Jackie's shoes would be hard to fill, but it seems that there's a steady line of excellent potential volunteer coaches, and next in line was Jay Clark's wife, Julie Ballard Clark—that's right, the Julie Ballard who was an All-American gymnast for the GymDogs from 1994 to 1998. Julie's job would become more important in her first season than anyone dreamed at the time she joined the team.

2001

While the GymDogs had dodged the bullet in 2000—after the team lost its best-ever seniors (1999) and struggled with injuries throughout the season—entering the 2001 season there was tremendous optimism because we only lost six positions from the 2000 Super Six lineup. But the major reason for enthusiastic anticipation was the entering freshman class. Five former national team members would give Georgia a freshman class some analysts ranked above the 1999 seniors—Chelsa Byrd, Cory Fritzinger, Kinsey Rowe, Sierra Sapunar, and Marline Stephens. Loren Simpson, from Atlanta, was a freshman walk-on. Add them to seniors Amanda Curry, Kristi Lichey, Suzanne Sears, and Kathleen Shrieves—for a total of eight former national team members and a returning national floor champion—and you really don't need anything else. And it's a good thing we didn't, because the rising sophomore class had been decimated. Anna Gingrich and Monica Flammar were forced to retire for medical reasons, and Breanne Rutherford had not been able to regain her national team-level performance since she enrolled at Georgia. Juniors Talya Vexler and Eileen Diaz would contend for three slots in the lineup.

As outstanding as Georgia's talent was entering the 2001 season, it was overshadowed in the media's assessment by defending champion UCLA's freshman class. We felt that our five freshmen were as talented, as a group, as UCLA's Olympians—Kristen Maloney, Jamie Dantzscher, and Alyssa Beckerman were from the U.S. team; Yvonne Tousek was on the 1996 and 2000 Canadian teams. Also among the UCLA freshmen was Jeanette Antolin, a five-time national team member. Having lost only two gymnasts—albeit both outstanding ones—from the 2000 national championship team, it wasn't surprising that UCLA garnered twenty-two of twenty-nine first-place votes in the preseason coaches' poll to Georgia's second-place three. Ken Short, publisher of *Gymnastics Insider*, tabbed UCLA's freshmen class "the most talented group of freshmen ever assembled." He went on to suggest that UCLA would be the favorite to win the NCAA Championship for the next four years. So the challenge for Georgia had been cast.

At the time of the preseason intrasquad meet in December, it appeared as if Georgia would be almost invincible. But on January 1, misfortune struck—Kinsey Rowe sustained an ACL injury, taking her out for the season. Then just before the Super Six Challenge, the first meet, my mom, Doris Allen, suffered a life-threatening cerebral aneurism. I missed the Super Six meet and several practices throughout the season. After the third meet, Sierra Sapunar injured her elbow, taking her out for the remainder of the season. In just three meets, Sierra had posted scores of 9.950 on vaulting and bars—winning both events in the second meet of the season against Florida—and 9.900 on floor. So now, three meets into the 2001 season, two gymnasts—each capable of scoring 9.90 to 9.95 or better on all four events—were out for the season, and I was concerned about my mom the entire season.

All successful head coaches have superior staffs, and my assistant coaches really stepped to the forefront when I missed so much time because of my mom's illness. Not only did Doug and Jay step up to the plate, but new volunteer coach, Julie, performed like a seasoned veteran.

I was already at Coleman Coliseum in Tuscaloosa, preparing for the Super Six Challenge, when my fiancé, Don Leeburn, came to the hotel to accompany me back to Athens to be at my mom's side. To their credit, Doug, Jay, and Julie held the team together to garner a tie with Alabama for the meet championship. Georgia counted two falls to Alabama's one. Doug McAvinn, speaking for the team, said that he was glad to get the tie for first place over Florida, Michigan, Penn State, and Stanford.

The GymDogs would go on, without Kinsey and Sierra, to lose only two meets during the regular season. Alabama would eke out a 197.500 to 197.350 in Tuscaloosa.

Forget, for a moment, who won the meet. This was college gymnastics at its best. Two of the best teams in the country going at it toe-to-toe for four rotations, hitting twenty-three routines each, with the lead changing hands each rotation, each team scoring its season high—over half-way through the season—compiling the highest dual meet combined score (394.850) of the year—maybe ever. The meet outcome was decided by the next-to-last gymnasts in the last rotation.

Six all-arounders (all three of ours) scored 39.400 or higher. And a frantic crowd of 8,588 people was recovering from tornadic weather just a couple of hours before. When is television ever going to wake up and learn that this would make for an absolutely electrifying live telecast? How can we be disappointed? And to Sarah's and my credit, neither the post-meet statements by the head coaches nor statements by the gymnasts reflected anything but graciousness and optimism about the remainder of the season. (Actually, we have both become a little exhausted by the constant references to our "personal rivalry.")

During the first six meets of the season, the GymDogs counted nine falls, placing us among the least consistent teams in the country. For the final six regular-season meets we counted one. This was largely because we were getting better—progressing through the season as all teams should.

The other loss came at Los Angeles against UCLA in the last regular-season meet. When looking at the talent of the two teams before the season, this meet was to be between the two Titans. The loss of Sierra and Kinsey left the team a different one from the preseason group. To add to the GymDogs' problems, Kristi Lichey, the team's top gymnast, sprained her ankle at Denver on Friday, before the UCLA meet on Sunday.

Coach Kondos Field was quoted in the UCLA campus newspaper about the upcoming meet: "'United we are intimidating and unbeatable,' Kondos Field said." She had a right to be proud of her team. They were good. The score: UCLA 197.475, GymDogs 197.375—without Kristi. It would be fitting if the two of us would meet again in the Super Six at the NCAA Championships.

Of course, we did meet in the Super Six. Georgia went on to win its ninth SEC Championship in eleven years with a score of 198.000. It was fitting that Cory Fritzinger, who won the all-around competition, was also named SEC Freshman-of-the-Year. The GymDogs easily won the regional championship, winning all five individual regional championships (four apparatus and team total). We won the first session of the NCAA Championships to put us in the Super Six.

Meanwhile, UCLA ran into a red-hot Stanford and came in a close second in the Pac-10 Championships. But they recovered nicely to win their regional and to win first session of the NCAA. So the "Titans" would meet again in the Super six—UCLA with two losses during the season and Georgia with two losses and a tie.

It was apparent to me after the preliminaries at the NCAA that there were only two teams who had a chance to win the Super Six, barring complete disintegrations by both teams: UCLA and Georgia. And the Super Six bore this assessment out, although Michigan came out of the shadows to win third place by a hefty 0.725 points over fourth-place Alabama, performing without its star Andree Pickens, who had torn an Achilles tendon the week before.

Going into the fifth rotation, the final rotation for both UCLA and Georgia, UCLA was leading Georgia by the thinnest of margins, 148.000 to 147.900. One would think that Georgia had the upper hand, going to our strongest event, vaulting, while UCLA had to confront the dreaded beam. To add pressure, the GymDogs finished first, really vaulted lights out, with a score of 49.500, leaving UCLA the seemingly impossible task of scoring 49.400 to tie. UCLA's RQS for beam was 49.255, lowest of any of their events. They were competing in Georgia's home arena. And it was for all the marbles.

After Georgia's fans finished their celebration at the end of the vaulting event, there was a hush over the crowd because they knew that the championship hinged on UCLA's beam performance. Valorie Kondos Field wisely took as much difficulty out of the beam routines her gymnasts were about to perform, as she could without lowering the start values below 10.0. Some observers claimed that some routines didn't add up to 10.0 start values due to the level of the dismounts, but the judges were not among those observers. Donnie Thompson was up first, and she performed a "bobbleless" routine for a 9.900 score. Then Malia Jones fell. The remaining four gymnasts all had to not only stay on the apparatus, but they could not afford more than one bobble among them. Can't be done! Or can it? Onnie Willis carded a 9.900, Kristen Maloney a 9.925, and Yvonne Tousek a 9.950. All without a bobble, all with precision and effortless execution. Mohini Bhardwaj, UCLA's lone senior in the lineup, was the final competitor, and she needed 9.750 to win the NCAA Championship for UCLA.

I turned to my gymnasts, who just a few minutes earlier might have been picturing themselves on the winners' platform, and said, "Get ready to go over and congratulate UCLA as soon as Mohini completes her routine. I've watched her for four years, and there is no way she'll score less than 9.750." And Mohini scored 9.900 to give UCLA a 0.175 margin of victory. UCLA had taken the national championship from Georgia on the same apparatus and in the same place they had given the championship to Georgia thirteen years earlier, in 1989.

After the meet, Kondos Field said, "All year long we've heard it would be a cakewalk for UCLA to take the championship, but it was extremely difficult." I couldn't have been terribly disappointed considering our team's battered condition, and I tried to reflect my pride in them to the press: "You saw how great UCLA is. We made them earn it. This is the greatest second-place finish my team has ever had." But deep down inside, we were hurting. This team had it all: leadership, respect, and team chemistry coupled with talent, determination, and competitiveness. This was a championship team finishing the season without the championship.

As dramatic and exciting as the finish was, neither team was at full strength because of injuries. Of UCLA's fabulous five freshmen, only Tousek, Dantzscher, and Maloney competed, as Beckerman and Antolin were injured. In addition to the loss of Sapunar and Rowe, Georgia's top gymnast, Kristi, was not able to compete on floor and was seriously hampered on beam by a sprained ankle.

If nothing else, the year and the championship clearly demonstrated that college gymnasts who did not compete in the Olympics could hold their own with those who did. And the Olympians were heard to say that the college experience was more fun, but also more nerve-racking, than the Olympics.

The end-of-the-year RQSs confirmed the closeness of the teams' strengths.

TEAM	RQS
UCLA	197.640
Georgia	197.520
Nebraska	197.285
Alabama	197.285
Utah	197.205

A spread of only 0.435 points between number one and number five. Contrast this difference, between one and five, with the average difference between number one and number two of 0.840 during the six years from 1994 through 1999, when Georgia was consistently on top.

Elise Ray (2000 U.S. Olympian from Michigan) won the individual all-around competition. Yvonne Tousek (UCLA) won the uneven bars, and Theresa Kulikowski (Utah) won balance beam. Floor exercise defending champion, Suzanne Sears (Georgia), had a repeat all wrapped up until her knee buckled slightly on the absolutely final skill of her collegiate career, costing her 0.05 point and the championship, which went to Mohini Bhardwaj (UCLA). During the regular season, Cory Fritzinger was Georgia's fourth-best vaulter, but the NCAA Individual Championship requires that a vaulter perform two different vaults, and Cory was equally strong on two vaults. This skill gave her the individual national championship in vaulting.

First team All-Americans for the GymDogs were: Cory Fritzinger (vault, floor, and beam), Suzanne Sears (vault, floor), Marline Stephens (vault, floor), and Kathleen Shrieves (bars). Kristi Lichy (all-around, bars), Amanda Curry (vault), Talya Vexler (beam), and Chelsa Byrd (bars) were named second team All-America. Kristi made second team All-America in her two weakest events. She was, by far, Georgia's strongest vaulter and balance beam performer, but her sprained ankle kept these honors and shots at two individual national championships away from her.

2002

The loss of Kristi Lichey, Suzanne Sears, Kathleen Shrieves, and Amanda Curry to graduation was a big one. They filled ten slots on the team that competed on the first night of the NCAA Championships. But eight of those slots could be filled by the return of Sierra Sapunar and Kinsey Rowe, if they both recovered fully from their injuries during the off-season. Add two of the top recruits in the country, Melinda Baimbridge and Michelle Emmons (both former national team members), and the 2002 team should be as strong as the 2001 team.

Again, the coaches were impressed by UCLA's national championship and by the talent on their team. The Bruins received twenty-nine of thirty-seven first-place votes in the preseason coaches' poll. Georgia was second to UCLA in total points received, but they received no first-place votes.

The GymDog's first meet of the season was a pretty close encounter with a surprisingly strong and well-prepared Nebraska team in Athens. Neither team counted a fall; Georgia had three and Nebraska just two. But the GymDogs won 196.875 to 196.350. It was the highest first-meet score for any team in the history of NCAA gymnastics. Kinsey Rowe, a redshirt freshman, made her collegiate debut with an all-around score of 39.475, but she was edged by Cory Fritzinger with a 39.525. The GymDogs were still without the services of Melinda Baimbridge and Sierra Sapunar because of injuries. As it turned out, Melinda would never compete for Georgia, succumbing to a painful shoulder injury, subsequent surgery, and finally taking a medical retirement (on scholarship for four years) in her freshman year.

The SEC Challenge (formerly the Super Six Challenge) in Gainesville, Florida would provide an assessment of the GymDogs' potential. Other teams included UCLA, Alabama, Florida, LSU, and Penn State. Georgia won by scoring a meet record 196.525; Alabama was second with 195.825; and UCLA was just behind Alabama at 195.650. Kinsey Rowe was beginning to show her potential by winning the all-around with a score of 39.425, edging Cory Fritzinger in their second head-to-head competition. UCLA was competing without Antolin and Maloney, who would sit out the entire season. Most of Alabama's gymnasts were recovering from injuries, most notably Andree Pickens, who was limited to three events. But Georgia's score was still a meet record, so we weren't handed the meet. Alabama did not count a fall, and UCLA counted one. UCLA's fall-adjusted score would have moved them into second place.

On Sunday, after the SEC Challenge on Friday, UCLA came to Athens for a repeat of the 2001 NCAA Super Six competition. This time they ran into the unbelievably hot GymDogs, who hit twenty-four routines in scoring 197.800—another national record for so early in the season—to UCLA's 196.875, tying Georgia's score against Nebraska for the second-highest score of the season. The Bruins counted no falls. Coach Kondos Field had said before the SEC Challenge that one of her team's goals was to go undefeated. After only two meets, they were staggering from three losses. But the bigger news was Georgia's record-breaking start. Kinsey Rowe continued her sky-high performance with a career-high 39.675 all-around, only to be out-pointed by Cory Fritzinger's 39.800. It appeared, after three meets, that the GymDogs would be the dominant team of the 2002 season.

But the GymDogs' sky-high position would last only until the following weekend in Tuscaloosa, Alabama. After starting with a lackluster performance on uneven bars—at least we didn't fall from the bars—disaster struck on vaulting. Kinsey Rowe suffered a severe injury to her foot, which not only knocked her out of the rest of the meet, but effectively the rest of the season. Then in the last rotation, Sierra Sapunar fell from the beam as the Alabama fans were chanting "Roll Tide" while she was performing. Her injury was excruciatingly painful, and sidelined her for several meets. Amazingly, even though Georgia counted no falls, we counted three scores under 9.6 and didn't have a good performance on any apparatus, resulting in our lowest score of the season, 195.025—2.775 points below our score the previous week. Alabama was only slightly better, at 195.675.

As the season progressed, Georgia's injury situation got worse, and Alabama's physical condition got progressively better. Alabama was progressing just like Coach Patterson said they would. Georgia did finish out the regular season with only one other loss, to Michigan in Ann Arbor. It was Michigan's first win over Georgia in fifteen attempts.

They were on a roll, hitting twenty-four routines for the second consecutive week. Georgia was beginning to come out of the doldrums.
We hit twenty-three routines and lost by 0.150 point. The score was
good enough to put us back on top of the national RQS rankings,
but later in the year, we fell back because we were unable to replace
enough of our poor road scores.

By SEC Championship time, we were struggling to find enough
gymnasts to put six on each apparatus, and many who competed were
at much less than full capability because of nagging injuries. The SEC
meet was held in Birmingham again, a strongly pro-Alabama environment. But somehow we were able to put a patched-up lineup on the
floor. Meanwhile, Alabama was getting healthier by the week. With all
the odds against it, we managed to win our tenth SEC Championship
in twelve years, squeaking by Alabama 197.025 to 196.925.

It appeared that the GymDogs might miss the NCAA
Championships for the first time since I came to Georgia in 1984.
You will recall that in the format adopted in 1999, the top-two teams
at each regional meet advance to the championships. At the North
Central Regional meet at Denver, Georgia tied with Stanford for
first place with another lack-luster performance of 196.125, but host
Denver scored 196.000, allowing Georgia to gain entrance to the
NCAA Nationals by the tiniest of margins. Had Denver scored higher
than Georgia and Stanford, Stanford would have gotten the bid on the
basis of counting all twenty-four scores to break a tie.

Again, spread between the first and fifth teams in the final RQS
standings was razor thin, 0.400 point:

TEAM	RQS
UCLA	197.230
Alabama	197.095
Georgia	197.085
Utah	196.920
Michigan	196.830

The NCAA Championships were held in Tuscaloosa, and Alabama had everything going for them. At regionals, they had hit twenty-four routines and broke the national record for the balance beam, 49.725 in taking first place. They were in peak physical condition, while UCLA and Georgia were struggling to find six gymnasts who could even compete on each apparatus. Postings on the Internet prior to the meet indicated that the Alabama fans felt it was incumbent on them to intimidate the other teams, and they wore T-shirts at the championship meets with "This is Our House" on them. Their pep band was positioned near the floor. Coach Patterson had made sure that the environment was right for Alabama to win. But the most important thing she had done was to keep them in the zone they went into in the regional meet. And she did!

Alabama hit twenty-four routines in winning their preliminary session and twenty-four more in winning the championship, bringing the total routines hit in the last three meets to seventy-two. Even so, going into the final rotation, Alabama was on beam while the GymDogs were on floor, with Alabama leading by only 0.250 over Georgia. Had each team hit its event RQS, Georgia would have won by over a tenth of a point. But Alabama's beam team was still in the zone they entered at regionals, and the best Georgia's hobblers could muster on floor was 0.075 point lower than the Crimson Tide's 49.375 on beam. Alabama won its fourth NCAA Championship by 0.325 point over Georgia, with a score of 197.575. The days of a team's counting a fall and winning the national championship are over. No team counted a fall in the Super Six. Had Alabama counted a fall, they would have come in fourth, that's how close the teams were to one another.

UCLA's Jamie Dantzscher won the all-around and vaulting individual championships; the uneven bars was won by Andree Pickens (Alabama); Elise Ray (Michigan) won beam; and Dantzscher shared the floor championship with LSU's Nicki Arnstad.

All-America honors went to the following GymDogs: Cassie Bair (beam★); Chelsa Byrd (vault, bars); Cory Fritzinger (all-around★, vault, bars★, beam); Sierra Sapunar (bars★, beam★); Loren Simpson (bars★); Marline Stephens (vault); and Talya Vexler (floor). (★denotes second team)

2003

Eileen Diaz and Talya Vexler contributed to two events each (one participation on each event) in the Super Six at the end of the 2002 season. They were the only seniors. The return of Kinsey Rowe, who won the all-around at the SEC Challenge in 2002, from a foot injury should more than compensate for the losses. In addition, four of the six freshmen—national team members Marie Fjordholm, Ashley Miller, and Brittany Smith and Jamie Ackerman, a promising level-10 performer—were considered among the best in the country. So there was reason for optimism about 2003. Alabama snagged a great recruiting class also, including Ashley Miles, the consensus USA top recruit; and UCLA brought in two more former Olympians, Holly Murdock from Ireland and Kate Richardson from Canada, giving them six former Olympians on the roster. It's little wonder that the coaches picked UCLA number one in the preseason coaches' poll, awarding them twenty of thirty-one first-place votes. The GymDogs were second, Alabama third, Utah fourth, Nebraska fifth, and Michigan sixth—the "usual suspects."

However, it didn't take long for tragedy to strike the GymDogs. Before the season, Marline Stephens had a season-ending Achilles injury. Then various physical problems occurred. With a pieced-together lineup, with only five gymnasts competing on floor, the GymDogs had no falls in our opening meet at Nebraska, but we counted seven scores of 9.7 or lower—to none the following week—losing by a point to Nebraska, who had a record-setting (for them) opening score of 196.45. By the following weekend, at the SEC challenge at Athens, the GymDogs recovered dramatically to win by over a half-point with a score of 197.325, over a tough set of teams—including Nebraska, who came in second. The GymDogs completed the remainder of the regular season without a loss, but in the SEC Championship we lost to Alabama by 0.05 point, at Birmingham again.

The final national RQS standings were close again, with UCLA hanging on to the first spot and the gap between number one and number six being only 0.500:

TEAM	RQS
UCLA	197.800
Nebraska	197.585
Arizona State	197.490
Georgia	197.485
Alabama	197.345
Stanford	197.300

The Southeastern Regional meet was held in Athens, and the GymDogs had a cakewalk, winning by over 2 points with a score 197.125, which was the third highest score of the thirty-six teams in the country participating in regionals. UCLA and Alabama were the two teams who scored higher.

Four SEC teams qualified for nationals—Alabama, Florida, Georgia, and LSU. Nebraska hosted the meet and scored the highest score in either qualifying round. The GymDogs had to count a 9.550 on beam and came in third in the second session, behind Nebraska and Utah.

Nebraska looked to be a bonafide contender for the championship, but they counted a fall in the Super Six to come in fourth. Of the top-four teams, UCLA had three falls, Georgia and Nebraska had two each, and Alabama had only one, but Nebraska was the only team in the top four to count a fall.

The final results:

TEAM	SCORE
UCLA	197.825
Alabama	197.275
Georgia	197.150
Nebraska	197.125
Michigan	196.050
Utah	195.300

If the six teams look familiar, they are the top six in the coaches' preseason poll.

Michigan counted a fall and Utah, uncharacteristically, counted two. Utah also lost to injury its top gymnast, Theresa Kulikowski, who was a rare fifth-year senior. Theresa was one of several gymnasts whose injuries took away much from what should have been even more impressive careers.

UCLA garnered three individual championships. Jamie Dantzscher and Kate Richardson tied for the bars championship, and Kate also won the beam. Rachelle Simpson from Nebraska took the floor and the all-around, and Alabama's Ashley Miles won the vaulting.

All-America honors for Georgia went to Chelsa Byrd on floor and vaulting, Brittany Smith on vaulting, Cassie Bair on beam, and Jamie Ackerman★ and Kinsey Rowe★ on bars. (★denotes second team)

2004

We lost only one senior from the 2003 team, Cassie Bair, who made All America on her specialty, beam, and filled in on bars for the entire 2003 season. Two elite-level gymnasts joined the team as freshmen: Ashley Kupets, considered by many the nation's top recruit and a national team member, and Brittany Thomé, a five-time national team member.

Two of the nation's top level-10 gymnasts also joined us: Kelsey Ericksen and Adrienne Dishman. Also coming in as freshmen were three outstanding gymnasts from the state of Georgia—Tiffany Gordon, Courtney Pratt, and Laura Thornsberry. With the return of Marline Stephens, who was out the entire 2003 season with an Achilles injury, things were looking up at the beginning of the season, and the coaches' poll reflected optimism for us, but we were second and not first. UCLA was voted (1), Georgia (2), Alabama (3), Utah (4), Michigan (5), Stanford (6).

The good fortune was short lived. Jamie Ackerman participated in only three routines before having to retire with a back injury, and Marie Fjordholm retired with a bad back without competing at all. As it turned out Marline was able to contribute on only vaulting and floor, and Sierra Sapunar could only do bars and beam and then only for the last two regular-season meets and the postseason.

Even with this patched-up team, after counting two falls and coming in third to Alabama and Florida at the Super-Six Challenge, the GymDogs ripped off ten consecutive scores between 196.900 and 198.050. Then we capped it off by winning the SEC Championship with a 198.175 after Kinsey Rowe tore her ACL in the first rotation. That performance showed the tenacity of this team. Kelsey Ericksen was named SEC Freshman of the Year. The final rankings, before regionals, based on RQS were:

UCLA	98.055
Stanford	97.64
Alabama	197.625
Georgia	197.620
Utah	97.575
BYU	97.525

UCLA had a modest lead over second place Stanford, but look at the spread between number 2 and number 6 (0.122 points). Man! That's close.

When the SEC was over, and we came back to practice for regionals it really set in that we had little left physically as a team. And then at regionals, Brittany Smith hurt her ankle warming up. We were down emotionally, physically—in every way. The GymDogs continued to claw away, without Kinsey, to score the second highest regional score in the country, behind Utah.

Because of the physical condition of the team we didn't have an opportunity to train sticking landings before nationals, and we missed enough landings to cost us a point cumulatively. At the Super Six, we missed nearly every landing on the first couple of events. Then we realized that UCLA was going to win no matter what we did the remainder of the meet. We didn't want to settle for second again, and we got worse instead of better. When Cory Fritzinger fell from beam in the last rotation, that said it all. We were a beaten team. She knew she was competing for second place, and her last chance for a national championship had gone up in smoke.

But, you must remember, UCLA was in a zone at nationals. They were at home at Pauli Pavilion, and they set a new UCLA Championship meet record of 198.125. It was their meet, and they deserved it. The scores at the Super Six:

UCLA	198.125
Georgia	197.200
Alabama	197.125
Stanford	197.125
Florida	196.800
Utah	195.775

Eleven falls were scattered among the Super Six teams, with only Utah counting a fall. And look what it did to them. You can't count a fall at Nationals and win any more.

Alabama's Jeana Rice won the all-around championship. Ashley Miles of Alabama won two individual championships: she won vaulting and tied with North Carolina's Courtney Bumpers for the floor exercise championship. Elise Ray, Michigan, won bars; and Ashley Kelly, Arizona, won balance beam.

Georgia's All-Americans were Chelsa Byrd (all-around, vault, floor, beam★), Cory Fritzinger (bars, beam★), Kelsey Ericksen (bars), and Ashley Kupets (bars★). (★ denotes second team)

You will recall our elation over signing the class of 2004 in the fall of 2000. I felt sure this class would win several national championships. But no, they became only the third class since the class of 1986 not to win a national championship while they were at Georgia. An incredible streak of injuries every year for four years made it impossible for them to win one. Even so, this group of tenacious fighters managed to win three SEC Championships and come in second in the fourth one. In the NCAA Super Six, they came in second three times and third once. But perhaps the biggest contribution from this group to Georgia gymnastics was teaching three classes behind them how to deal with adversity and how to compete to win.

2005

The 2005 season was a new beginning. Not only were six seniors gone, but Marie Fjordholm, Jamie Ackerman, and Ashley Miller were no longer on the team. And two of the 2004 freshmen from Georgia decided not to return—eleven of eighteen members gone from the 2004 team! That's like a new beginning.

But what a way to begin—with five freshmen who would have to figure prominently in our program! Katie Heenan, a six-time national team member, was a bronze medalist at the 2001 World Championships. Samantha Sheehan, a three-time national team member, was a bronze medalist at the 2002 World Championships. Nikki Childs and Megan Dowlen were national team members, and Audrey Bowers was on the level-10 Junior Olympic National Championship team for three years.

The year 2005 was the first one that all judges, throughout the nation, were selected by regional assigners. I thought it worked great. Unquestionably it ended the major problem of biased judging, when judges were selected by the coaches. There were a lot of complaints at first, but in the end the best teams were at the national championships. At first there were some discrepancies from region-to-region, but as the year went on the regions got closer together. The region-to-region discrepancies might have accounted for the fact that four different teams were ranked number one at one point of the season or another.

From my standpoint, we were scored a little bit lower than teams in some other regions, and it made us a better team. At the beginning we were doing pretty well and still scoring lower than a lot of the other teams in the country in other regions. The team didn't like that. The difficulty of our schedule helped us become a strong team. We competed against every top team in the country week after week.

In 2005, our coaches went into the season feeling like we needed to change some things. We felt that injuries and UCLA's talent had a lot to do with why we didn't win a national championship. But changes needed to be made, and it was difficult to change when our team was dominated by seniors in 2004. With them gone, we went to conditioning early in the morning. We had everybody's class schedule changed so they could attend conditioning exercises.

We really focused on team chemistry as our top priority. The chemistry was good from the beginning. The graduation of the six 2004 seniors was like a flower's opening in terms of our lone senior, Michelle Emmons, and our only junior, Brittany Smith. The entire team wanted information, they listened to us, they trusted us. In the fall, we said each gymnast had to develop three things: (1) confidence in the program—in the coaches, in what we said, and in what we were doing. (2) confidence in herself and her routines and (3) confidence in each other.

The whole 2005 team, not just the freshmen, were so positive. Katie Heenan was such a positive force at the Olympic trials in 2004 that she was invited to the Olympic camp to spread that positive force, even though her gymnastics performance didn't qualify her for the camp. Katie's as far from being a prima donna as anyone I've ever coached. She's so nice you can't be jealous of her.

The coaches throughout the nation seemed to discount all of our personnel losses when they predicted the way teams would finish the year in the coaches' poll. UCLA was voted (1), Georgia (2), Stanford (3), Alabama (4), Utah (5), Florida (6).

At first it looked as though we would be bitten by the injury bug again. Adrienne Dishman injured her Achilles and was out for the season, and Brittany Thomé had to retire from gymnastics after competing only one routine. But fortunately, we had no more serious injuries.

We started the season as if we might live up to the coaches' confidence in us. Although all teams were pretty sloppy at the Super Six Challenge, we won, and went on undefeated until we hit Florida in Athens. We counted two falls in the Florida meet and counted falls in the next three meets as well, losing four in a row. Losing four meets in a row was a first for me in twenty-two years at Georgia. We hadn't even lost two meets in a row since 1991.

I took full responsibility for the falls when we lost the four meets in a row. I changed the beam routines and the beam lineup what seemed like a hundred times—more than I ever changed it in twenty-two years. Because we had so many freshmen I couldn't get it right. What was great about working things out, what made it work, was that the girls believed in the system. Every time I made a change they were completely receptive. There was no resistance. In fact, the team members felt solving the problem was as much their responsibility as it was anyone's. For example, Kelsey Ericksen volunteered to go first on beam, perhaps sacrificing a tenth or so on her individual score in order to make sure the team was off to a solid start. Kelsey's unselfish move set the tone for leadership from that point on.

The falls accounted for all of the losses except the loss to Alabama, so the coaches and the team still had confidence that we could finish strong. And we did. After the Alabama loss, we defeated Utah, UCLA, N.C. State, and Michigan to end the regular season. Three of those teams were in the Super Six at Nationals.

With no falls, we won the SEC Championship with our second highest score of the season, 197.250, just edging LSU, who came into the meet ranked second in the nation. Coach D. D. Breaux was gracious after the meet saying that LSU had a good meet and pushed Georgia to excel. They did. Katie Heenan, 39.625, and Ashley Kupets, 39.550 came in first and second in the all-around.

The final national rankings, based on RQS were:

Utah	197.320
UCLA	197.090
LSU	197.025
Alabama	196.815
Georgia	196.800
Nebraska	196.750

The fifth-place ranking was our highest of the season. The teams are the same teams that would later reach the Super Six, except that

Michigan replaced LSU. The small spread between number one and number six has become the usual now, reflecting the level of parity among the top teams.

At regionals, we had a complete breakdown on beam, counting two falls and a score of 9.550 for the lowest beam score I can remember in my years at Georgia. Denver had a great chance to push us out of Nationals, but they faltered on beam, too, and came in over a point below our second place 195.150, the lowest qualifying score in the nation. LSU's 197.125 regional score was the highest. So the two teams were first and last.

Another characteristic of college gymnastics was evident in Stanford's experience. You may recall that they were ranked third in the preseason coaches' poll. But they had an almost unbelievable rash of injuries and ended the season ranked seventeenth. Of course they didn't make nationals. And LSU failed to make the Super Six by 0.075 point. They counted no falls in the preliminary round, but they had three falls and were forced to count nine scores below 9.800.

Before the national championships, I said, "This is not going to be a competition of talent; this is going to be a competition of the minds. The team that is strongest mentally is the team that will win this championship." And that's exactly what happened. It was all mental. We won it because we were a total team bonded together, perhaps more than any other team we've ever had. Everybody was "on." It was the fourth and fifth scores that made the difference.

In the preliminary round, we scored the highest score in either session, 197.350, the GymDogs' highest score of the season, so far. We were as strong mentally as any team I've ever coached.

In the championship session, we had to start on beam, the apparatus that had been our downfall at regionals. After the draw for starting apparatus and before the meet, I told the team that if we scored a 49.3 on beam, we would win the national championship. The GymDogs scored a 49.350, the highest beam score of any team in the Super Six. We stuck landings throughout the meet. Our lowest score of twenty-four was 9.800. In the two sessions we posted fourteen season highs or ties for highs—phenomenal for late in the season. Our winning final score was our highest of the season.

No team counted a fall in the Super Six. There were only 3 falls among the 144 routines. The final scores:

Georgia	197.825
Alabama	197.400
Utah	197.275
UCLA	197.150
Michigan	196.575
Nebraska	196.425

Tasha Schwikert, UCLA, won the all around championship; Kristen Maloney, UCLA, won vaulting and balance beam; Terin Humphrey, Alabama, won uneven bars, and Courtney Bumpers, North Carolina, repeated on floor exercise. In the Super Six, Kristen Maloney and Georgia's Katie Heenan tied Tasha Schwikert's all-around championship score of 39.725, which is awarded during the preliminary sessions.

Although no GymDog won an individual championship, we had more All-America citations (17) than any other team, indicating the importance of the third, fourth, and fifth scores on each apparatus. GymDog All-Americans: Kelsey Ericksen (AA,UB, FX,BB★) Katie Heenan (all-around, vault, beam, bars★), Brittany Smith (vault, bars★), Ashley Kupets (all-around, floor, bars★), Michelle Emmons (floor, vault★), and Nikki Childs (bars★, beam★). (★ denotes second team)

This may sound like a broken record, but I can't emphasize enough how important team chemistry was at the 2005 NCAA Championships.

In 1983 when I came to Georgia to my first college coaching job, I dreamed that someday mature gymnasts would do Olympic-level skills in the vibrant college atmosphere. In the twenty-two years since then, hundreds of club gyms have sprung up like mushrooms all over the country, producing thousands of talented young gymnasts. NCAA scoring standards have become much more challenging over the years.

But, even so, as these exceptional gymnasts have come into the college ranks, the winning scores at the national championship have risen about 10 points. And the lowest scores in the Super Six of 2005 were higher than the winning scores in the championship meets twenty years ago. My dreams have been fulfilled and surpassed. Women's collegiate gymnastics is the best gymnastics in the world today.

COACHES WHOSE TEAMS WON NCAA
NATIONAL CHAMPIONSHIPS 1982–2005
Greg Marsden, Utah, 9
Suzanne Yoculan, Georgia, 6
Valorie Kondos Field, UCLA, 5
Sarah Patterson, Alabama, 4

COACHES WHOSE TEAMS FINISHED IN
THE TOP 6 AT NCAAS 1982–2005
Sarah Patterson (Alabama)1983, 1984, 1985, 1986, 1987, 1988, 1989, 1990, 1991, 1992, 1993, 1994. 1995, 1996, 1998, 1999, 2000, 2001, 2002, 2003, 2004, 2005—22 times
Greg Marsden (Utah) 1982, 1983, 1984, 1985, 1986, 1987, 1988, 1989, 1990, 1991, 1992, 1993, 1994, 1995, 1996, 1998, 2000, 2001, 2002, 2003, 2004, 2005—22 times
Suzanne Yoculan (Georgia) 1986, 1987, 1988, 1989, 1990, 1991, 1992, 1993, 1994, 1995, 1996, 1997, 1998, 1999, 2000, 2001, 2002, 2003, 2004, 2005—20 times
Valorie Kondos Field (UCLA) 1993, 1994. 1995, 1996, 1997, 1998, 1999, 2000, 2001, 2002, 2003, 2004, 2005—13 times
Dan Kendig (Nebraska) 1989, 1990, 1997, 1999, 2000, 2001, 2002, 2003, 2005—9 times
Beverly Plocky (Michigan) 1994, 1995, 1996, 1997, 1999, 2000, 2001, 2003, 2005--9 times
John Spini (Arizona St.) 1982, 1983, 1984, 1985, 1986, 1987, 1997, 1998, 1999—9 times

Judi Avener / Judy Markel (Penn. St. / Florida) 1982, 1986, 1991, 1992, 1994, 1997, 1998—7 times

Jerry Tomlinson (UCLA) 1982, 1983, 1984, 1987, 1988, 1989, 1990—7 times

Lynn Rogers (Cal. St. Fullerton) 1982, 1983, 1984, 1985, 1986, 1989—6 times

Ernestine Weaver (Florida) 1983, 1984, 1985, 1987, 1988, 1991—6 times

Jim Turpin (Oregon St.) 1991, 1992, 1995, 1996--4 times

D.D. Pollock/D.D. Breaux (LSU) 1983, 1988, 1990—3 times

Jim Gault (Arizona) 1992, 1993—2 times

Ron Ludwig (Oregon St.) 1982, 1985—2 times

Kristen Smith (Stanford) 2002, 2004—2 times

Robert Dillard (Auburn) 1993—1 time

Rhonda Faehn (Florida) 2004—1 time

TOP LEFT
Meredith Willard, Alabama.
(UA Media Relations)

TOP RIGHT
Alabama Team, 1996; Left to Right, Front
Row: Heather Nasser, Lisa Gianni, Gwen
Spidle, Kim Kelly, Middle Row: Meredith
Willard, Kim Bonaventura, Stephanie Woods,
Shay Murphy, Top Row: Mandy Chapman,
Merritt Booth, Marna Neubauer, Danielle
McAdams.
(UA Media Relations)

BOTTOM
Lori Strong, Georgia.
(UGA Sports Communications)

TOP
Georgia Team, 1998 NCAA National
Champions: Left to Right, Front Row:
Sam Muhleman, Caroline Harris,
Suzanne Sears, Julie Ballard, and Stacey
Galloway; Middle Row: Amanda Curry,
Courtney Whittle, Kim Arnold, Kristi
Lichey, and Brooke Andersen; Back
Row: Jenni Beathard, Kathleen Shrieves,
and Karin Lichey.
(UGA Sports Communications)

LEFT
Cony Fritzinger, Georgia.
(UGA Sports Communications)

LEFT
Theresa Kulikowski, Utah.
(U of U Staff Photos)

BELOW
Georgia Team, 1999 NCAA
National Champions: Left to
Right, Front Row: Kathleen
Shrieves, Sam Muhleman,
Karin Lichey, Jenni Beathard,
Stacey Galloway; Middle Row:
Suzanne Sears, Eileen Diaz,
Caroline Harris, Emily Chell,
April Hoellman, Talya Vexler,
Danielle Maurone; Back
Row: Brooke Andersen, Kristi
Lichey, Amanda Curry.
(UGA Sports Communications)

UCLA Team, 2003, Left to Right,
Front Row: Katie Richardson,
Christie Tedmon, Jeanette Antolin,
Middle Row: Malia Jones, Kristin
Parker, Jamie Dantzscher, Kristen
Maloney, Christy Erickson, Trishna
Patel, Back Row: Yvonne Tousek,
Alyssa Beckerman, Jamie Williams,
Carly Raab, Onnie Willis, Donni
Thompson, Holly Mucock.
(UCLA Sports Informations)

Mohini Bhardwaj, UCLA.
(UCLA Sports Information)

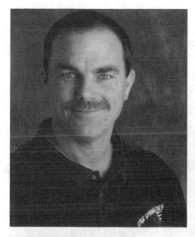

TOP LEFT
Greg Marsden, Utah coach, nine
NCAA Championships.
(U of U Staff Photos)

TOP RIGTH
Me, proud to be the Georgia coach for
six NCAA Championships.
(UGA Sports Communications)

MIDDLE LEFT
Valorie Kondos-Field, UCLA coach,
five NCAA Championships.
(UCLA Sports Information)

BOTTOM LEFT
Sarah Patterson, Alabama coach, four
NCAA Championships.
(UA Media Relations)

TOP
Clapping with the team at our SEC Championship win, 2004.
(UGA Sports Communications)

MIDDLE LEFT
Watching the GymDogs with Assistant Coach Doug McAvinn, left, and Associate Head Coach Jay Clark, center, 2005.
(UGA Sports Communications)

BOTTOM LEFT
Georgia Team, 2005 NCAA National Champions: From Left to Right, Front Row: Michelle Emmons, Brittany Smith; Middle Row: Courtney Pratt, Ashley Kupets, Katie Heenan, Kelsey Ericksen; Back Row: Nikki Childs, Megan Dowlen, Brittany Thome, Audrey Bowers, Sam Sheehan, Adrienne Dishman.
(© Rodi Nabuki)

Gender Equity

In 2001, Brian Schrader came from the University of Iowa swimming program to become an assistant coach with Georgia's three-time-national-championship women's swimming team. He said publicly that Georgia was the perfect place for him: "It is one of the few schools in the country where all the sports get an incredible amount of support."

"All the sports," of course, includes women's sports. And the University of Georgia, indeed, has a remarkable record in women's athletics. Georgia won the SEC women's all-sports trophy six times between the year of its inception, 1984, and 1994, when the conference decided to combine men's and women's sports for the trophy, as is done for the Sears Cup. It is awarded to the school whose overall athletic program ranks highest in the nation, based largely on the national rankings of its teams. Since 1987, UGA has won thirteen national championships in four women's sports. Without question, Liz Murphey, who was Georgia's first coordinator for women's athletics, deserves a major share of the credit. But Liz will insist that Athletic Director Vince Dooley and the coaches she hired deserve the credit.

As significant as the contributions of Murphey, Dooley, and the coaches are, the strongest force behind the emergence of women's intercollegiate sports at the University of Georgia was the enactment of Title IX of the Educational Amendments of 1972 to the Civil Rights Act. Title IX bans sex discrimination within schools in academics and athletics. In short, it calls for equality of financial assistance (athletic scholarships), awarding of scholarships in proportion to the numbers of males and females in the total student enrollment, and providing equivalent benefits in other areas of college athletics—coaching, equipment, travel, medical, and training support.

Georgia hasn't always been a leader in women's sports. In the 1970s UGA was slow—and that's being generous—to react to Title IX. It took six years after the enactment of Title IX for the university to award the first athletic scholarship to a female in 1978. At the time there was a ratio of about 150 male scholarships to the lone female scholarship. In 2000, the numbers were 141.2 for males to 108 for females. These numbers demonstrate that women have made substantial progress in the number of scholarships and in other areas, but it was not without prodding from the courts. And it was in an environment that was, and still is to some extent, one of the most chauvinistic of any profession—a college athletic department. Liz provides background on the women's sports situation before Title IX and during the early years after enactment:

When I came here in 1967 as physical education teacher and golf coach, there were no scholarships for women athletes. We were club teams. You really wouldn't call the organizations, teams. They were just clubs. In the women's physical education department, we volunteered to be coaches. In the department staff meetings, we'd ask, "Who'll work with the gymnasts?" And we'd say, "We're building a university golf course. Don't you think we ought to have a golf team?" Since I was teaching golf, becoming the golf coach was a logical position for me. But the clubs were funded only through student activities funds. There were no athletic department funds. We had to go to the allocations committee of the student activities program and present our club constitution and officers to get any money whatsoever, just like the other clubs on campus. And the largest budget for any of the clubs was like $500 for the year.

All of the coaches taught. No one was paid for coaching. It was a voluntary activity. In fact, the golf team did a lot of camping out when we traveled because we had no travel budget. We'd go down to Rollins College in Florida to play in a tournament during spring break and stay at Yogi Bear campground.

It was a while after the passage of Title IX before we awarded the first athletic scholarship to a woman. And it was like pulling eyeteeth to get it. The Office of Civil Rights (OCR) came to look at our program after Title IX was passed. A lot of our women athletes would sign a petition and hand-carry it over to the OCR in Atlanta, pointing out that the men were getting all the scholarships, and the women were getting none. The OCR said, "You've got to start giving scholarships to women." In 1977, six years after enactment of Title IX, we granted the first scholarship for women's athletics. That year we were given $10,000 for scholarships for the entire women's program.

The $10,000 didn't go very far. So the girls wrote another appeal to the OCR, pointing out that the men get full scholarships, and the best we can do is for a few women on each team to get in-state tuition. But it was a beginning.

I asked Coach Eaves, the Georgia Athletic Director at the time, "How do we ever give a full scholarship?" He said, "If you can prove to me that any athlete you are recruiting is the most highly rated athlete in the nation in her sport, I'll find the money for a full scholarship." I thought I knew how I could answer his challenge. All of the letters of intent had to be filed with the Association for Intercollegiate Athletics for Women (AIAW). So I called the AIAW and asked them about Terri Moody, a high school senior from right here in Athens, who was a terrific golfer. She led the nation in the number of schools who wanted to offer her a scholarship. When I showed the results to Coach Eaves, Terri became our first full scholarship female athlete. She lived up to her billing. Terri won the AIAW Individual National Championship in 1981.

But it's obvious that the athletic department was still only paying lip service, if even that, to the women's programs.

After a bitter fight, the NCAA took over women's college athletics from the AIAW in 1982. To become more Title IX compliant, the NCAA began providing money for tournaments and championships. The women's program at Georgia was moved from coordination in the department of physical education to the athletic department. The coaches' offices were moved from the women's physical education building to a little cubbyhole on the concourse in the coliseum. I was already beginning to ruffle the feathers a little. "It was Suzanne's idea that we move upstairs later, when the football coaches moved to Butts-Mehre," according to Liz.

Athletic Director Joel Eaves made a tremendous contribution to Georgia athletics. He was a man of unquestioned integrity. But he wasn't quite ready for Title IX. The demands he made on Liz before he would finance the first full-time scholarship for a female athlete exemplify his attitude. He certainly had no similar restrictions for scholarships in men's athletics. Liz had shown incredible patience during the early years of Title IX implementation—"in-implementation" is more accurate. She is soft-spoken, and she's a complete lady. But she felt that she had to question some of the athletic department's actions in order to carry out her responsibilities. For example, while she was in Los Angeles attending an AIAW convention, a women's tennis coach and a men's basketball coach (both males and both former Georgia athletes) had been approved by the all-male Athletic Board without even consulting Liz. When Coach Eaves called to tell her, Liz responded, "Wait a minute, this is not quite right. You couldn't wait until I got back to select these people? I think I need to have a little input here. I think we should do a search, not just appoint former athletes to be our coaches."

In the same telephone conversation, Coach Eaves informed Liz that the athletic board decided to have a national search for a women's athletic director. Liz had remained the coordinator of women's athletics until then. According to all accounts from the people she represented, Liz had been doing an outstanding job for several years. It didn't really make sense to have a national search. Faculty member Dr. Louise McBee, who later served in the Georgia State Legislature, exercised some of her legislative skills while still on the faculty. She thought the search was a slap in the face to Liz, and pointed out, "Look, we've got the best person we could find right here."

A sports writer who was following Title IX picked up on some of Liz's concerns and wrote about them, putting pictures of Coach Eaves and Liz on the front page of the sports section. Liz had been uncharacteristically vocal about what was going on. The athletic board indicated that they didn't like the kind of attitude she was displaying. Of course they didn't. How dare a woman ask for fair treatment of women in college athletics? She told me, "I could feel it all around me. It was really hard to get the job." But to their credit, the athletic board made one of the wisest decisions they've made, and Liz became the women's athletic director.

In the summer of 1979, Joel Eaves retired after a brilliant career as athletic director, and Vince Dooley assumed the position while remaining the football coach. Liz recalls, "At that time we were the most out-of-compliance Division I school in America." And for a few moments in Vince Dooley's first meeting with Liz, she thought women's athletics was in for more of the same treatment:

> Coach Dooley came to be me and said, "I don't understand Title IX. I don't have time for all this. I'm right in the middle of the football season." I thought, "Here we go again." But then Coach Dooley added, "Tell me what you need and we'll make things right." Could I believe what I was hearing? Did he really want to "make things right?" Then he said, "We need to hire a full-time coach. Which sport do you want to hire one for?" After discussion, he agreed with me that the first coach should be for basketball because it was the number-one high school sport for girls in Georgia.
>
> Then Coach Dooley said, "I want us to interview ten people." I said, "That's a lot of folks. You're practicing

football." He responded, "I would like to be involved with the first search for a full-time coach, however." That was pretty exciting. He really spent a lot of energy. A lot of the applicants were assistant coaches somewhere. And he agreed with me that we've got to find the most qualified person.

That was a great experience because Coach Dooley learned so much about what was going on in this country in women's sports and how far behind we were. And I soon learned that he doesn't like to be behind in anything. One of the applicants was assistant coach at UCLA—a lot of them were high school coaches. I had a lot of criticism during the early years because we hired more men coaches than we did women. But none of the women who applied had any idea of what recruiting was like because AIAW didn't allow recruiting. Nevertheless, we were going after the most qualified person.

Three years later, we were almost in complete compliance—with scholarships, with coaches, with locker rooms, etc. There was a real transformation between Eaves and Dooley. We had gone from the bottom to near the top in just three years.

Liz was right—unfortunately, only partially right. The University of Georgia had gone from the bottom to near the top in terms of many tangible assets, but women's sports at Georgia were still far behind men's sports in terms of attitudes toward women's sports shown by some men in the athletic department and in the media, which the sports information office influenced significantly. They were inexnperienced in working with women in sports. I was the first woman hired as a head coach, in 1983. In 1986, Beans Kelly came onboard to coach golf, but a third female coach was not hired until 1996, well after Beans and I had fought and won a lot of battles for the recognition of women's sports. During those years, some men in the athletic department gave me a hard time and were anything but supportive. They said things about me and treated me in a way that they would have fought any man for treating their wives. I pushed for more for my team, questioned decisions, and rarely accepted "No" from them without an explanation. According to an *Atlanta Constitution* article, they frequently referred to me as a "bitch."

Before I go into more detail, I must add that the University of Georgia Athletic Department is probably one of the better ones in the nation in terms of compliance with Title IX, and in terms of success in winning championships in women's sports.

But there's a vast chasm between compliance with Title IX and developing a culture in which the administration embraces women's sports as they do men's and allows them to promote the sports they— for whatever reasons—want to promote. And this chasm exists at nearly every university in the United States. So it's an NCAA problem.

UGA President Michael Adams holds prominent positions among college presidents in the administration of athletic programs. He's a member of the Knight Foundation Commission on Intercollegiate Athletics, he headed the search committee for a new Southeastern Conference Commissioner, and is the current president of the SEC. With the rapidly changing role of women's intercollegiate athletics, one in such a position needs to demonstrate his awareness of these changes and his equal support for both men's and women's sports by his public statements and, more important, by his actions. And frequently, he does. For example, in his newsletter to prominent alumni, the Board of Regents, and university staff, Dr. Adams had this to say: "Just last Saturday evening, a number of us watched as the university's women's gymnastics team edged out Alabama for the SEC Championship in one of the most hotly contested athletic events I have ever witnessed. Coach Suzanne Yoculan and the team are due our hearty congratulations as they move now to the regionals at Penn State, and hopefully, the national championships at UCLA." More comments like this one will begin to close the chasm.

While the University of Georgia is among the top-three or top-four schools in the country—maybe the top—in providing resources for women's athletics, and the success of its women's teams reflects this support, the athletic organization is still stacked with males. For example, in 2003 all seven of the alumni on the athletic board were males—four of them former football players. To be objective, I must point out that male members can be as supportive of women's sports as females. Member Jack Turner is a major supporter of gymnastics. He, his late wife, Nancy, and son, Jimmy, have endowed two gymnastics scholarships. They attend every meet and every national championship, wherever it is. Also, member Don Leebern III joined his father in endowing one of the scholarships Don Jr. started. But, reflecting the board's history, none of the twenty-three athletic board emeriti was a woman. Only among the faculty representatives do you find women— three of the nine are women. Only two women are listed among the thirteen-member "senior staff" in the athletic department.

Board members and senior staff should be selected on the basis of qualifications, without regard to gender. With the sudden rise in popularity of women's sports coming only recently, it's understandable that fewer women than men are currently qualified to fill positions of higher responsibility in the athletic hierarchy, and the gender ratio may legitimately never be in favor of women. But, at present, women are significantly under-represented in these important positions. Until women are better-represented in the governing bodies, suspicion will persist that their sports continue to get the short end of the stick.

I can remember when I got into the coaches car dealer program. Many coaches, including both football and men's basketball coaches, had tried to get a complimentary car from the local Ford dealer, Bill Winter. Bill owned Trussel Ford at the time, and he was a Georgia Tech grad. He was not interested in participating in the program until I went to Mr. Winter with a business plan. He explained to me why it wasn't a good business move to provide me or any coach with a car—to have someone put 3,000 to 5,000 miles on a car that he had to turn around and try to sell. His customers felt like they weren't buying new cars and wanted to pay a lot less for them, and he was losing money on the whole thing.

So I said, "Well, you lease cars. I don't have to have a new car. Why not give me something from the rental fleet that's already got miles on it. You can get your association with the university, thus supporting the community, get your tickets, and have a tax deduction." I just used a different approach, other than, "I'm a football coach, and you should want to supply me with this car," which was the approach then, over twenty years ago.

Well, I got the car, and I went back to Butts-Mehre to tell everyone, and they said, "No way, how did you accomplish that?" And they made comments such as, "How long were you in the room with him? What were you wearing?" I'm sure they were just kidding around, but they didn't give me any credit for having a plan or sales strategy. They didn't ask, "Congratulations, what did you say? How did you convince them?" It was just smart alec sexual comments. And everybody was laughing, thinking it was funny. And the men making the comments weren't the only ones laughing; others stood around and laughed with them. To me, they're just as guilty as the men who made the comments. But how could they explain how a woman could accomplish something that they could not? Naturally, it had to be sexual. It was insulting.

And then there were all the years spent trying to get the coliseum floor early enough on a Friday afternoon to set up for a competition that night. Andy Landers had basketball practice from 1 to 3 p.m. and Hugh Durham, our men's coach at the time, had practice from 3 to 5 p.m. We needed to be set-up by 3:30 p.m. in order to have the equipment ready for warm-ups. Coach Dooley did not want to get involved. I was told to work it out with the coaches. For ten years, I dealt with the problem myself. When we had a competition, Andy was willing to practice somewhere else, or practice before class, but Hugh Durham would not budge. He would agree to start a little earlier, maybe 2:30, but that was it. My assistant coaches and I would have the mats and equipment ready on the side of the basketball court and would stand there at 3:30 and wait until it suited Hugh Durham to finish. He would continue his practice as long as he felt like it, and no one from the administration would intervene on my behalf. As a matter of fact, in 1992, the UGA Athletic Department's policy on priority usage of the coliseum floor still read: (1) Men's basketball games (2) Women's basketball games (3) Men's basketball practice (4) Women's basketball practice (5) Women's gymnastics meets.

Every gymnastics coach in the SEC had a similar problem at the time. In Kentucky, our gym meets would sometimes start an hour late because of men's basketball practice. Finally, the SEC baseball coaches took a similar problem to Commissioner Roy Cramer, and he sent out a letter to athletic directors saying that gymnastics meets would take precedence over basketball practice. In February of 1991, Hugh Durham sent a memo to then Assistant Athletic Director Lee Hayley saying he would move basketball practice up to 11:30 a.m. to be of assistance to Lewis Gainey, but that it was a "tremendous inconvenience." His players would miss lunch at McWhorter Hall, so he wanted $230 transferred from the women's gym budget to his account to cover the cost of eighteen players per diem. Lewis, our staff member in charge of event management, had gone to Coach Durham concerning his practice and our meet that night. Lewis was always trying to help. I find it appalling that Durham would move his practice "as a favor to Lewis Gainey"! How about moving it because it is the right thing to do? That darn gymnastics, it just interferes with everything. How dare we have a meet? Lee Hayley, by the way, did not move money from my budget.

And then came the potential job offer at Florida. Long-time and highly successful gymnastics coach Ernestine Weaver resigned. I still, to this day, don't know all that happened. Ann Marie Rogers (now Ann Marie Lawler), recently retired associate athletic director for women's sports at Florida, contacted me about replacing Ernestine. I was told by people in the Georgia Athletic Department who knew people at Florida that I was the number one candidate for the Florida job. I'd been at Georgia just eight years and won two national championships. It was the Georgia contacts' opinion that it was just a matter of me naming my price. The people at Florida told me on the phone that by law they had to interview two or three people. They sent me my plane ticket to come for the interview.

Then Liz Murphey came to talk with me. This is the way Coach Dooley works; he never meets you face-to-face when there's anything controversial or personal. He sends somebody else to find out what's going on for him. Liz said, "Are you leaning towards Florida?" And then she'd report back to him. That's his management style, even concerning Andy Lander's recent job offer from Vanderbilt. Coach Dooley never called him and said, "We really want you to stay." President Adams called him, but not Coach Dooley. So the whole time I was sitting here with Liz Murphey, whom I trust and respect saying, "You know I really want the job. I think I'm gonna take it." It wasn't a bluff to get more money. Florida didn't make an offer; they wanted me to draw up the figures. I said, "Ann Marie Rogers expressed that she *wanted* me, and Georgia obviously didn't as Coach Dooley never called me to discuss it with me or to say, 'We want you to stay.'" It wasn't about the money. He could have probably given me very little if he had just said, "I want you to stay." It would have been over. But there was no phone call—nothing. So I told Liz I really felt like I was going to accept Florida's offer, and I was.

Then came the weekend of the SEC meeting at Destin, Florida, for football coaches and athletic directors. Liz Murphy went down to the meeting, and Ann Marie Lawler was there. The next thing I knew, while I was at home that weekend, preparing to leave for the Florida interview, I got a phone call from Liz saying Ann Marie told her they had hired the Penn State coach and they were canceling my interview. I don't know what changed. Ann Marie had told me they were interviewing three people. Liz said, "You don't need to go down there. They've already hired another coach." And then Claude Felton (Georgia's Sports Information Director) called me fifteen minutes later and said, "Coach Dooley's gonna give you a $6,000 raise, and he says it's okay for you to say to the paper that you've withdrawn your name because you love it here so much. We'll give a real positive spin to this, and you don't have to say that they hired someone else. You can save face, and Florida has agreed that you could say this."

I said, "No! I'm not doing that. Coach Dooley's willing to offer me $6,000 more when I didn't even get the job? Why is he giving me $6,000 more now? They canceled the interview. Why didn't he give me $6,000 more two weeks ago to show his desire to keep me?" The timing seemed weird to me.

I called Liz Murphey back and said, "You'll have to tell Ann Marie, she'll have to call me herself or I'll be on her doorstep Tuesday morning, because I have a ticket. Her commitment was with me, not you. Why are you involved?" So Ann Marie did call me and said they had hired Judy Avener (now Judy Markel), but gave no explanation.

Here's the statement the University of Georgia released to the media in June 1992:

> Athens—Georgia gymnastics coach, Suzanne Yoculan, who has been a finalist for the Florida coaching job, received a $6,000 raise to about $46,000 a year.
>
> The move came about partially because of the team's runner-up finish in the NCAA Championships and because the program has been designated a "special emphasis" sport.
>
> "The idea was born several months ago and finalized a few weeks ago," Associate Athletic Director Claude Felton said. "It's really a matter of equity [between men's and women's sports]." Felton said the special emphasis designation could mean additional support staff and promotional emphasis.
>
> "I was surprised [about the raise] initially because I didn't have the interview at Florida and Georgia didn't have to give me anything," said Yoculan, 38. "It just reaffirmed their commitment to the gymnastics program."

The "special emphasis sport" was primarily a media ploy. Coach Dooley sent a memo to the head coaches announcing that gymnastics had been made the second "major emphasis sport" (he used the term, "major," instead of "special," as was reported in the media. Women's basketball had been designated one several years before.) But aside from getting our own secretaries and a few pages added to our media guides, the "major emphasis" designation didn't change much—no significant changes in salaries, travel, and other promotional activities. It was still the case that if a nonrevenue-producing sport was to be promoted, the coach had to do it.

A little later, I learned the University of Georgia Athletic Association wanted me to stay. The senior associate athletic director had spoken with a friend on the Florida staff and suggested that Florida not start hiring coaches from other conference teams. Up until that time, it had not been done. Apparently, the Florida people heeded the suggestion.

I'm sure someone interfered. I think what happened on the Georgia end was that they felt if I went down there and Florida offered me $10,000 or $20,000 more, which they were going to do, Georgia would have to counter with a substantial raise and it would throw everything off-kilter here with the other coaches. At the time, Florida was paying all their coaches of all sports the highest salaries in the country if those coaches had successful records. Florida paid top dollar to get and keep the best coaches. Some coaches feel there has been an agreement going on for years that they don't want to get into bidding wars for coaches of nonrevenue-producing sports. Some athletic directors still cooperate in holding down salaries. Coaches should be rewarded for the job they do, based on merit and longevity. Sarah Patterson, Greg Marsden, and I are the market for college gymnastics coaches, so if you hold us down, you hold down the market.

Our current football coach has his first season, and he does what he's supposed to do. He wins. He has an eight and three record. Coach Dooley initiates a $60,000 raise for him. Great! Smart move. Giving him a raise at the beginning of his career demonstrates confidence in the job he is doing and instills loyalty and commitment from him to the University of Georgia. But on the other hand, the coaches of nontraditional sports who are winning championships are told it is our job to win and that our bonus package compensates us for our NCAA titles, so we never get a substantial raise for merit. This is not equitable.

I was still smarting a year later, following our record-breaking 1993 national championship. I got my regular bonus for winning the championship and naturally no raise. I never got a raise because we did well. On March 13, 1994, Scott Reid wrote an article in the *Atlanta*

Constitution titled, "Special Report: Women's Coaching Salaries: What Price Fairness?: Landers pay: The next Kemp case?" As the title implies, Andy Landers was questioning his salary. He was making only about 60 percent of the salary made by several SEC coaches who were less successful than he was and 45 percent of what Pat Summitt, the head basketball coach at Tennessee, was making. In responding to the press question about Andy's salary relative to Pat Summitt's salary, Coach Dooley spoke too hastily: "Has Andy won three NCAA Championships like Summitt has? We don't draw six, seven-thousand people like they do." UGA gymnastics had won three NCAA Championships, and average attendance at Georgia's gymnastics meets was exceeding attendance at Tennessee's women's basketball games at the time. I think this exchange exposed Coach Dooley's failure to keep up with what was happening in women's athletics—some of it right under his nose—despite Liz Murphey's appeals for better pay for her coaches. And what about my salary? It was less than that of the Georgia head coaches for men's golf, baseball, and track, yet none of them had won a national championship.

In the article, Pat Summitt was quoted, referring to Andy: "He's long been considered one of the country's top coaches. He's got to be really frustrated." More important, Liz Murphey said, "I think Sue Gunter of LSU and Andy may be two of the more experienced coaches in the conference, and they may be the worst paid. I'm sure we have the worst-paid assistant coaches in this part of the country. My amazement is why do they stay?" Liz, who had been totally loyal to Coach Dooley in appreciation for his supporting her in gaining scholarships and facilities, finally spoke publicly in criticism of his salary policy. She had obviously been frustrated, too, in her failed attempts to help her coaches gain better pay. And she showed courage.

While all of this was being written in the press, I dropped by Andy's office. We were both frustrated, and we started discussing the situation. His contract was up, and I asked if he was going to get a substantial raise, and we shared information. I told him I knew a lawyer, Alan Manheim, who worked on gender equity issues. I told Andy I was going to call

Alan and see if he would negotiate my contract, and I offered Andy the opportunity to meet with him too. Eventually, Alan went to Coach Dooley on behalf of Andy and me, but it didn't have anything to do with suing the university, as was widely rumored. Coach Dooley asked Alan to leave and stated that he did not negotiate contracts with outside representatives. But at the time, Coach Dooley had an attorney who negotiated his contract with the athletic association board.

Neither Andy nor I ever authorized Alan Manheim to sue the university. We wanted him to negotiate our contracts. As a matter of fact, I just wanted Coach Dooley to do what was right and raise my salary up to what it should be, based on merit, compared to the coaches of the men's sports at Georgia. Coach Dooley, once again, never called Andy or me; he maneuvered his position through the media and made it look like we were hurting the university for personal gain. King and Spalding's attorneys advised Coach Dooley to settle the matter, as our salaries were clearly a problem from a gender equity standpoint. In particular, because Coach Dooley himself had named women's basketball and women's gymnastic as Georgia's "major emphasis sports" for the sole reason of being in compliance with Title IX, but our salaries were not raised in accordance. So one afternoon in President Knapp's office, Coach Dooley, the UGA president, and Andy and I agreed on our salaries. It was comical; Andy and I had to run back and forth to the library during negotiations in order to talk with Alan Manheim. Coach Dooley still would not have our attorney in the room with him during the process.

I never considered what I did daring, but others point out that threatening legal action against a recalcitrant athletic department was a courageous move. Just a year earlier, Marianne Stanley, the highly successful basketball coach at the University of Southern California, sued USC over her salary. The suit resulted in her losing her job and being blackballed by the athletic administration community so she couldn't get a job elsewhere. Eventually she lost her suit.

Although I was not trying to lead a crusade, apparently my case ended up helping a lot of people across the country. It had a trickle-down effect—first of all, here at Georgia. Coach Dooley wasn't going to raise my salary and not do something about Jack Bauerle,'s and Jeff Wallace's and all the other coaches' salaries. They all got considerable raises too. And then, secondly, it helped coaches at other schools. Sarah Patterson wasn't going to stand back knowing I was making $40,000 more than her. I got calls and other means of communication from coaches all over the country in all sports telling me how much they appreciated my opening the door.

The negotiation process took its toll on me. It came while I was preparing my team to defend its national championship at Salt Lake City in just a couple of weeks. Because Coach Dooley would not meet with me and Andy together to discuss our salaries and would not allow our attorney to be present, I had to face an older, more experienced, powerful man alone. He had obviously been angered by Alan Manheim's approach. My entire future was at stake. The meeting was almost routine for him. During the media accounts of the negotiations, I received threatening phone calls from high-level university administrators. And after the salary negotiations, the already cold shoulders got colder.

On April 17, Scott Reid, the same reporter who wrote the article about Andy, asked to interview me in my office. He caught me at a time when I was particularly harried, and in the middle of the interview, I just let go. With tears in my eyes I told him:

> It's very lonely. The last two years I've just sort of holed up here in my office by myself. I'm not happy. I'm not happy here at all. The only thing that makes me happy here is that gymnastics team. I would do absolutely anything for them.
>
> Some of the people at Georgia outright don't like me. Sure I'm aggressive. Sometimes I have tunnel vision. Sure I've probably stepped on some toes along the way. What coach hasn't? So why does that make me a bitch? I just want to be treated fairly.
>
> I've chosen a certain path to take, and with that I've made a lot of enemies. But I resent being called a bitch. I resent

being judged by someone who doesn't even know me. I'm not going to let any of this slow me down. It's not going to stop me. No way.

My interview upset Coach Dooley. As usual, he didn't arrange to talk to me and ask how he could help. Instead, he arranged for Blake Giles, a local sports writer, to interview me as I was boarding the plane to go to nationals at Salt Lake City. Coach Dooley instructed me before the interview to essentially rescind the statements I'd made to Scott Reid in my interview with Blake. I was too tired of confrontation to cry, "Where's the first amendment?" I complied with Coach Dooley's request. Can you imagine a worse time for a coach's boss to publicly reprimand her—while she's preparing to lead her team in the defense of the national title. I'm not blaming Coach Dooley for my not-so-calm decisions in the final rotation of the national championships. A coach should be able to overcome adversity and deal with unexpected problems. But I was still feeling like the red-headed stepchild when I got back to Athens after coming in third at the national championships, when every statistic indicated clearly that we were the best team in the country.

Just think for a minute. Can you imagine Coach Dooley telling the head football coach or the head men's basketball coach that he'd arranged an interview for him to rescind a statement he'd made in an interview with the press?

Then a dramatic occurrence took place. When I walked into my office on Monday morning following nationals, there were stacks and stacks of letters in envelopes with all sorts of different shapes and colors. Some were addressed by hand. Others were typed with business decals on the envelopes. After the way I'd been treated, I expected the letters to be carbon copies of letters to Coach Dooley calling for him to fire me. I almost considered just pulling up a big trash can and brushing the stacks into it without opening them. But I decided to sample a couple of them. The first was not a carbon copy of a letter to Coach Dooley. It was addressed to me. And it was sympathetic and supportive in a way that brought a different type of tears to my eyes. That gave me courage to open another. And it was the same. Then I opened another. The same. I just sat there opening one supportive letter after another, crying with appreciation as I read each of them.

Of the three or four hundred letters, only one or two were critical. Several letters were from "heavy hitters." Specifically, I recall letters from James White of Birmingham, Alabama, who had served on the Athletic Board, and Stephen Selig III, from the family for whom Selig Circle in front of Butts-Mehre is named, in support of my salary increase.

Hundreds of fans had read the interview with Scott Reid and were so appreciative of what our team had done over the course of ten years that they took the time to write letters—mostly by hand—to tell me they supported me and our program.

The letters gave me a new sense of belonging—not to the Athletic Administration but to the hundreds of gymnastics fans and supporters throughout the southeast. They gave me new confidence and determination to keep the University of Georgia's gymnastics program at the top of the heap. My final words in the interview with Scott Reid were reinforced: "But it's not going to stop me. No way."

This experience was helping me size up the gender inequities at Georgia, which mirrored the situation at other schools across the country. Title IX had impacted the granting of scholarships, so that most institutions had at least half as many scholarships for women as they did for men. It had impacted the quality of facilities, too. Women's facilities were being upgraded to at least adequate condition. But even though significant improvements have been made in women's sports programs, treatment of women's sports and the staffs associated with them is still as different as night and day from that of the traditional sports of football and men's basketball. For example, when the football team wins a conference championship, the head trainer gets a bonus, along with the other football coaches. When we win a championship, our trainer doesn't get a bonus. And travel in chartered planes was unheard of for gymnastics teams until recently, while football and men's basketball teams traveled in chartered planes almost routinely.

More important than the differences in tangible benefits was what Title IX couldn't do—change the century-old culture in the athletic departments across the country, where there was general resentment of women's sports similar to the resentment I'd felt at Georgia. You just can't legislate attitudes and culture. Many athletic administrators have been brought up in a culture where women did not participate in sports. So, for them, change takes time.

Some influential Georgia loyalists cannot swallow the equality of women's sports. Loran Smith—longtime executive secretary of the Georgia Bulldog Club, who does the sidelines comments for the Georgia football radio broadcasts and writes two columns in the local newspaper—is paid by the University of Georgia Athletic Association. But he almost always writes only about men's sports. I was in my sixteenth season and had won four national championships before he wrote about my team for the first and only time. He attended the Georgia-Alabama meet in 1999. Loran's article indicated that it was his first time attending a gymnastics meet. After dropping the names of several prominent spectators—name-dropping is a trademark of Loran's columns—his article focused almost entirely on my success at promotion and the "spectacle" in the coliseum.

But there were belittling comments throughout the piece. For example, he implied that a men's basketball game with Kentucky would draw more fans. How can that be? We had a sellout. The best the basketball game could do would be to draw an equal number of fans. And he suggested that the event might not really have been a sellout: "That many of the tickets were complimentary is not important." There were no more complimentary tickets than there would have been for that Georgia-Kentucky basketball game. Why was he compelled to compare us to basketball anyway? The only mention of the gymnasts was, "First of all, there's something exciting about pretty girls dressed like they were heading to the beach in a one-piece bathing suit."

Loran's columns about men's sports—and there are many—usually mention something about athletics. The closest he came in this article was, "I haven't said anything about her ability to coach. I'm not knowledgeable about such things, but I do know she can promote and recruit." For a journalist, who is supposed to be knowledgeable about sports (the piece was on the sports page), to write that he's not knowledgeable about a coach's ability to coach is ludicrous. Most journalists aren't coaches or experts in coaching themselves, so they rely on the established accomplishments of coaches to evaluate them. Would Loran say he's not knowledgeable about the coaching of Mike Krzyzewski at Duke, Bobby Bowden at Florida State, or Georgia's own Jack Bauerle and Manuel Diaz? Of course not. He knows from their accomplishments that they are all great coaches, and a cursory examination of the media guide—available to all journalists—reveals that my accomplishments speak for themselves. His reluctance to acknowledge my coaching achievements reflects the worst in biased journalism, and more important, it reflects his attitude towards women's sports. Why would a respected journalist write such an article?

Bill Hartman Jr., father of the Atlanta television sports commentator, Bill Hartman III, has been one of the icons of Georgia sports history. He is one of the greatest football players ever to play for Georgia and has long been associated with the athletic department, coaching kickers as a volunteer coach for the football team and heading the Georgia Student Educational Fund. His contributions to the athletic program at Georgia over many years are monumental. But in 1995, when I was appearing on a call-in television show, Bill phoned and chastised me in a most ungentlemanly fashion—certainly not characteristic of his usual demeanor. Someone had called in and asked me if our attendance was better than men's basketball. I replied that our average attendance was higher. Mr. Hartman did not like my saying that, but it was a fact.

Chauvinism can be a deep-seeded characteristic, reflective of one's life experiences over many years. And sometimes the person exhibiting chauvinism can be totally surprised when his attitudes are revealed. A case in point is what Dan Magill experienced. Dan is the most respected and winningest college tennis coach in history. After he turned over the reins of coaching the men's team to Manuel Diaz, Dan remained active as the coordinator of both men's and women's tennis. He had raised money over the years to build the finest and most aesthetically beautiful varsity tennis stadium in the country. It is the site of about 90 percent of the NCAA National Championships. When the women's tennis coach asked that his team be allowed to play its home matches in the stadium, instead of on the women's practice courts, Dan refused, pointing to the stadium's long association with the men's team. Of course, Dan was forced to give in, but he took a thrashing in the press. One woman, writing to the editor, pointed out that he referred to the teams in an article as the "men's team and the girls' team." Perhaps it's a subtle distinction but one that reflects his thinking—not "men and women" or "boys and girls," but "men and girls." Here is a highly revered man, one of my personal heroes, having difficulty adjusting to fair treatment for men and women in tennis.

And it's not only individuals who display chauvinism, it's the Athletic Administration. The incidents I'm about to describe probably did not affect the nontraditional sports directly, or perhaps they did. But they illustrate the point that the three traditional sports, all men's sports, of course, remain in the minds of the Georgia athletic hierarchy as the only ones of importance. In the same athletic year, 1998–1999, four University of Georgia teams won national championships: men's golf (Coach Chris Haack), women's gymnastics (Suzanne Yoculan), women's swimming and diving (Jack Bauerle), and men's tennis (Manuel Diaz). This was unprecedented in Georgia history. The performances of these teams led the University of Georgia to second in the nation in the Sears Cup race, our highest finish ever. Coach Dooley was extremely proud of this feat, and he gave it considerable publicity. He even had a large colorful picture framed of the four championship rings and distributed copies to coaches and supporters. As a part of the recognition, he asked the four coaches to make three-minute presentations at the meeting of the prestigious Atlanta Bulldog Club, a stop on the annual tour by Coach Dooley and the head football coach to larger booster clubs to promote the upcoming football season. We were all excited because two or three thousand people attend the Atlanta meeting. It would give us an excellent opportunity to tell them something about our sports—a great promotional experience.

We entered the hall in Colony Square, where the meeting was held, and sat together in the lower part of the dais. Coach Dooley came over to the four of us and said that we were not going to speak. My bubble was burst. I had looked forward to speaking to this group with tremendous excitement. But I think, as disappointed as we were, we could have understood that the schedule was tight and there just wasn't time for our collective twelve minutes of presentation. But then it happened. Both the new basketball coach and the new baseball coach (coaches of traditional sports), neither of whom had ever won even one game for the University of Georgia—much less a national championship—were introduced and asked to speak from the upper dais. We were only introduced as the coaches of the four teams that had won national championships in the same year and allowed to stand and wave at the audience. We were definitely subordinated to the two new coaches—both of whom have already left the University of Georgia.

In appreciation of this accomplishment and to give our football fans an opportunity to see the coaches of these other sports, Coach Dooley invited the four coaches to travel to the Georgia-Florida football game (traditionally held in Jacksonville, Florida) with the football team entourage. All four of us were thrilled again to be included and honored. We traveled from the airport to the team hotel on the staff bus, and when we got off, fans were yelling "GymDogs" and cheering for me—football fans yelling, "GymDogs." Imagine that. It felt great!

To add to the insult again, when we arrived at the athletic association pregame dinner, we discovered that no arrangements had been made for us to be introduced and no special seating arrangements had been made for us. The athletic association had given big publicity to its four-in-one-year NCAA Championship teams, but they did a halfway, at best, job of paying tribute to us, where it would have really meant something. I think the fans and other guests would have enjoyed the opportunity to meet and talk with us. They certainly indicated that as we got off the bus.

But instead of being honored, the four coaches who had won the national titles and who were most responsible for the second-place finish in the Sears Cup competition were left to entertain ourselves. While I roamed the lobby of the hotel looking for something to do, Coach Dooley was entertaining special friends of the athletic association at a breakfast for our new basketball coach, Jim Harrick. We, of course, were not invited.

And then there are the locker rooms at Stegeman Coliseum. The athletic association has renovated the men's basketball locker room three times in the last ten years and paid for everything. Simultaneously, Andy Landers, our women's basketball coach, renovated his own locker room. I mean literally, he did it himself. With help from some donors and friends, especially Vickie and Leon Farmer, Andy laid the tile, ripped out walls, and bargained for services and materials.

I didn't fully realize the depth of the tradition of men's sports in college, particularly football, until 1999 when I read a series of articles about chauvinism in sports in Georgia by two *Atlanta Journal-Constitution* reporters. One article, titled, "Georgia treats girl athletes, second-class," revealed the unbelievable situation controlling high school sports in Georgia. The State Department of Education totally abdicated responsibility for high school sports, turning it over to a private organization founded in 1905—that's no typo, nineteen hundred and five, almost a hundred years ago—called the Georgia High School Association (GHSA). It is run by a committee, and currently out of 39 members, 2 are women. From 1905 until 1999, 5 women had been among the 2,500 committee members who served.

The worst part about this system is that the GHSA is responsible for all extracurricular activities, including music, drama, etc. But it has only one interest: you guessed it, football—to the exclusion of every other sport and extracurricular endeavor. So far, the GHSA has gotten away with this enormous hoax—having it both ways—claiming immunity from Title IX because it is private and claiming immunity from a lawsuit against its activities because it is "quasi-public." The Georgia State School Superintendent says she has no control since it receives no state funds. But it does, indirectly. And all the activities it oversees participate in one way or another on school-system-owned property and are supported by school system employees. Do you see why I use the term "criminal"? The deeply imbedded culture of football as the only important sport, of course, is carried over into college.

Football gets us to the other most discussed topic about Title IX, the "unintended consequences." Sadly, as financially strapped college athletic departments have tried to comply with the requirements of Title IX, a number have eliminated some men's sports, most notably wrestling and gymnastics. And they have provided more scholarships for women than for men on teams where the women's and men's teams are similar—tennis, golf, swimming, and basketball, for example. The chauvinists are quick to place the blame on Title IX, even though most programs still have more men on athletic scholarships, as does Georgia, than women. Why eliminate men's sports? The answer is simple. They don't distribute the men's scholarships in a sane manner. The number of men's basketball players on scholarship is about two and one half times the minimum number of players required to play the game. The same is true of women's basketball and women's gymnastics. This seems fair for these sports, which require different talent for different positions and have a reasonably high injury frequency. Perhaps tennis could get by with only one and a half times the number required for a match because the players compete as individuals, and there are no "positions" in tennis. So why are there almost eight times more scholarships for football than the number of players required to play the game?

Mary Jo Kane, at the University of Minnesota, puts it this way: "It's a very clever strategy to have men's minor sports pitted against women. The irony in all this is that if men's nonrevenue sports would team up with women's sports and go after football, reducing the size and expenditures in football, you could add sports for women and very comfortably support men's nonrevenue sports."

Before I go further, let me reiterate that I love football. And some of my closest friends are football coaches or work for the football program at Georgia. My fiancé Don Leebern played tackle for Georgia on the

1959 SEC Championship Team. But regardless of my love for football, I am convinced that reducing scholarships for football is at least worth serious examination. I'm afraid it's not easy to implement Mary Jo's idea. Whenever one suggests reducing the number of football scholarships, there are spontaneous cries from members of the "football family" that reducing the number would ruin the game and consequently kill the cash cow that helps finance the other sports at the university. They don't—they can't—explain how reducing scholarships will ruin the sport.

Representation of women is even worse in the sports media. The *Athens Banner-Herald* has no women sports writers, although there are as many high school and college women's teams among the local sports they cover as there are men's teams. There are no former gymnasts on the staff, so they can't cover gymnastics with the same first-hand feel that they can football, men's basketball, and baseball. Although the GymDogs' average attendance is second to football among all sports at Georgia, men's basketball and baseball receive much more space in the papers. There is no coverage of gymnastics teams other than Georgia's as there is for the three traditional men's sports. And they never write about gymnastics during the off-season, as they do the traditional men's sports.

In the fall of 2003, the number-one gymnastics recruit in the country gave an oral commitment to attend the University of Georgia. The same weekend a basketball player, ranked about one-hundredth, gave an oral commitment. A significant article was written about his commitment in the local paper. Nothing was reported about the gymnast. A week later another top-five gymnast orally committed to Georgia and another about one-hundredth basketball player committed. The same thing happened. I repeat, over nine thousand people attend gymnastics meets at Georgia; six or seven thousand attend men's basketball games. I have tons of files illustrating the bias in the press, but this one example should show that it exists—big time.

The bias is evident even in the coverage of high school sports. When both a boys' high school soccer game and a girls' game are covered, the boys' game is written about first, with the girls' game coverage cut short because space runs out. The easiest way to edit is just to cut the latter part of the article. My daughter Alexis scored fifty-four goals in high school soccer one year and was named player of the year, but the boy who was named player of the year and scored only half as many goals was mentioned first in the article about their selection.

Now get this. The new sports editor for *The Red and Black*, the University of Georgia student newspaper, recently wrote an opinion piece, on the editorial page, indicating that he didn't like women's sports. With an attitude like that, how can he be sports editor for a paper representing a school with more women's varsity sports than men's? At least the kid was honest.

One of the myths espoused by the anti-women sports activists is that women really aren't interested in participating in organized sports. On the contrary, perhaps the biggest surprise resulting from providing young women opportunities to participate in organized sports is that young girls, high school girls, and college women have stampeded into programs as they open. And this stampede has been almost totally without prodding. Given the rapid rate of growth in participation up until now, it is likely that within a few years the number of women participating in high school and college sports will exceed the number of men. At Athens Academy, a local private school where my daughter played basketball and soccer, it's already happened. Over 90 percent of all high school girls are on organized interscholastic teams while the percentage of boys is in the eighties. The headmaster tells me that there was no more encouragement for the girls than there was for the boys.

The varsity soccer team at the University of Georgia can't accommodate the number of women who want to participate in collegiate soccer—even as walk-ons. In addition to the varsity team, whose participants receive scholarships, there is a totally volunteer club team. The club team receives only the level of financial support afforded by the student activities program, so the participants augment the funds to pay for equipment and travel. They travel over several states, participating in intercollegiate club-level competition.

Jack Bauerle coaches both men's and women's swimming and diving at Georgia, so he's in an authoritative position to judge women's and men's interests in participating in college sports. Jack says that after the impact of Title IX was fully in place, the interests of men and women in swimming and diving at the college level are essentially the same. When you see the results of opening opportunities for young women to participate in organized sports, you recognize how wrong it was to deny them these opportunities for so many years.

In many respects—largely because of Coach Dooley's leadership— the culture chasm at Georgia is less severe than at almost any other school. Coach Dooley and I have had our confrontational moments during the years. But I'd be terribly remiss not to praise him for all that he has done for the University of Georgia and for women's athletics. He retired after forty years of service to the university, building one of the top college athletic programs in the country—tops in every respect. You read Liz Murphey's assessment of how he changed women's athletics, going from near the bottom in Title IX compliance to near the top in just three years. He's effected changes from a position of strength, which results in change to stay ahead of, not just to stay up with, your competitors. Women's sports will continue to benefit from plans he has already laid.

And Coach Dooley has made certain that the program at Georgia not only stays as good as it is, but that it continues to improve. He did this by supporting President Adams' selection of Damon Evans, Coach Dooley's protégé for six years, to succeed him as the UGA Athletic Director. Damon has been an astute student under Coach Dooley, and he's developed some great ideas to implement as he takes over. For example, Damon has said that every senior staff member and every head coach in the athletic department must attend at least one event every year of every team in the Georgia Athletic Association—all twenty of them. He knows, from the inside, the places where we can improve. He knows the people—their strengths and their weaknesses. And, as far as the gymnastics program is concerned, he already has in place plans to renovate and expand Stegeman Coliseum to include a new gymnastics practice facility.

Damon says he wants to restore the closeness of coaches and

athletes of different sports that we had back in the days when we were in our cubbyholes in the coliseum. Getting more coaches, better facilities, and more support staff has been wonderful, but it has taken us away from each other, and Damon wants us to come together as a family. I believe this will help move toward bridging that culture gap.

But even all of these moves won't completely bring women's sports to where they should be unless we all work at it. As stated earlier, it's a culture problem, and you can't legislate culture. Culture changes slowly. It usually takes people, who have grown up in a culture similar to the new culture you're trying to develop, coming into an area. But as an individual—as a coach—you can do what I'm doing. Build your team to be the best it can be. Promote attendance at your sport to reach the full potential that interest in the sport suggests. Continually remind the media and college and school administrators to look at women's and men's sports objectively. If we do this, someday women's sports will get what they deserve. It may be less than men's sports. It may be greater. But it will be fair.

And finally, every chance you get, remind the university administrators that this is an institution of higher education, not professional sports.

Problems and Progress

College women's gymnastics has undergone major changes in the past twenty years, with substantially higher average-meet attendance, more skilled gymnasts doing more exciting routines, and greater popularity overall. Understandably, there are still some kinks to work out. But we're making progress. Here are some forthcoming improvements that address things we had previously identified as changes that should be made.

First, the rules for scoring in college gymnastics: There are various levels of rules ranging from those for judging beginners up to those for the elite level. The NCAA gymnastics committee, working in concert with the college coaches, develops the rules for judging college gymnastics. In general, college rules are a slight modification of the Junior Olympics Level-10 rules. I've definitely changed my opinion about the rules. Obviously in the early years, Georgia was one of the few teams doing considerably more difficulty than what was required by the collegiate rules. I never thought, as some coaches do, that we should have our own set of rules for collegiate gymnastics; I wanted to use the J.O. Level-10 code without modification. I thought we shouldn't make it easier for collegiate gymnasts to have a 10.0 start value. I felt like we, at Georgia, were not rewarded enough for the difficulty that we were doing—in most cases, far in excess of the college rules requirements for a 10.0 start value (maximum score). But even when I was expressing my feelings, I wasn't expressing them because we were losing—we weren't losing; we were still winning. But I felt that we should have been rewarded more; that a greater differentiation should have been given between scores—even within our own team—when a gymnast performed a more difficult routine.

But there are many conflicting factors to consider in deciding which rules we should adopt. First, of course, is the safety of the gymnasts. We don't want to encourage gymnasts to attempt routines they can't perform with reasonable safety. Then there is the desire to establish rules that provide the better teams a fair chance of winning. But, in contrast to this, there is a need to develop a reasonable level of parity, so that just a few teams don't dominate the sport to the degree that competition is reduced too much. The judges don't want to see all gymnasts with 10.0 start values, because with no separation in start values the only separation among gymnasts' scores would be based on execution, with no credit given for performing more challenging routines. But the fans want the excitement of the occasional perfect 10.0, the "home run" in college gymnastics, so the code of points should not make 10.0 scores unattainable, as they have become in elite-level competition and in men's gymnastics. And, of course, coaches must select routines that gymnasts can perform with a high level of consistency; otherwise, deductions for mistakes would outweigh the advantage of the higher start value.

So now I've really almost taken a 180-degree turn on this. The reason is that the choice of the difficulty is just that, a choice the coach makes. It's a strategy. You don't have to choose it. So for a coach to argue the point that his or her team is doing more difficulty and they're not going to be rewarded is the result of a choice he or she makes. If you don't want to do the more difficult skills, don't do them. It's part of the strategy of collegiate gymnastics. As you can see, my opinion has changed.

I've seen injuries hit us hard during the past few years. Some of them have been on the more difficult skills, like Sierra's front double twist when she tore her ACL. It's an elite-level she didn't have to do. But on the other side, Marline Stephens tore her Achilles tendon doing a simple skill. So it would have happened anyway. It had nothing to do with the difficulty of the skill, at least at the time she was hurt. Certainly the risk of injury is greater when you attempt a higher level of difficulty, because you have to train more hours.

After being here for twenty years and seeing the response of the fans when we score a "Perfect 10.0," I think it would be the worst thing that could happen to collegiate gymnastics if the 10.0 were essentially taken out of the sport because we make the requirements for a 10.0 so difficult. The home run for everybody to experience would be taken away. That's the way the fans look at gymnastics. The home run in gymnastics is the 10.0. We have to have it. And the best way to continue having the occasional 10.0 is by continuing with the current system, J.O. rules as modified for college.

I think the J.O. rules, the rules that are used for the 9-and 10-level gymnasts in competition, make for a perfect situation as long as we retain some modifications. The elites can drop back to those rules. Some gymnasts like to cut back, and some want to continue to do more difficulty. Heather Stepp said, "There's no way I'm gonna cut back," and Lucy Wener didn't like to do double backs off the beam and said, "I'm never gonna do double back dismounts again. I hate it. I don't want to do it. I only did it because I had to do it in elite gymnastics. I don't wanna do it in college." And Lucy did very well for four years here and stayed healthy by doing lower level skills on some apparatus. I think when former elite gymnasts first come to college, it's a pride thing. But after a while, when you're in a competition and you see you're doing more difficulty than gymnasts who are doing a lot less and they are beating you because their execution's better and they stuck their dismounts, you begin to question the level of difficulty you choose to include in your routines. Your opponent did a shorter bars routine, and they stuck their dismount, and they scored higher than you. You had three D-level release moves to their one, yet they scored higher.

From the very beginning, I believed in the least amount of difficulty possible on balance beam. No difficult mount. Get on the beam with an easy mount. Don't start off with a problem or mistake. Georgia has been doing that for twenty years. And I saw our current U.S. National Team just adopted that. At the USA Championships, where they were picking the team for the World's Championships, Marta Karolyi was not allowing them to do difficult mounts. She wanted them to start out easy. I've always felt like that. And on bars, I've felt that a short bars routine reduces your chance of a lot of execution deductions. Meet the requirements and have a big dismount. We would get our difficulty in the dismount. That's the last thing the judge sees, and that's what he or she remembers.

For years, Michigan and Utah were doing much better on bars than we were doing from the standpoint of total composition, and we were beating them. Depending on the event and depending on the gymnast, I like to play it both ways. It fits in with my general philosophy that I don't want to clone the gymnasts in terms of the types of girls we have on our team, and I don't want to clone how we do things. It's different for different girls. Kimmie Arnold had the most difficult balance beam of anyone, but she could hit it every time. She didn't miss. It depends on what they want to do and whether they can do it safely and consistently.

It makes it tough on the judges when so many gymnasts perform the Yurchenko full vault. So many parts of the vault are overlooked with the emphasis on sticking. On vaulting, especially, I'd like to see lower start values assigned to some vaults. But most college coaches want to make it easier. Their argument is, and I can certainly see this, the more 10.0 start values you have, the more competition there is among the teams, so different teams have a chance of winning. That's good for our sport. What's not good for our sport is if we only have a certain number of teams that dominate. Only four teams have won a national championship in twenty-two years. We need to have upsets in gymnastics like you have in basketball and soccer. Now, with the modified rules and one vault, we have a lot more upsets. For example, a tenth-ranked team today can beat a second-ranked team.

Biased judges: In general, gymnastics judges are exceptionally skilled. They have to go through a rigorous training, testing, and apprentice process before they are qualified to judge. But they are human, and they can be biased in one of four ways: (1) Judges can show favor for a specific team. To me, this is the worst example of biased judging, and it is probably the least prevalent. (2) They can be biased in scoring all gymnasts higher than the guidelines would suggest—or lower. (3) Judges in one region can, as a group, score higher or lower than judges in another region. (4) Judges can be influenced by the reputations of teams or individual gymnasts to favor those with better rankings. Ten years ago, biased judging was a tremendous problem and remained so up through the 2004 season—when judges were selected by the coaches. The bottom line is that to some degree gymnastics is a subjective sport. All in all, I believe that the judges have a lot of integrity. They're put in difficult situations to judge and separate their personal relationships with team members or coaches from their judging. The problem has been that, except for a few conferences, the coaches have decided who can judge and who cannot during the regular season. In some instances, if judges didn't judge a certain way, they didn't get asked back. Selection of judges should have been taken entirely out of the coaches' hands. It's as simple as that.

And now it has been. At the annual meeting of the National Association of Collegiate Gymnastics Coaches-Women, held in St. Louis after the 2004 season, it was decided that beginning with the 2005 season all judges will be assigned by regional assigners (voluntary participation for the first year) and will be coordinated by Carole Ide of the National Association of Women's Gymnastic's Judges (NAWGJ). This practice will apply to all regions. Judges can be selected from more than one region, which should help standardize judging differences from region to region.

Having judges assigned by a national committee should open the door to remedy another problem. Because of past inconsistent and biased judging, various practices have been established for computing a team's Regional Qualifying Score (RQS) in an attempt to mitigate the inconsistencies. I'd like to see 100 percent of all meets count in a team's qualifying score rather than the current RQS system where it's two away and two at home or two other, etc. Drop the high. Average four, then average five, then average six. I don't even know anymore; it changes so often. I try to be consistent in the coaches' meetings. I try to make my decisions on the basis of making the sport easier to understand by the press and the fans. The way gymnastics teams qualify for nationals is so messed up. The RQS should be an average of all your scores for the entire season. In basketball, when you have a hurt player and you lose a game, it counts on your record. I think the qualifying score should be based on the team average of all meets. Average them all, regardless of how many meets you have and how many are at home. Having assigned judges for all meets should allow us to do that.

Crowd behavior: Improper crowd conduct is not a problem at every school. But at those where it is, coaches need to take steps to correct it. As thousands of fans have discovered the excitement of college women's gymnastics, it has been great for the sport, in general. But as the number of fans has increased, some have brought with them the demeanor they exhibit in attending other sports, particularly when the competing gymnastics teams represent schools who also are intense rivals in football, basketball, or ice hockey—where it's considered part of the sport to intimidate the opponent. In bringing to the arena the "football mentality," fans have booed visiting coaches and gymnasts when introduced, intentionally tried to cause gymnasts to fall from the apparatus, yelled insults at visiting gymnasts, and exhibited other inappropriate behavior.

Unfortunately, at the SEC Championship Meet in 2002, some fans even booed gymnasts and coaches from an opposing team who were recognized for achievement during the awards ceremony. While this imposed no danger to the award recipients, it characterized those who booed as ignorant and tasteless—not the kind of image we want for gymnastics fans.

Far worse than booing or showing pleasure for a gymnast's misfortune is orchestrating noise during performance, for example, conducting a chant in unison while a gymnast is performing on the balance beam. Performing on the beam requires a longer period of sustained, intense concentration than performance of any other activity in sports—about a minute and a half. The gymnast is from four to eight feet in the air, doing flips and turns above a four-inch-wide wooden beam, four feet from the floor. If she falls, she can be seriously injured, and it has happened too many times. Purposely doing anything to distract her is cruel. It reflects badly on the fans involved, the gymnasts they are supporting, and the school they represent. Fans who do this should be barred from attendance, and a coach who permits supporters to do this should be reprimanded.

The comments of fans on Internet message boards indicate that some believe distracting and intimidating activities are part of their obligations as fans to enhance the home-gym advantage. Performance results indicate that there is, indeed, a home-gym advantage. But it should be an unavoidable consequence of the rigors of travel and the strange environment and equipment. It should not result from fan intimidation of the visiting team.

But how do you encourage enthusiasm—loud positive cheering—without inviting inappropriate behavior? I believe that coaches have both the capability and obligation to take a proactive posture in encouraging appropriate fan behavior and eliminating improper behavior. Coaches have lots of tools to help them educate fans and monitor their behavior. For example, the meet announcer can remind the crowd right at the beginning of a meet, before he introduces the visiting team, how proud its team and coaches are of their hospitality and demeanor, including loudly voiced enthusiasm—but at appropriate times. Coaches also have control over cheerleaders, both the cheer team from the school and the self-appointed ones in the crowd. And these leaders may be the most effective crowd control device of all.

But coaches don't have to stop there. They can distribute instructions on crowd behavior at meets and publish encouragement for proper fan behavior in publications the fans read. Several years ago, I published the following code of conduct:

"Gymnastics Fans' Code of Conduct for College Gymnastics"
(1) Always Greet Our Guests (Our Opponents And Their Supporters) With Genuine Hospitality.

They love their team, just as we love ours, and they can be valued guests if we extend a hospitable hand. Their gymnasts are much like ours, having dedicated years of intense and disciplined practice to develop the skills they will exhibit in entertaining us. Their coaches are the kinds of people we want leading our youth. And they are all our guests. Your greetings should be highly vocal and positive.

(2) Demonstrate Your Appreciation For Good Gymnastics

Demonstrate your appreciation for good gymnastics with applause and cheers—loud and enthusiastic—for good performance by gymnasts from all teams. Our gymnasts want you to show our guests that you are appreciative and knowledgeable. It reflects well on you and our school, and it makes them proud to be members of our team and representatives of our school.

(3) Never Conduct Organized Activities (By the Cheer Team Or By "Ad Hoc Cheer Leaders") That Would Be Distractive To The Gymnasts While They Are On The Apparatus.

To perform safely, gymnasts have to remain totally focused for longer periods of time than do athletes in any other sport. Distractions may cause loss of focus, and they have resulted in falls and serious injuries. It is entirely inappropriate—even cruel—to attempt to distract or to intimidate gymnasts.

(4) Never Applaud Or Cheer For A Gymnast When She Makes A Mistake During Her Performance—Particularly After A Fall From The Apparatus.

Such conduct is simply insensitive and reflective of coarse behavior. Just as you would not applaud a golfer for missing a putt or a diver for hitting his head on the springboard, you should *never* show demonstrative pleasure at a gymnast's misfortune. Pull for your team—not against the opponent.

(5) Never Boo Or Yell Derogatory Remarks.

Don't boo opponents. Don't boo coaches. Don't boo judges. The opponents are your guests. Treat them as such. The judges are much better trained and more capable of awarding proper scores than fans. Most of them are conscientious and dedicated.

In summary, coaches can and should take leadership rolls in educating fans and in controlling their behavior.

Recruiting: One of our biggest problems is that some individual gym coaches still don't help their gymnasts learn all they need to know about potential opportunities in college gymnastics. For example, they don't pass on information from colleges. We have trouble finding recruits' home addresses in order to contact them, so we send our mail for recruits to the coaches, who frequently don't pass it on because they are not interested in college gymnastics. We can't call the recruits until July 1 following their junior year, but we can send them information. Often when we call them they'll say they never received anything from their coach. Sometimes it's unintentional, and sometimes it's intentional. If you call some clubs, they won't give a college recruiter the addresses of their gymnasts. This is all symptomatic of a lack of interest by the club coach or his or her bias toward another school.

Last year, Jay Clark was supposed to visit a gymnast who lived several hundred miles away. He made arrangements to meet with her and her family. When he arrived, she told him that her coach had instructed her that she could only make official visits to three teams instead of the five that the NCAA allows. Georgia was not one of the three. We had wasted a lot of time and money. It would have been nice to know this before he traveled up there. Some club coaches focus almost exclusively on the national team and the Olympics. They really aren't putting the best interest of the gymnasts first. Only seven kids make the Olympics every four years. One thousand kids get college scholarships every four years. Gym coaches should recognize that where a student goes to college is important, and, like high school football coaches, do all they can to help their athletes get information on the schools they might consider attending.

Unfortunately, some coaches advise gymnasts about schools based on their own prejudices. I know one coach who thinks that there is only one college in the country that her gymnasts should attend. Some coaches discount college gymnastics as a factor in choosing a school. They are partially right in that the most important thing about going to college is getting an education, but there are many other factors that, cumulatively, may be more important than just the academic ranking of a school. Gym coaches should let decisions about college be decided by the gymnasts and their parents. For the vast majority of gymnasts, I think this is the case. Club coaches are not experts in the selection of colleges, particularly since they seem to disdain college gymnastics. This is changing now that more and more former college gymnasts are becoming coaches and now that Olympians are extending their gymnastic careers into college.

Those coaches who think that the Olympics is the only important factor in gymnastics are living in the dark ages. Mary Lee Tracy, who is as familiar with Olympic competition as anyone else, targets college for her gymnasts. She's had more than her share of both Olympians and of girls who excelled in college, either after the Olympics or in place of the Olympics.

Greg Marsden, who's been successful for a long time in dealing with club coaches, gave me an assessment of their attitudes:

> Like any other group with strong wills and strong per-sonalities, each club coach is different. Some are great and go out of their way to be helpful, some are laissez faire, some just don't care and don't want to be to involved. And a very few just want us to stay away. Most of this depends on the timing and how considerate the college coach is about what the club coaches are trying to accomplish with their athletes.
>
> Some club coaches actually tend to steer their gymnasts toward college teams they like and away from teams they dislike. And again, some do and some don't.

Of course, we'd all profit from close cooperation, but for the most part I think we do that.

Promotion: Most college athletic administrators don't promote gymnastics. But that's not the only sport they don't promote. They don't promote any sports other than men's basketball and football. In 2003, on the main page of the USA Web site it said, "Ask Mark Richt (head football coach) and Dennis Felton (head men's basketball coach) questions on the Internet." Why weren't there other coaches on the page? In 2004, this was fianally corrected. As recent as 2003, the athletic administration at Georgia installed a new automated phone-answering system with messages about football and men's basketball tickets, but nothing about other sports. This, too, has been corrected. Was it because the athletic association assumed that there was no interest? Well, what came first, the chicken or the egg? Maybe there was not as much interest in other sports as there was in football and basketball, but the athletic association should have considered that there might have been. I fought these same battles every year. For several years, the University of Georgia published a special edition of the *Georgia Bulldog* magazine that came out every November featuring men's and women's basketball. I asked why they didn't feature women's gymnastics also. I had to argue for three years. Finally, we were included.

From the standpoint of assisting in promoting college sports, the USAG could do more to promote college gymnastics. Sometimes, I think they seem to view college gymnastics as not important and even exhibit a feeling that they are competing with college gymnastics. Greg Marsden is less critical of them than I am:

> I think they do a relatively good job. They sponsor the USAG collegiate championships for lower division schools. This has helped save some of those programs. I have always found their staff to be helpful and responsive.
>
> However, you must keep in mind that college gymnastics is not their main charge, and therefore not a strong focus.

I think the same could be said for other national governing bodies as well.

We must rely on ourselves, our universities, our coaches association, and the NCAA to promote and foster collegiate gymnastics.

Greg is right. College gymnastics is not the USAG's main charge, but we could all profit from more cooperation. For example, USAG sponsored meets are frequently scheduled to coincide with the NCAA Regional meets, hurting attendance at both sets of meets.

Apparently, the perceived lack of coordination between the USAG and college gymnastics programs has resulted in the United States Association of Independent Gymnastics Clubs (USAIGC) explicitly emphasizing its interest in working with college gymnastics programs. In a recent letter to college coaches, Paul Spadaro, vice president of the USAIGC, said, "The most profound change in the direction of the new USAIGC is that we have 'hitched our competitive star' to the NCAA collegiate program." Among other promotional activities to link club and college programs, the USAIGC sponsors the annual college-bound invitational meet to help link college coaches and gymnasts seeking opportunities to compete in college gymnastics.

I can go on mentioning areas in which we need to improve. But we have a pretty full plate if we work on solving the problems associated with the scoring system, non-uniformity of judges, crowd conduct, lack of involvement from club coaches, and lack of support from college administrators, the NCAA, and the USAG. But even though we still have problems—what sport doesn't—more and more people are beginning to realize that women's college gymnastics, with mature gymnasts performing Olympic-level skills in the exciting college environment, is unsurpassed in collegiate athletics. If you haven't experienced it yet, make sure you do next season.

Acknowledgements

First and foremost I would like to thank my family.

Sam Yoculan who supported and encouraged me from the beginning to pursue my passion for coaching.

My mom and dad, Bill and Doris Allen, who followed me to Georgia to help raise my children as I pursued my passion for coaching.

My children, Alexis and Adam, who sacrificed their time with me so I could pursue my passion for coaching.

And my fiancé, Don Leebern Jr., who has balanced my life as I continue to pursue my passion for coaching!

I am living proof that "The world belongs to the discontented."

Second, I want to acknowledge two individuals who are responsible for my being at the University of Georgia. Ed Isabelle who gave me the confidence to begin this journey and Liz Murphey who gave me the opportunity.

A special thanks is extended to all college gymnasts especially those who were "GymDogs" whose successes are the reason there is this book.

I would also like to thank the coaches throughout the country who were kind enough to talk to my coauthor, Bill Donaldson. I especially thank Greg Marsden, whose contributions throughout the book are significant, and a very special coach, my assistant and friend, Doug McAvinn, who has been with me for twenty-one years and six National Championships.

And last but not least, thank you is not enough to say to Bill Donaldson, my coauthor, whose relentless pursuit to complete this book is the reason it is finally finished. He personally collected all of the data and statistics in the book and then coerced me to do my part.

And thank you to Judy Long, our editor, who saw the value of having a book on college gymnastics. I hope this is the first of many!

SUZANNE YOCULAN

First and foremost I thank my wife, Barbara, who shared many hundreds of hours of my time with *Perfect 10* during a crucial period in our lives. Liz Murphey, Kelly Macy Roberson, Kathy McMinn, and Becky Switzer enthusiastically provided extensive and essential input to several chapters. Ken and Garie Lee Short's *Gymnastics Insider* made acquiring significant statistical information possible. Editor Judy Long demonstrated a rare combination of attributes; she was demanding and considerate. Tom Payton brought his vast knowledge of publishing to hone the book's marketable qualities. And, of course, without Suzanne Yoculan there would be no book and little to write about.

BILL DONALDSON

Index

Abel, Shannon, 21
Ackerman, Jamie, 197, 199, 202
Adams, Michael, 91, 215, 199
Alabama, University of, ix, xii-xiii, 2-4, 11, 14, 16-19, 21-23, 26-35, 39, 43, 48, 70, 108-09, 113-14, 120, 124, 126, 130, 135-36, 138-39, 158, 159-67, 169-72, 175-76, 178-83, 185-86, 188, 190, 192-201, 203-04, 206-07, 215, 227
Alfano, Elaine, 13, 16
Alicea, Lisa, 29
Allen, Bill, 37
Allen, Doris (Carlisle), 37, 188
Andersen, Brooke, 136, 171, 179, 185
Anderson, Heidi, 14
Andrews, Jill, 22, 25
Angeles, Leslie, 132, 157, 165, 168, 173, 174
Anthony, Kim, 24
Antolin, Jeanette, 187
Anz, Maria, 14
Arizona, University of, 14, 35, 171, 201
Arizona State University, xii, 13-14, 16-19, 22-23, 29, 70, 132, 172, 173, 181, 198
Arnold, Kim, 47, 49, 152, 162, 169, 172, 173, 175, 176, 177
Arnstad, Nicki, 196
Auburn University, 8, 15, 31, 35, 168, 208

Avener (Markell), Judi, 14, 208
Ayotte-Law, Mary, 13
Baimbridge, Melinda, 52, 95, 193
Bair, Cassie, 179, 196, 199
Ballard (Clark), Julie, 87, 138, 147, 152, 162, 167, 175, 176, 177, 186
Ballard, Steve, 144, 171, 177
Balk, Arnold, 138
Bañales, Gina, 15-17, 31, 45, 89
Barber, Alan, 44
Barker, Bill, 138
Barks, Kelley, 152
Basile, Gina, 31
Bauerle, Jack, 8, 224, 228, 229, 234
Beathard, Jenni, 120, 166, 168, 173, 175, 179
Beckerman, Alyssa, 62, 187
Beecham, Stan, 152
Bhardwaj, Mohini, 68, 185, 191, 192, 193
Bienvenu, Melissa, 118
Bluett, Kristi, 167
Boguinskaia, Svetlana, 65, 66
Bohler, Clyde, 2
Bonham, Steve, 5, 7
Borden, Amanda, v, 61, 166, 171
Bowden, Bobby, 228
Brennan, Stephen, 103
Brigham Young University, 29, 160
Brink, Heather, 185
Brown, Leah, 49, 132, 157, 160, 168, 169, 171-74

Brummer, Jackie, 14, 18
Bryant, Michele, 28
Bull, Scott, 21, 28, 144, 161, 167
Buwick (Switzer), Becky, 63
Byrd, Chelsa, 88, 187, 192, 196, 199, 201
California State University-Fullerton, 13-14, 17, 23, 208
Cameron, Jeri, 13
Cappuzzo, Jennifer, 89, 149
Carbone, Jennifer, 26, 29, 30, 157
Carley, Gerald, 69
Carter, Jimmy, 5
Chell, Emily, 141, 142, 177, 179
Chow, Amy, 62, 171
Clark, Jay, v, 28, 144, 166, 177, 245
Clifton (Estes), Jackie, 43, 186
Clifton, Judy, 43
Comaneci, Nadia, xi, 47-48, 76
Cook, Stacy, 10
Cunningham, Lee, 6, 42
Curry, Amanda, 66, 175-77, 179, 183-85, 187, 192
Daggett, Tim, 107
Dantzscher, Jamie, 187, 191, 196, 199
Darst, Delene, 28, 144, 146
Davison, Fred, 43, 44
Dawes, Dominique, 62
Denver, University of, 189, 195, 205
Desteva, Lena, 185

DeMasi, Debbie, 21
DePaoli, Melissa, 23
Dewey, Andrea, 32, 34, 36, 157
Diaz, Eileen, 177, 185, 187, 197
Diaz, Manuel, 228-29
Dill, Wayne, 154
Dobransky, Dana, 33, 35
Donaldson, Bill, viii, 103, 120
Dooley, Vince, 4, 209, 213
Durham, Amy, 35
Durham, Hugh, 217-18
Dwyer, Kathy, 23
Eaves, Joel, 212-13
Eckert, Terri, 9-11, 14, 16, 19, 21, 39-40, 45
Ericksen, Kelsey, 155, 199-201, 204, 206
Etchison, Herbert, 15
Evans, Damon, 154, 235
Fears, Eric, 150
Feldman, Sid, 7
Felton, Claude, 199-220
Felton, Dennis, 247
Flammer, Monica, 95, 179, 185
Florida, University of, xii, 5, 8, 11-12, 14-17, 19-24, 26, 31-32, 70-71, 99, 112, 120, 129, 135, 139, 159, 160, 164, 166-167, 170, 173, 175-176, 180-81, 188, 193, 198, 200-01, 203, 208, 218-21, 228, 230
Fjordholm, Marie, 197, 199, 202
Fontaine, Larissa, 176
Foster, Dee Dee, 28
Fritzinger, Cory, 129, 187, 189, 192, 193, 196, 200-01
Galloway, Linda, 139
Galloway, Stacey, 50, 139, 166, 179

Galvin, Becky, 154
Garrison, Kelly, 19, 22, 63
Gault, Jim, 14, 208
Gelfand, Kurt, 29
Gelin, Dana, 167, 168
Georgia, University of, v, vi, ix, xi-iii, xv, 1-6, 8-31, 33-37, 39-46, 48, 50-53, 55-56, 58-59, 61, 63-66, 69-71, 73-78, 80, 82-84, 88-89, 92-97, 99, 102-04, 107-09, 112-14, 116-126, 128, 132, 134, 136-141, 145, 147, 150, 152-53, 155-56, 158-160, 162-66, 168-176, 179-196, 198-207, 209-16, 218-24, 226-35, 237, 239, 245, 247
Giles, Blake, 225
Gilbert, Sarah, 1
Gingrich, Anna, 179, 187
Goewey, Julie, 13
Greco, Debbie, 17, 26
Gunter, Sue, 222
GymDogs, vi, xi, xv, 2-4, 11, 14-18, 21-26, 28-32, 34-36, 45, 49, 50-52, 55, 58, 61-62, 66, 72, 87, 96, 104-05, 108-11, 113-17, 119, 122, 128-31, 135-36, 138-40, 148, 150, 155, 157-177, 179-90, 192-200, 205, 230, 233
Haack, Chris, 229
Haley, Lee, 154
Hallman, Donna, 148
Hamilton, Kim, 19, 22, 24, 25
Hamm, Betsy, 176
Hanley, Beth, 38
Hansen, Jenny, 161, 165, 171
Harris, Caroline, 149, 171
Hartman, Bill Jr., 228
Hartman, Bill III, 228
Hastey, Jackie, 15

Hatch, Brooks, 1, 36
Hayashi, Kiralee, 179
Hauschild, Penny, 16, 18, 39, 48
Henrich, Christi, 69, 74-75, 84
Herman, Leigh, 21
Hines, Susan, 173, 176
Hornbeek, Heidi, 171
Horvat, Glada, 154
Hummer, Steve, 119
Isabelle, Ed, xvi, 249
Ito, Bob, 14
Jackson, Jana, 9-10, 15
Johnson, David Allen, 141
Johnson, Kathy, 107
Jones, Laurie, 10, 45
Jones, Malia, 190
Jordan, Michael, ix
Kane, Mary Jo, 232
Keleti, Agnes, 46
Kelly, Beans, 214
Kelly, Kim, 171
Kenoyer, Kristen, 33
Kentucky, University of, ix, 21, 29, 35, 161, 165, 167-69, 171, 173-174, 218, 227
Klick, Julie, 15, 17, 19, 46
Knapp, Charles, 117, 223
Knysh, Renald, 47
Kondos-Field, Valorie, 184, 189, 190, 191, 194, 207
Karolyi, Bela, 47-48, 65
Karolyi, Marta, 240
Korbut, Olga, xi, 3, 46-47
Kramer, Roy, 163
Krzyzewski, Mike, 228
Kulikowski, Theresa, 179, 192, 199
Kurc, Lisa, 130, 173-74
Lahey, Susan, 154
Laing, Emma, 49
Landers, Andy, 123, 217, 222, 231
Lawler (Rogers), Ann Marie,

218-19
Lawrence, Karlene, 122
Lawson, Ludlow, 154
Leebern, Don Jr., 123, 216, 232
Leebern, Don III, 216
Leland, Carl, 5, 21, 143
Leonard, Angie, 179
Lewis, Morgan, 15
Lewis, Rick, 49, 152
Lichey, Kristi, 175-76, 179, 184-85, 187, 189, 192
Lichey, Karin, 166-67, 169, 176, 179
Lombardi, Vince, 91
Loree, Pam, 18
Logan, Nneka, 31, 34, 36, 159, 162
Louisiana State University, xii, 19, 21, 28, 31, 113, 120, 124, 129, 135, 159, 164, 167, 173, 178, 182, 193, 196, 198, 204-05, 208, 222
Macy (Roberson), Kelly, 28, 30
Macy, Linda, 82
Macy, Mike, 82
Magill, Dan, 228
Maheu, Paula, 15, 17, 26
Maloney, Kristen, 187, 190-91, 193, 206
Manheim, Alan, 222-223
Marlowe, Chris, xvi
Marlowe, Missy, 31, 33, 48
Marsden, Greg, 2, 9, 13-14, 17, 32, 36, 53, 56, 125, 184, 207, 221, 246-47, 250
Marsden (McCunniff), Megan, 13-14, 48
Marshall, Tammy, 33, 35
Martinelli, Pete, 64
Maurone, Danielle, 136, 177
McAllister, Sydney, 15
McAvinn, Doug, 16, 138, 143, 167, 188, 250

McBee, Louise, 213
McCallum, Heather Whitstone, 9
McLean, Avery, 123
McMinn, Kathy, 5-6, 10, 13-15, 41-42, 45, 250
Messer, Lynn, 21
Michigan, University of, xii, 3, 26, 35, 99, 136, 138, 140, 159, 161, 164-66, 169-170, 172, 175-76, 178, 181, 183, 185, 188, 190, 192, 194-999, 201, 204-07, 240
Miles, Ashley, 197, 199, 201
Miller, Ashley, 197, 202
Miller, Shannon, 62
Mitzel, Lisa, 16
Mobley, Lisa, 147
Moceanu, Dominique, 62
Moneymaker, Heidi, 176, 179
Moody, Terri, 211
Mordre, Yumi, 19
Muhleman, Sam, v, 50, 61, 66, 133, 151, 166, 173, 176, 179
Mulvahill, Dick, 39
Murdock, Holly, 197
Murphey, Liz, 8, 41-42, 107, 209, 218-20, 222, 249-50
Neal, Kim, 13, 18
Nebraska, University of, xii, 4, 14, 28, 39, 40-41, 149, 181, 183, 185, 192-94, 197-99, 204, 206-07
Normile, Dwight, 16
North Carolina, University of, ix
North Carolina State University, 40,
O'Neill, Katie, 167
Ohio State University, 11, 19, 125
Origer, Susie, 15
Oestrang, Marny, 179

Patterson, Sarah, 14, 17, 20, 109, 207, 221, 224
Phelps, Jaycie, 61
Phillips, Kristi, 63
Pickens, Andree, 179, 190, 193, 196
Ponstein, Julie, 23
Prestigiacomo, Kelli, 175
Ray, Elise, 192, 196, 201
Reid, Elizabeth, 173
Reid, Scott, 221, 224-26
Reid, Summer, 171, 173
Reiff, Laurie, 10, 45
Rice, Grantland, xiv
Richardson, Kate, 197, 199
Richt, Mark, 247
Roberson, Brad, 82
Rodis, Chris, 23, 25, 28, 31, 34, 115
Roethlisberger, Marie, 28
Rogers, Lynn, 14, 210
Rosetta, Dick, 2
Rowe, Kinsey, 94, 156-57, 189-90, 195-96, 199, 201-02
Rowlette, Sandy, 26, 31, 36, 155, 157
Russell, Bill, 128
Rutherford, Breanne, 179, 187
Ryan, Joan, 49
Sabo, Tyler, 156
Sang, Lan, 140
Sanders, Red, 91
Sapunar, Sierra, 94, 155, 187, 189, 191, 193-194, 196, 199
Schrader, Bryan, 209
Schuler, Tanya, 15, 17, 26
Sears, Suzanne, 175-76, 179, 185, 187, 192, 209, 229, 231
Selig, Joy, 25, 28
Selig, Stephen, III, 226
Sessions, Michelle, 15

Service (Chaplin), Tanya, 24
Shafer, John, 154
Shephard, Steve, 86
Shirk, Lisa, 13
Short, Ken, 158, 166, 183, 187
Shrieves, Kathleen, 66, 136, 175-76, 180, 185, 187, 192
Spini, John, 14, 207
Simpkins, Agina, 31, 34-36, 146, 157, 160, 162, 171
Simpson, Loren, 187, 196
Simpson, Rachelle, 199
Smith, Brittany, 62, 197, 199-200, 203, 206
Smith, Kirk, 113
Smith, Loran, 227
Smith, Rankin, 93
Snyder, Courtney, 34
Spadaro, Paul, 248
Spivey, Hope, 3, 28, 30-31, 33-36, 49, 70, 72, 84, 157, 161, 163
Stanford University, xii, 99, 116, 154, 171, 178, 188, 190, 195, 198-99, 200-01, 203, 205, 208
Stanley, Marianne, 223
Stednitz, Sue, 13
Stevenson, Mark, 40
Stephens, Marline, 94, 187, 192, 196-197, 199, 238
Stepp, Heather, 3, 26, 29-30, 32-36, 49, 72, 157, 239
Still, Debbie, 26
Stokes, Erica, 70
Strong, Lori, xiii, 34, 36, 39, 65, 144, 147, 157, 161, 165, 168-69, 172, 174, 177
Strug, Kerri, 171
Stryker, Sherri, 15
Summitt, Pat, 220
Tagtmayer, Kim, 147, 167
Thomas, Andrea, 18-19, 25, 28, 33, 89

Thompson, Donnie, 190
Thompson, Jenni, 62
Thompson, Jodi, 9, 10
Tibbetts, Alan, 119
Tilton, Traci, 26
Tomlinson, Jerry, 14, 23, 208
Tousek, Yvonne, 187, 190-191, 193
Tracy, Mary Lee, viii, 61-62, 147, 246
Trensch, Kit, 121
Trippi, Charlie, ix
Twoey, Jodie, 39
Umeh, Stella, 165, 176
University of California at Los Angeles, xii, 24-25, 28, 29, 35, 68, 71, 99, 105-06, 114, 130, 134-35, 158, 160-61, 163-66, 170-76, 178-79, 181-87, 189-204, 206-08, 214-15
Utah, University of, xii, 1-4, 12-14, 16-17, 19-22, 27, 29, 31-33, 35-36, 44, 48, 70, 122, 125-26, 159-62, 164-66, 170-73, 176, 178-79, 181-85, 192, 195, 197-201, 203-04, 206-07, 240
Vexler, Anne, xvi
Vexler, Talya, 38, 104, 141, 177, 180, 185, 187, 192, 196-197
Walker, Herschel, ix, xii, 5
Wallace, Jeff, 224
Walton, Bill, 36
Walton, Rick, 4, 9, 14, 40
Warbutton, Danny, 39
Ward, Kelly, 151
Warfield, Russell, 155, 156
Washington, University of, 14, 19, 29, 39, 134-35
Weaver, Ernestine, 12, 14, 16, 112, 208, 218
Weider, Don, 38
Wener, Lucy, 17, 19, 22,

25-26, 33, 46, 48-49, 89, 110-111, 130, 239
White, Craig, 153
White, James, 226
White, Morgan, 62
Whittle, Courtney, 171
Willard, Meredith, 171
Winter, Bill, 216
Woods, Stephanie, 171
Woodward Gymnastics Camp, xvi, 5, 40, 42, 155
Woolsey, Sandy, 161
Wright, Corrinne, 18, 19, 25, 28, 130
Wymer, Beth, 35, 161
Yoculan, Adam, 4, 5, 6, 40
Yoculan, Alexis, 18, 51, 234
Yoculan, Sam, 4, 5, 9, 39
Yoculan, Suzanne, v, xi, xv, xvi, xviii, 2, 16-17, 22, 24-27, 35, 116-17, 123, 163, 181-82, 184, 207, 215, 220, 229
Zeis, Lisa, 16, 18
Zmeskal, Kim, 70